The Worst Jobs
in History

THE WORST JOBS IN HISTORY

TWO THOUSAND YEARS OF MISERABLE EMPLOYMENT

Tony Robinson
David Willcock

Dedication

For Lucy, Jo and Andrew

First published 2004 by Boxtree
an imprint of Pan Macmillan Ltd
Pan Macmillan, 20 New Wharf Road, London N1 9RR
Associated companies throughout the world

0 7522 1533 7

9 8 7 6 5 4

A CIP catalogue record for this book is available from the
British Library

Designed and typeset by Perfect Bound Ltd
Commissioned and project managed by Emma Marriott
Colour Reproduction by Aylesbury Studios (Bromley) Ltd
Printed by The Bath Press

This book accompanies the television series *Worst Jobs in
History* made by Spire Films for Channel 4
Writer and Presenter: Tony Robinson
Executive Producer: David Willcock

Picture Credits

While every effort has been made to trace the copyright
holders for illustrations featured in this book, the publishers
will be glad to make proper acknowledgements in future
editions in the event that any regrettable omissions have
occurred at the time of going to press.

Adam Hart-Davis 85
AKG London 61
The Bridgeman Art Library/www.bridgeman.co.uk: page 10
Cott Nero DIV f.139 The beginning of St. Lukes' Gospel
Lindisfarne Gospels, (c.698 AD),British Library, London;
page 13 Preparing for a banquet, 4th century BC (mural
painting) by Palace of the Popes, Orvieto, Italy; page 29
Cott Nero DIV f.25v Portrait of St. Matthew Lindisfarne
Gospels, (c.698 AD) British Library, London, UK; page 34
Penny of Offa, King of Mercia, 757-96 (obverse) (silver)
(for reverse see 168072) by English School (8th century)
Fitzwilliam Museum, University of Cambridge, UK; page
71 Historiated initial 'N' depicting sheep shearing, from
'The Natural History of Pliny the Elder' (23-79 AD)
(vellum) by Italian School (15th century) Historia
Naturalis, (15th century)Biblioteca Marciana, Venice; page
74 Interior of the Kitchen, the Supper at Emmaus (oil on
panel) by Flemish School (16th century) Musee des Beaux-
Arts, Lille, France; page 83 Meeting at the Field of the
Cloth of Gold, 7th June 1520, after Hans Holbein the
Elder (1460/5-1524) (oil on canvas) by Friedrich
Bouterwek (1806- 67) Chateau de Versailles, France; page
89 John Hunt, Nightman and Rubbish Carter, near the
Wagon and Horses in Goswell Street, near Mount Mill,
London (engraving) by English School (18th century)
Private Collection/The Stapleton Collection; page 95 The
Globe Theatre on the Bankside as it appeared in the reign
of James I (1566-1625), after an engraving c.1612,
published 1810 (engraving) by English School (19th
century) Private Collection/The Stapleton Collection; page
96 Portrait of Nathan Field (1587-c.1634), Elizabethan
actor (panel) by English School (17th century) Dulwich
Picture Gallery, London, UK; page 100 La Vie Seigneuriale:
Embroidery, c.1500 (tapestry) by French School (16th
century) Musee National du Moyen Age et des Thermes de
Cluny, Paris; page 111 A Rake's Progress IV: The Arrested,
Going to Court, 1733 by William Hogarth (1697-1764)
Courtesy of the Trustees of Sir John Soane's Museum,
London; page 113 The Death Warrant of Charles I, 29th
January 1648 (actually 1649) pub. 1750 (engraving) (b&w
photo) by English School (18th century) Private
Collection; page 127 Sir James Thornhill (1676-1734)
(engraving) (b&w photo) by Joseph Highmore (1692-
1780) (after) Private Collection; page 131 Antonio
Stradivari, 1893 (panel) by Edgar Bundy (1862-1922)
Bonhams, London, UK; page 143 Mr and Mrs Andrews,
c.1748-9 (oil on canvas) by Thomas Gainsborough (1727-
88) National Gallery, London, UK; page 161 An Interesting
Scene on board an East-Indiaman, showing the Effects of a
Heavy Lunch, published by G. Humphrey, London, 1818
(coloured etching) by George Cruikshank (1792-1878)
Private Collection/The Stapleton Collection.
British Leather Confederation 201
The British Library 90
© Colin Hinson 43
Corbis Images 17, 21, 24, 36, 39, 41, 128, 151 (bottom), 181,
184, 196, 202
David Alexander 142
Guildhall Library, Corporation of London 102, 114, 132, 181
Henry Mayhew, *London Labour and the London Poor* (Penguin
Classics) 179, 191, 193, 198
London Borough of Hackney Archives Department 187
Manchester Library 165
The Mary Evans Picture Library 14, 23, 35, 44, 47, 51, 53, 55,
77, 79, 81, 86, 104, 107, 115, 117, 119, 123, 137, 149, 154,
170, 171, 177
Museum of Welsh Life 205, 206
The National Trust/Quarry Bank Mill 166
Osterreichische Nationalbibliotheck Bildarchive 63
Dr Peter Giles, Castrato expert and consultant to *The Worst
Jobs in History* television series 150
Peter Higginbotham 188, 190
The Record Office for Leicestershire, Leicester and Rutland
168, 173
© The Royal College of Surgeons of Edinburgh 146
Science & Society Picture Library 174
St James' Hospital, Leeds 186
Tony Robinson 94
Victorian & Albert Museum Picture Library 151 (top)
All other images supplied by and © Spire Films

Contents

Introduction

The history I learnt in school was all kings and queens, battles, generals and prime ministers. But I've always known that was only half the story. For the vast majority of people, living British history has been a very different experience. Behind all the great men and women who made the headlines has been an unseen army doing all the really hard, dangerous and unpleasant work.

Archaeology demonstrates this vividly. Most finds aren't the treasures of the Great and the Good, but the detritus of ordinary people. Working on *Time Team* I'm constantly brought face to face with the touching reality of ancient lives: people who survived despite the events of history rather than because of them.

For a long time I've wanted to give a voice to such people, but struggled to find a way that would portray their lives vividly and entertainingly. Then a couple of years ago I had a conversation with historian Dr Mike Jones about the realities of the battle in the Age of Chivalry: how a medieval knight would have coped with the rigours of eight-hour fighting, given the several hundred-weight of armour he'd have been wearing. My interviewee described in lurid detail the Formula-One-type backup team that kept a knight-in-armour operational. My favourite team member was the Arming Squire, the lowest rung on the ladder, who had to sluice out the sweat, urine and excrement that had accumulated in his master's armour after a day in the saddle. It seemed like the Worst Job in the world to me, but Mike insisted – as in the famous Monty Python sketch – that 'he was lucky. There were many worse ways to earn a living in the Middle Ages.'

Equal opportunities Tudor-style. A world of Fishwives and ducking stools sounds rather jolly until you find yourself about to be plunged into near-freezing river water.

But were there really? I decided to to find the Worst Jobs there have ever been. Officially I suppose I've written a social history, but anyone who has ever read any social history books will know why I shy away from using the term. Intense study of manorial rolls to document the change from ox-drawn to horse-drawn ploughs, or statistical analysis of fresh-fish consumption in a Kentish village may be important academic work, but it doesn't make for a

riveting read. Social historians rarely give their anonymous subjects the colour and imagination that biographers allow their more famous heroes and heroines.

As to my selection of jobs, I have to admit it's ultimately subjective. There is no objective way of measuring human misery. And you could say I've avoided the very worst of the worst. At any time before the twentieth century just being a woman and giving birth was as unpleasant as anything in this book, and throughout history countless adults and children have been sold and abused by the rich.

Instead I wanted to tread the wilder shores of employment. The very names Toad Eater, Powder Monkey and Searcher of the Dead underline the fact that the past is a different and fairly disgusting country. Of course, my choices are made with the benefit of squeamish, mollycoddled twenty-first-century hindsight. No doubt, in years gone by, stomachs and nerves were stronger. Folk were far more concerned with how much they were going to get paid than with how stinky the job was. Nevertheless, although the Groomer of the Stool at the Tudor court was a highly prized position that brought one into close contact with the King, I'm sure there were a thousand and one things the successful applicant would rather have done than wipe Henry VIII's capacious bottom.

Tony in a Scold's Bridle. Being pulled through the streets of Alnwick in a dress by a bunch of young Geordie males may be a bizarre way to discover the agonies of the Scold's Bridle – but someone's got to do it!

But not all the jobs are mucky. I've taken into account other elements, such as risk – the eighteenth-century Riding Officer lumbered with the Canute-like task of holding back a violent crime wave armed with only a pony and pistol. There are safe but excruciatingly tedious jobs like the Pipe Roll Transcriber who had to copy out each year's royal accounts by hand. This was a task so painstakingly finicky that it took a full twelve months to complete, so by the time he'd finished, he had a fresh year's accounts already waiting for him so he could start all over again.

Occasionally I've been inspired by the great events of history. For instance, the Gunpowder Plot drew me to the role of the Saltpetre Man who collected human waste for its nitrate content to turn into gunpowder. These were strangely powerful figures in their time. They had the authority of the state to enter old houses, and take up the floorboards without consent to access the 'night-soil' beneath.

In the same vein, there's a look at some of the Worst Jobs behind the building of the great medieval cathedrals. We look at life in Admiral Nelson's navy. Most seamen didn't have the fuss over their death that Nelson enjoyed at Trafalgar. No 'kiss me Hardy' valedictories for them. They were simply sewn into their hammocks with a couple of cannonballs and dropped over the side (unlike Nelson, whose body was pickled in rum for safe keeping). Then there's the impact of the Industrial Revolution, a source of wealth and power for the few, but a cornucopia of lousy jobs for the huddled masses represented by the Mule Scavenger.

By the Victorian era, as health and safety laws and social legislation began to bite, the number of arcane and awful jobs began to decrease, and workers like the Match Girls of London began to demand improvements. But many horrific tasks continued into modern times. The Viking job of Guillemot Egg Collector, which to us sounds so weird, lasted at Flamborough Head in Yorkshire right into the early twentieth century under the job-title 'climmer'!

The fact that you've got time and education to read this book means, almost by definition, your life is not as tough as those people we'll be meeting within these pages. I hope you learn a little from this book but, especially if you've just had a lousy day at work and are feeling a bit put upon, please be thankful you aren't one of the countless millions throughout history who've had jobs far more awful than yours will ever be.

Tony Robinson
June 2004

THE BEST & WORST OF TIMES

Note You'll notice a timeline running through this book, in boxes like this. Timelines usually record events surrounding the Great and the Good. In ours we have combined the usual markers of history with various inventions and issues which really impacted on the lives of ordinary people, but which are seldom given prominence.

CHAPTER ONE

The First Worst Jobs

B ritain has been transformed by migration and invasion just as surely as the coastline has been shaped by the waves of the North Sea and Atlantic. Its original inhabitants were supplanted by Celtic peoples who arrived around 3500 BC. In 80 BC a new wave of sophisticated Belgic tribes settled in southern England. Then in AD 43, the stuttering Roman Emperor Claudius ordered the permanent invasion and occupation of Britain to win himself better PR at home. Despite the bloody revolt of Queen Boudicca against Claudius's successor, Nero, this invasion was the start of nearly 400 years of continuous rule. Roman values and Roman culture thoroughly permeated British life.

Roman Worst Jobs

The Lindisfarne Gospels picture St Matthew with the same sort of bound vellum book that the monks were making in the drafty scriptorium.

Prior to the Roman invasion, the word 'job' was a pretty hazy concept. Basically, work was the thing you got on with when you weren't fighting. But when a nation's culture becomes more sophisticated, work tends to become divided up into specific tasks. The Romans knew exactly which jobs were the worst. By and large they were the ones they made the slaves do. Terrible conditions and lives of profound suffering underpinned all the technological advances the Romans brought with them. For example, the superb engineering that gave the Romans underfloor heating had to be serviced by a lad acting as a hypocaust cleaner, wiggling along under ground in pitch blackness cleaning out the pipes: an early version of the Victorian Chimney Sweep (see page 176).

Can you call the work slaves did a 'job'? Probably not; they had no choice about what they did, or where they did it. But a few tasks have been included that were done by slaves, because free men and women did them too. In Roman times, who did what, and what the perks were, wasn't quite as black and white as it might seem. To add to the confusion, household slaves were paid pocket money and could win their freedom. There was a hierarchy of good and bad slave jobs, and through good work and good behaviour you could work your way through the ranks. One of the aristocracy's complaints about the Emperor Nero was that he surrounded himself with high-ranking officials who were all ex-slaves rather than patricians.

You were more likely to gain advancement as a slave if you worked in the house of the family that owned you, rather than if you were stuck miles away on their estate. Nevertheless this book begins with a slave job that was the preserve of someone very close to their master. In fact, too close.

The Romans brought to Britain the sophistication of Mediterranean culture and cuisine. When King Togidubnus in his villa at Fishbourne wanted to give a truly sumptuous Roman feast, he needed a slave to do something pretty disgusting for him.

Fine dining expressed social status for the Romans. A noble household would try and bag the equivalent of a Michelin-starred chef who would work with a platoon of kitchen slaves like this one on a mural painting from the fourth century BC.

Puke Collector

There are two facts that most people know about Roman banquets. One, that the participants ate dormice in honey, and two, that they popped off to a room called the vomitorium to throw the dormice up, in order to make room for the next course.

Actually only one of these so-called facts is true. The Romans did eat dormice drizzled with honey and lightly garnished with poppy seeds, after a slave had gutted and stuffed them. But there was no such place as a vomitorium in a Roman house. A vomitorium was a corridor in an amphitheatre, so called because it enabled thousands of Romans to spew out on to the street in a matter of minutes.

Roman aristocrats may not have had a specially named room to throw up in, but throw up they did. Nero's mentor, the philosopher Seneca, said of the Romans that 'they vomit so that they may eat and eat so that they may vomit'.

Cicero, in one of his letters, describes how Caesar avoided an assassination attempt. He 'expressed a desire to vomit after dinner' (vomere post cenam te velle dixisses), but instead of going to the bathroom where his assassins were lying in wait, he went to his bedroom and threw up there.

Much of the evidence suggests that Roman diners didn't even bother to leave the room when they wanted to make themselves sick. They vomited into specially provided bowls that had been thoughtfully laid out for them, or else

THE BEST & WORST OF TIMES

AD43 The Romans launch a full-scale invasion under the Emperor Claudius, landing in Kent.

AD61 Boudicca leads an uprising of Britons but is defeated.

AD77 Wales is defeated by the Romans, who secure the Dolaucothi Gold mines.

AD122 Hadrian's Wall is built.

they simply spewed on the floor. And trotting round after the guests, or crawling under the couches on which they reclined, was the Puke Collector. This isn't simply the writer's over-vivid imagination. Another passage of Seneca refers to the charmingly sophisticated habit of spitting and throwing up at table. 'Cum ad cenandum discubuimus, alius sputa deterget, alius reliquias temulentorum subditus colligit': 'When we recline at a banquet, one [slave] wipes up the spittle; another, situated beneath, collects the leavings [i.e. vomit] of the drunks' (Epistulae Morales 47.5).

What a truly revolting job, wiping up acrid-smelling cocktails of food, lumpy mixtures of Falernian wine, roast meats, the ubiquitous Roman sauce made of fermented fish and, of course, semi-digested dormice.

'Trimalchio's Banquet' is one of the most famous parts of the *Satyricon* by Petronius. It is a comic romance that was composed during the reign of Nero (i.e. at the same time Roman culture was being introduced to Britain), and was intended to poke fun at the excesses of the vulgar freedman Trimalchio, an ex-slave with money. It is a prime source for our information about dormice in honey. It also gives a vivid picture of the way slaves had to do everything for their masters.

Menelaus had scarcely ceased speaking when Trimalchio snapped his fingers; the eunuch, hearing the signal, held the chamber-pot for him while he still continued playing. After relieving his bladder, he called for water to wash his hands, barely moistened his fingers, and dried them upon a boy's head.

… Marvelling greatly, we followed, and met Agamemnon at the outer door, to the post of which was fastened a small tablet bearing this inscription:

> *NO SLAVE TO LEAVE THE PREMISES*
> *WITHOUT PERMISSION FROM THE MASTER.*
> *PENALTY ONE HUNDRED LASHES.*

… At length we reclined, and slave boys from Alexandria poured water cooled with snow upon our hands, while others following, attended to our feet and removed the hangnails with wonderful dexterity, nor were they silent even during this disagreeable operation, but they all kept singing at their work.

… On the tray stood a donkey made of Corinthian bronze, bearing panniers containing olives, white in one and black in the other. Two platters flanked the figure, on the margins of which were engraved Trimalchio's name and the weight of the silver in each. Dormice sprinkled with poppy seed and honey were served on little bridges soldered fast to the platter, and hot sausages on a silver grid-iron, underneath which were damson plums and pomegranate seeds.

… Trimalchio came in; mopping his forehead and washing his hands in perfume, he said, after a short pause, 'Pardon me, gentlemen, but my stomach's been on strike for the past few days and the doctors disagreed about the cause… So if anyone wants to do his business, there's no call to be bashful about it. None of us was born solid!… I never objected yet to anyone in my dining-room relieving himself when he wanted to, and the doctors forbid our holding it in. Everything's ready outside, if the call's more serious, water, close-stool, and anything else you'll need.'

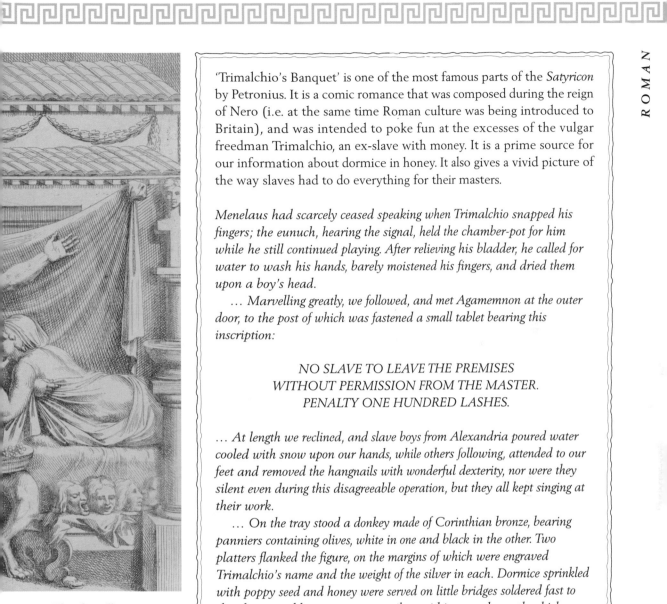

The absurdly extravagant feast given by the Roman parvenu Trimalchio, in the Satyricon **by Petronius.**

But at least the puke collectors had a roof over their heads and the luxury of Roman central heating. When the last bloated guests had finally retired for the night, and the puke collectors were scrubbing the last blobs of congealed dormouse fat from their masters' golden tableware, did they perhaps spare a thought for those even less fortunate than themselves – the wet, shivering wretches in some far-off land who mined the raw materials used to make their golden washing-up?

Gold Miner

One of the main reasons the Romans invaded Britain was to get their hands on our metals and minerals. Lead was highly sought-after. It was used for water pipes, and once liquefied it could be mixed with tin to make pewter. In addition, the silver also found in the ore could be extracted to make coins and tableware. By AD 70, Britain was the Empire's biggest supplier of lead and silver. The writer Pliny the Elder in his *Natural History* describes its abundance in the new colony: 'The lead we use in the manufacture of pipes and sheets is mined with considerable effort in Spain and the Gallic provinces; in Britain, however, it is found on the surface in such large quantities that there is a law limiting production.' (This quota was imposed after the Spanish lodged a complaint with the Emperor – an early version of an EC directive!) To obtain this level of productivity, even though the mines were open-cast, demanded harsh work. Over 10 per cent of the work force died each year.

But there was a far worse mining job in Roman Britain: looking for the most precious metal of all – gold. It was worse because finding gold meant deep-cast mining. Going underground was very risky. You might assume that this was a job for slaves, but there is evidence from elsewhere in Europe that freemen did the job too.

There was a Roman gold mine at Dolaucothi in Wales. Using their famed technology, the Romans channelled water for miles via a system of aqueducts to two great reservoirs on top of a nearby hill. This water was then released in a powerful flood to denude the hillside of greenery and soil and expose the quartz-rich rock in which gold could be found. After this sudden and spectacular demonstration of the power of Roman engineering, the rest of the gold-mining process was simply a question of very hard graft. It's estimated that the Romans removed half a million tons of rock from Dolaucothi in the 300 years the mine was operational. And it was all done by hand.

The slaves had only the most rudimentary tools to do this: simple hand-picks and baskets, and wooden carriers to transport the ore. The reason so much rock had to be shifted lies in the way gold-bearing quartz is laid down. A mineral like coal is comparatively simple to extract. It lies in a seam, a geological stratum

THE BEST & WORST OF TIMES

c.325 Iron foundry is built at Silchester in Hampshire. More work for Bog Iron Hunters.

402 One of the two Roman legions in Britain is withdrawn to help defend Rome.

406 Barbarians sweep into Gaul, cutting off Britain from the Roman Empire. The remaining legion mutinies and is withdrawn.

A gold tiara, the height of Roman civilisation, but only possible because of the worst job of Gold Miner.

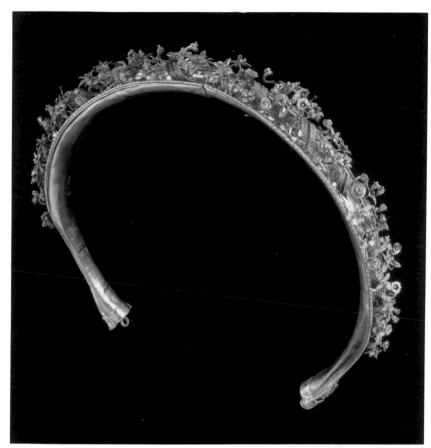

that can sometimes be diagonal to the surface, but always lies in an identifiable strand between the same strata of rock above and below. Quartz, though, is produced by ancient volcanic activity. It is the solidified result of molten ore shooting into irregular fissures in the rock. So it lies not in seams, but in veins that run higgledy-piggledy through a mountain. Sometimes they go up, sometimes down. They may widen into a great expanse of ore, or peter out into nothing. Following the veins is a frustrating game of trial and error.

The Miners worked in a labyrinth of tunnels. The roofs of the shafts were propped up by wood, but the natural movement of the earth could crack the props like matchwood. The conditions were cramped, dangerous and dark. Very dark. Although the miners had lamps fuelled by animal fat or olive oil, they were smoky and gave off little light. It is possible that the miners often hacked away in the pitch black, only able to tell the difference between the smooth shale and sharp quartz by touch.

In order to clear the rock around the seam, they banked faggots of wood against the rock face, set fire to them and then kept them burning for a couple of days in order to heat the rock to a high temperature. As it heated up and the smoke drifted along the tunnel, the conditions must have been intolerable for those charged with keeping the fires alight. In the choking smoke, their dim lamps would have been virtually useless. But the most dangerous part was yet to come.

When the rock was so hot it began to glow, it was suddenly cooled by throwing water or vinegar on to it. The sudden contraction caused by this change in temperature created violent explosions. The Miners, choking in the smoke of two days' worth of fire, had to deal with collapsing rock face and flying debris in virtual darkness.

All this waste rock was then carted out down the long tunnels by hand and dumped, before the miners could start chipping away at the newly exposed quartz with their picks.

---

70. *The third method used for extracting gold rivals the achievements of the Giants. By the light of lamps, long galleries are cut into the mountain. Men work in long shifts measured by lamps, and may not see daylight for months on end. Local people call these mines 'deep-vein'. The roofs of these are liable to give way and crush the miners, which makes diving for pearls or getting purple fish from the depths of the sea seem comparatively safe. So much more dangerous have we made the earth. Arches are left at frequent intervals to support the mountains above.*

71. *In open-cast and deep-vein mining masses of flint are encountered. These can be split by fire-setting, which involves the use of vinegar. Fire-setting in galleries usually makes them suffocatingly hot and smoke-filled. Instead, therefore, the rocks are split by means of crushers which carry 150 pounds of iron. The miners then carry the ore out of the workings on their shoulders, each man forming part of a human chain working in the dark; only those at the end of the line see daylight.*

Pliny the Elder, *Natural History*, Chapter XXXIII

But quarrying the veins was just the start. They had to be broken into smaller chunks until they were portable. Then they too were carried out into the open. Quartz is very hard and brittle, and the specks of gold in it are tiny. So the quartz was smashed as finely as possible, and put on to woollen fleeces. The stone was then washed away, leaving the gold (which is heavier) on the bottom of the fleece. This was then burnt, and among the ashes were the tiny gold flecks.

We don't know how many Miners died at Dolaucothi extracting gold to be turned into fine ornaments for wealthy citizens around the Empire. Anyone who has been to the Welsh mountains in the winter will know how harsh the conditions can be. The fort at Dolaucothi was too small to accommodate the workforce, so the slaves were housed, possibly shackled, in their own huts. Few of them would have shed a tear when, at the beginning of the fifth century, the mine was finally abandoned – to be left dormant until the Victorian era.

But if the gold mine at Dolaucothi was a symbol of harsh colonialism, it was also a symbol of the sophistication of Roman economics and culture. What followed when they left Britain was hardly an improvement.

Worst Jobs in the Dark Ages

In AD 410 Alaric the Goth stood at the gates of Rome. The Western Empire was being overrun by a succession of aggressive tribes from the East. The legions were stretched to breaking-point, so its forces were recalled from the farthest boundaries of the Empire to defend the Italian heartland.

That left a power vacuum in Britain. Faced with attacks from Picts, Scots and the Irish, the Romano-British tried to replace the legions with hired mercenaries from the Germanic tribes of the Saxons.

The warriors Hengst and Horsa were among the first. In 450 they arrived with 'three keels' of warriors. Vortigern, who was leading the Britons, fell in love with Hengst's daughter, and gave him Kent in return for her hand in marriage. The trouble was, the mercenaries liked the place so much, they told their friends. A year later, there were Saxon raids on British towns and cities.

Despite fierce resistance by the Romano-British, the country was rapidly settled by a flood of tribes from northern Europe. The Jutes settled in the south; the Angles flooded the north and east, giving their name to East Anglia and Angle-land – or England. The Saxons implemented their saxerule in southern East Anglia (Essex), as well as the west (Wessex), the south (Sussex) and the bit in between (Middlesex). Much of our language is derived from the lesser-known Frisians who arrived from the Netherlands.

Under the onslaught of this pagan warrior culture, the remnants of Roman Britain capitulated. The native Celtic population was forced into the hills, and classical culture was almost forgotten, eclipsed by the period we call the Dark Ages.

The new invaders lived in tribal settlements. They shunned the towns and temples. The great Roman buildings and public works fell into disrepair, and those who built them were forgotten. A tenth-century poem, 'The Ruin', ponders on the remains: 'Wondrous is the masonry shattered by fate, the fallen city buildings; the work of giants has decayed. The roofs have caved in, the towers are in ruins, the barred gates destroyed, there is frost on the mortar, the gaping shelters collapsed and torn apart, undermined by age.'

THE BEST & WORST OF TIMES

410 Rome falls to the Visigoths.

446 The Romano-British overlord Vortigern authorizes the use of Saxon mercenaries to defend northern England from raiders. Bad idea. Saxons led by Horsa and Hengst arrive in ever-increasing numbers.

480 –547 In Italy St Benedict establishes his rule for monastic communities.

What is now England gradually became dominated by three power-blocks: Wessex in the south, Mercia in the midlands, and Northumbria stretching north to the Scottish border. Each so-called kingdom had a highly complex and structured society. At the top was the King. Below him was an aristocracy of powerful warriors who did the fighting and administered his will. Then there were the peasants, who did everything else. A peasant was known as a ceorl (pronounced 'Churl' – from which we get our word 'churlish') and, for them, life itself was a Worst Job.

597 Augustine arrives from Rome to convert Saxon pagans.

664 The Synod of Whitby synchronizes Celtic Christianity with Roman rules.

687 St Cuthbert dies and his cult is established at Lindisfarne.

700 Creation of the Lindisfarne Gospels.

Churl

The Churl carried the economic weight of England on his shoulders. He was a free peasant farmer but ironically, throughout the Dark Ages, his situation became worse and worse. In the sixth century he might have a piece of land of his own and be answerable only to the King. But by the time of the Norman Conquest, he had to provide a whole range of services to his lord and, on his death, his land passed back to the lord of the manor.

A Churl's life was stuffed full with repetitive, taxing labour. But let's get this into perspective. He wasn't a one-man band. He was the hard-working foreman of an extended family unit. The Churl at least had the dignity of a title. His wife, his children and probably a couple of slaves who shared the chores weren't so lucky. They were as much the Churl's property as his spade or his axe. Every Churl was a woodsman, a farmer, a miller and a builder. But his wife was a miller, weaver, tailor and cook. And besides giving unanaesthetized birth most years of her fertile life, she'd be expected to farm and butcher, reap and winnow, lug and slog. And the Churl's illiterate children were cowherds, swineherds, shepherds, fetchers and carriers and general assistants. And despite his unpaid and unrecognized band of helpers, it was the Churl who had the responsibility of providing for his family group. Even the simplest tasks required endless hours of gut-wrenching effort; like the business of simply keeping warm.

Cutting wood was a constant burden in Saxon times. Wood was necessary to keep the home-fire burning. It could take four hours a day to cut down the amount of fuel needed back home. The Churl also needed wood for building. If he needed a home, he had to make one. The technique used was the famous wattle and daub. For the wattle he used straight, thin sticks of coppiced hazel, which were bent and woven inch by painstaking inch into hurdles. He then had to fasten the woven sections together to create a wall. And because the wattle let the wind through, it had to be coated with a solid covering of daub. For this, he needed mud, water, straw and a special magic ingredient – horse dung. Lots of it. He mushed it all up into a mud-pie consistency and slapped it on the wattle with his bare hands. Why dung? The naturally digested fibre in dung acts as a binding agent. Mud alone would drop off the walls as it dried.

But even with brand-new walls around him and a roof over his head, our Churl still had to say alive, and the simplest tasks took time and energy. Not his energy, of course. This is where Mrs Churl came in. To make the cakes of barley bread that were the staple diet, first the raw barley had to be ground by the women by hand on a quern stone, then kneaded and baked on the fire. It took at least three hours to grind enough grain to make cakes for a family of twelve. No wonder that the legend of the Saxon King Alfred the Great had such resonance for a tenth-century audience. Letting those precious cakes burn meant hours of hard work had gone up in smoke.

But being a Churl wasn't just a question of self-employment. On top of the back-breaking work of keeping his family alive, he had to do work for his lord too. And, as the centuries went by, this burden of service grew heavier and heavier.

Throughout most of Saxon England the basic land division was a hide – the area that a Churl might expect to survive on. A statute for a ten-hide area of Wessex demanded that the Churls supply their lord with 10 vats of honey, 300 loaves, 12 ambers of British ale (we think an amber was about 6 gallons), 30 ambers of clear ale, 2 oxen, 10 geese, 20 hens, 10 cheeses, an amber of butter, 5 salmon, 20 pounds weight of fodder and 100 eels. The Churls of Hurstbourne

This medieval illumination shows a landlord overseeing harvesting peasants – the inheritors of the Churl's mantle.

Priors in Hampshire had to pay a rent of 40 pennies per year for every hide, work three days a week for forty-nine weeks of the year for their lord, plough and sow 3 acres of the lord's land, and mow (with scythe and sickle) half an acre of his meadow all in their own time. They also had to wash and shear his sheep, deliver 4 cartloads of cut and split wood and 16 poles of fencing, as well as handing over sheep, lambs, ale, barley and wheat.

But there was one job in particular that lay at the root of agriculture. It was a task that required both strength and skill. If your name is Plowman, or Ploughman, you have an ancestor who trudged the fields of England providing the basics of Saxon and medieval life.

Churls from the later medieval period tend sheep and gather the harvest. Abundant harvests like these were the very best life could offer the Churl.

Ploughman

If you didn't plough in the Dark Ages, you didn't live. A failed harvest because of an inadequately ploughed field meant famine. Hunger was a fact of life. Times could be so bad that Anglo-Saxon law allowed for a father to sell his son into slavery if it brought in much-needed income. The Saxon historian and monk Bede refers to suicide pacts in famine-struck seventh-century Sussex, where 'Frequently 40 or 50 emaciated and starving people would go to a cliff, or to the edge of the sea, where they would join hands and leap over, to die by the fall or by the drowning.'

> *Master:*   *What do you say, ploughman? How do you carry out your work?*
>
> *Ploughman:*   *Oh, I work very hard, dear lord. I go out at daybreak driving the oxen to the field, and yoke them to the plough, for fear of my lord, there is no winter so severe that I dare hide at home; but the oxen, having been yoked and the share and coulter fastened to the plough, I must plough a full acre or more every day.*
>
> *Master:*   *Have you any companion?*
>
> *Ploughman:*   *I have a lad driving the oxen with a goad, who is now also hoarse because of the cold and shouting.*
>
> *Master:*   *What else do you do in the day?*
>
> *Ploughman:*   *I do more than that, certainly. I have to fill the oxen's bins with hay and water them, and carry their muck outside.*
>
> *Master:*   *Oh, oh! It's hard work.*
>
> *Ploughman:*   *It's hard work sir, because I am not free.*
>
> **Aelfric's *Colloquy*, written towards the end of the tenth century**

THE BEST & WORST OF TIMES

731 The Venerable Bede writes his *Ecclesiastical History*, giving us a valuable picture of Dark Ages Britain.

765 The first English penny is issued, presumably struck by a Coin Thrall.

793 Vikings raid Lindisfarne. These raids will continue for the next three centuries.

*ulaiper eft quærffumicæ ut umær
magno lætbofsquæspinæ æblncolændo*

Ploughing nowadays is pretty easy, and not only because we have tractors. The modern metal ploughshare is perfectly shaped to cut through soil and turn it over with ease. In the Dark Ages the technology was more primitive and needed more skill to operate. The Anglo-Saxon ploughshare was known as an 'ard'. It was made of a very long log, with a wooden blade or 'share' coming out from beneath it. It was difficult to control and constant pressure was required to keep it at the right depth in the furrow.

Two peasants plough with the long wooden 'ard' behind the frisky-looking oxen.

The power for the plough was supplied by oxen. The horse was a much more prestigious beast used in warfare – see page 46 in the Middle Ages for an explanation of the revolution in harnesses that allowed horses to be yoked to the plough. Oxen were slow but sure, and needed careful training and control. Once you'd got them moving, the trick was to keep going in a straight line without stopping. A straight furrow didn't just look smart, it got you maximum efficiency from the soil.

Ploughing in the open air was slow and cold. While one man kept the ard in the ground, another led the oxen. In an illustration on the Anglo-Saxon calendar, the man who led the cattle is barefoot. We don't know whether this was standard practice, but if you've ever got your feet soaked and your shoes caked in mud in a boggy autumn field, you'll understand that, before the invention of wellingtons, going barefoot might have been preferable to sloshing around in rudimentary leather plimsolls.

Small wonder that some of the most promising youngsters from better-off families got out of the agricultural cycle by being sent off to study with the monks, who promised an education and a better life – because, although pagan Saxon ways dominated for a century after the Romans left, Roman culture and the Latin language did survive. This heritage was preserved in tiny Celtic monastic communities in Ireland and on Scottish islands such as Iona. From these remote rocky outposts, monkish missionaries set out to convert the pagan incomers, and formed other communities such as the one on Lindisfarne in Northumbria. Some evangelical monks even went back into Europe to preach the Christian message there. By AD 600 the move to re-Christianize Britain was well under way.

Celtic monastic Christianity was deliberately heroic. The monks realized that if they were going to convert a warrior people, they would have to show that the representatives of Jesus Christ were just as tough as them. So the monastic life, which became so luxurious and debased in medieval times, was in the Anglo-Saxon era one of the very Worst Jobs.

Novice Monk

We have relatively little detail about the life of Celtic monks, because their rules were passed on by word of mouth, and remained unwritten. But the austerity and hardship of the Celtic communities were legendary. We certainly know that they fasted and submitted to harsh mortification of the flesh, a practice that is still present in Irish spiritual life.

We also know that Celtic monks looked very different from the archetypal image we have of the regular monastic brethren. If 'monk' conjures up a picture of a jolly Toby-jug man with a bald bit on top of his head and a black habit with a cowl, singing medieval plainsong in a big church, think again. Celtic monks wore garments of undyed sheep wool. They had their own Celtic chants for singing the psalms. They worshipped in buildings that were closer to scout huts than cathedrals. And their tonsure was different. This bizarre haircut was a hangover from Roman culture. Roman slaves had been shaved, so monks now did likewise to show they were slaves of Christ. But whereas later monks shaved the crown of their heads, their Celtic equivalents removed their hair from the forehead back to a line which went from ear to ear, like an exaggerated receding hairline.

The hut a novice would have lived in on entering a monastery would have been as rudimentary as the one he had left behind him. Bede says that 'there were very few houses beside the church… indeed, no more than were barely sufficient for their daily residence'. It would doubtless have been made from wood, wattle and daub, and would have been bitterly cold in winter. He would have had his own bed, but definitely no Slumberland mattress. A monk called Adomnan said he had 'for his couch the bare rock, and for his pillow a stone'.

Not that there was time for much rest. This was a life of prayer that makes boot camp look like Club Med. The drowsy monks left the comparative luxury of their hard beds at two o'clock in the morning for matins, a service that went on for about an hour. In bigger monasteries there were wakers who prowled round carrying lamps to shine in the faces of those who were dozing off. The monks then went back to their cells for a few winks before lauds at dawn, followed by mass, then terce, sext at noon, nones at three in the afternoon, vespers at six, and compline just before going to bed again at eight or nine. All these services were lengthy and in Latin. No wonder that even a stone pillow didn't stop the monks getting off to sleep!

Their life was not only hard – the monks were also subject to rigorous discipline. There were set punishments for a variety of offences, including snatching an extra half-hour of sleep. Judging from the Rule of St Benedict, these could range from a beating to having to prostrate yourself in front of the brethren – 'lie stretched, face down in silence before the door of the oratory at the feet of all who pass out. And let him do this until the Abbot judgeth that it is enough. When he then cometh at the Abbot's bidding, let him cast himself at the Abbot's feet, then at the feet of all, that they may pray for him.'

But much of their discipline was self-administered. Monks believed that the body was a hindrance to the life of the spirit. Some submitted themselves to acts of mortification of the flesh. Others practised 'white martyrdom', whereby they retired into solitude and a life of fasting and prayer. But a few went even further. St Cuthbert of Lindisfarne was famous for his acts of endurance, which won respect from the tough Saxons.

> *Here also, as elsewhere, he* [Cuthbert] *would go forth, when others were asleep, and having spent the night in watchfulness return home at the hour of morning-prayer. Now one night, a brother of the monastery, seeing him go out alone followed him privately to see what he should do. But when he left the monastery, he went down to the sea, which flows beneath, and going into it, until the water reached his neck and arms, spent the night in praising God. When the dawn of day approached, he came out of the water, and, falling on his knees, began to pray again. Whilst he was doing this, two quadrupeds, called otters, came up from the sea, and, lying down before him on the sand, breathed upon his feet, and wiped them with their hair after which, having received his blessing, they returned to their native element. Cuthbert himself returned home in time to join in the accustomed hymns with the other brethren.*
>
> **Bede's *Life of St Cuthbert***

If a novice, fresh from the country, thought that this massive dose of spirituality and churchgoing would get him out of the daily chores that were the Churl's lot, he was sadly mistaken. St Benedict's Rule was based on the insight that too much spirituality was a bad thing unless it was grounded in reality. Work was fundamental to a monk's life. So he had to throw himself into wood-cutting, sheep-rearing, ploughing and harvesting as well as indulging in more monkish pursuits. For practical reasons, the hours of work changed with the seasons, as stipulated by the Rule of St Benedict:

> From Easter till the calends of October, they go out in the morning from the first till about the fourth hour, to do the necessary work, but that from the fourth till about the sixth hour they devote to reading. After the sixth hour, however, when they have risen from table, let them rest in their beds in complete silence; or if, perhaps, anyone desireth to read for himself, let him so read that he doth not disturb others. Let None[s] be said somewhat earlier, about the middle of the eighth hour; and then let them work again at what is necessary until Vespers.

Apart from the general business of everyday survival, there was a specialist task the monks did that must qualify as a Worst Job.

Illuminator

The abbeys of Lindisfarne and Iona are best known for their illuminated manuscripts. Every monastery had a scriptorium, or writing room, where books were made and copied. Like the other buildings in the monastery, this was usually a simple thatched-roofed construction, and it was in such simple huts that western learning was preserved for posterity. In the dark days of the sixth and seventh centuries, making copies of books was part of the great missionary effort to keep Christian culture alive, and it was assigned to the less practical brethren.

The Gospels were vital to the missionary activities of the Church. Although much preaching and conversion were done via the spoken word, churches and monasteries needed to ensure doctrinal uniformity. This stimulated a great demand for written texts. British missionaries to the Continent were constantly sending urgent requests to foundations back home for basic works. It's the elaborate so-called carpet pages of the Celtic manuscripts that get all the attention, but the real hard work was in laboriously copying out page after page of text. The monks reproduced all sorts of books: not only bibles and liturgical works, theology, and the works of the Church Fathers, but also classical texts by authors such as Cicero, Plato and Aristotle. If it seems an easy option compared to ploughing, think again.

THE BEST & WORST OF TIMES

878 Battle of Edington. Alfred defeats the Vikings.

978 The Saxon King Edward the Martyr is murdered. Ethelred the Unready takes over.

Medieval portraits show monks writing in books that were bound. This is an artistic fiction. Writing was done on individual sheets of vellum, which were only later incorporated into a book. They worked on benches, and used animal horns for inkwells. They literally carved the letters on to the page. Once lines had been ruled to ensure the writing was straight, the monks pricked the vellum to provide a join-the-dots guide to the letters. It was more like tattooing than writing with a fountain pen. The ink was hard to erase, so this fiddly work was vital because it avoided mistakes.

Everything they needed had to be made first. For the ink, they needed to hunt out a suitable oak tree and find some wasp eggs in it. The wasps inject their eggs into the bark of the tree. They die soon afterwards but, when the eggs hatch, they release saliva. The bark reacts, producing a hard layer around the larvae known as a 'gall'. These galls have an outer wall, a spongy fibre layer and a hard, seed-like structure in which the gall wasp grub develops. The monks collected these galls from the tree, crushed them with a pestle and mortar, mixed in vitriol (iron sulphate) and gum Arabic and added vinegar, egg white, rain water, beer or wine to get the consistency and acid balance right.

Thus equipped, the hard work could begin. The north-east of England is not a place to sit for hours on end without heating, but that is what the monks on Lindisfarne had to do. They needed the daylight to save their eyesight, but windows weren't glazed in the Dark Ages. Monks constantly complained of the difficulty of writing in their draughty huts. Copying was painstakingly slow and required enormous concentration. Minor mistakes could be scraped off with a knife, but a big splodge meant starting the whole page again. And, although they were sitting still, the scribes' work was physically demanding.

Anonymous monks have left us a record of what this Worst Job felt like. In later medieval manuscripts they doodled in the margins of their texts, leaving us tantalizing human insights into what went into the preservation of western culture before the age of printing. 'The art of writing is difficult,' one moans. 'It tires the eyes, wearies the back and sends cramps through the arms and legs.' Another simply says, 'My God, it's cold.' While a third celebrates the end of a day in the scriptorium with 'I have finished my work, now give me a bottle of wine!'

These shivering scribes produced unforgettable works that were also highly valuable. The top manuscripts were given covers encrusted with jewels and precious metals. This meant that the monasteries became targets for invaders. In the eighth century the Vikings began to raid the British mainland. Many hundreds of hours of labour were either stolen for their cover or ransomed back to the community. In AD 793 the Vikings destroyed Lindisfarne and purloined the famous Gospels, though they were thankfully recovered after a dip in the sea.

Over the next hundred years these attacks got worse and worse. In AD 865 the Viking 'Great Army' landed in East Anglia. By AD 875 the Scandinavian invaders had conquered the kingdoms of Mercia and Northumbria. Then in

Besides preserving Latin civilization, literacy and Christianity, the Celtic monastic communities made their own unique contribution to western art. Illuminated manuscripts are some of the greatest works of art produced in western Europe and are certainly among the best created in Britain prior to the Renaissance. The magnificent Book of Kells was made in Iona, and the Lindisfarne Gospels were produced in honour of St Cuthbert by Eadfrith around AD 700 on Holy Island. This is the opening page of St Luke's Gospel – but works like this are simply the tip of a manuscript iceberg.

877, they attacked Wessex, and King Alfred had to flee to the Somerset marshes to regroup his forces. (This is the period from which the story of the burnt cakes comes.) But the next year he decisively beat the Viking army at the Battle of Edington, and forced them to confine themselves to the so-called Danelaw in the north and east of England.

But all this carnage couldn't have happened without someone being prepared to splosh around in a bog looking for the raw materials from which all the axes, swords and spears were made.

Bog Iron Hunter

The Bog Iron Hunter did exactly what it says on the tin. He hunted for iron in a bog. Imagine the wettest and coldest your feet have ever been. Now think of that as a constant state, and you have the daily grind of some of the least fortunate people in Anglo-Saxon England.

The Bog Iron Hunter was near the bottom of the social pecking order, either a lowly paid servant or a slave working to the command of a smith or iron smelter. Iron ore was found in lumps in bogs and marshes among tussocky grass and squishy mud. The demand was huge. In some areas smiths needed 30 or 40 kilos of bog ore a day. The ore was found in 1- or 2-kilo lumps dispersed round marshy areas. Which added up to a lot of hunting.

Armed with a long metal spike, the Bog Iron Hunter trudged through the mud, sticking it into likely looking places. Out in all weathers, his only reward was the sound of metal hitting bog ore. When he heard the tell-tale clunk, he would get down on his hands and knees, thrust his hand into the mire, haul out the lump, put it in a basket and carry on. If he got enough ore, he knew he'd be given a meal.

But smelted iron ore was useless if the metal couldn't be heated to a sufficiently high temperature. Wood didn't produce enough heat. You needed charcoal, and for that you needed another tedious, and unpleasant, job. You've heard scare stories about the hours junior doctors work. They were mere part-timers compared to the Saxon Charcoal Burner.

Charcoal Burner

The Saxon word col meant charcoal. Coal as we know it wasn't mined until the very end of the Saxon period in 1054, when monks in South Wales began digging for it at Margam. Before that, the only 'coal' apart from charcoal that the Saxons knew was 'sea-coal': the strange black lumps that got washed up on the seashore from subterranean seams. It was an extra fuel-for-free, but there just wasn't enough of it to be used as a staple fuel.

Charcoal is essentially concentrated wood. The process of charcoal-burning involved taking fresh wood, and baking the water out of it. This was done by charring it at a slow, controlled rate, so it didn't catch fire and turn to ash. To make sure this didn't happen, the amount of air feeding the fire was controlled, by covering the charring wood in an earth kiln known as a clamp.

Charcoal was the only combustible substance that generated enough heat for blacksmiths and other craftsmen to do their valuable work. So it had to be made in vast quantities – a time-consuming, difficult process.

The Worst Job of Charcoal Burner involved staying awake for four or five days and nights at a stretch. Come rain or shine, the Burners would sit monitoring a vast pile of smouldering wood, waiting for the white smoke issuing from the earth kiln to turn blue. One moment of inattention could mean missing a crack in the kiln. A sleepy Charcoal Burner who woke up to find flames shooting up in the air would lose tons of charcoal and days of heavy work. To avoid this, they sat on one-legged stools, so that if they nodded off, they toppled over.

They lived a semi-nomadic life in the woods. They camped where they worked, their quarters determined by the need to watch the kiln constantly. They worked alongside woodsmen, using the wood that was too small or misshapen to be used in building. They had to collect 12 tons of wood – coppiced hazel, ash or hornbeam – to make a 3-ton clamp of charcoal. Then they spent another day or so shifting enough earth to make a large mound up to 7 metres across. Only once this was complete were they ready to start the burn.

A Charcoal Burner's work was extremely tiring. Even if he had a son or assistant to take turns on watch, it meant an entirely unnatural sleep pattern. It was unhealthy too. He was constantly breathing in wood smoke.

Once the process was completed, he had to empty the kiln. It was essential to make sure that the charcoal was properly cold, otherwise it could reignite without warning. After his seventy-two- or ninety-six-hour shift, the Charcoal Burner had to wait to do this at night. In the day, hot charcoal looks white, but in the dark you can see its red glow.

There was one final job before he moved on to the next settlement in need of his labour. He had to dig up and bag the burnt soil from the base of the clamp. This dusty, burnt earth was a more valuable resource than the charcoal itself. It was the only material that provided a truly efficient seal for his next kiln; fresh soil was too porous.

For all this work there was little reward, but it was a very common occupation. Charcoal Burners were a familiar sight throughout two millennia of British history. In fact charcoal burning is one of the longest-lived Worst Jobs in this book. Even today there are Charcoal Burners. Buy a bag of traditional British charcoal for your barbecue in your local DIY store, and it will have been made by one of around a thousand charcoal burners still active in the woods and forests of Britain today.

THE BEST & WORST OF TIMES

1012 Ethelred pays the Vikings the equivalent of 20,000 kilos of gold to prevent them sacking his kingdom. Much of the Coin Thralls' work now ends up in Scandinavia.

1013 Ethelred is driven off the throne and replaced by the Viking King Canute.

1066 King Harold, the last Saxon king, is crowned. Nine months later he defeats the Vikings, but Saxon rule comes to an end with the Battle of Hastings and the Norman invasion.

How to Burn Charcoal

You need thirty to forty hours of spare time, some wideawake pills and four tons of wood. The result will be a ton of charcoal and some unique additions to your vocabulary.

1 Make your pitstead: *Remove the turf from a circle with a diameter of approximately 3 metres. Sieve out any stones, as these will explode in the heat.*

2 Build your clamp: *Erect a large pile of wood around a central stake, using branches and secondary wood, not the main trunks of trees. Put a 'motty peg' in the top. This is a peg that has a hole in it so that it can be removed easily. Collect bracken and ferns. Pack this over the wood. Sieve the previously burnt topsoil, to make an outer coating for the whole mound. This coating is known as the 'sammel'. Pack it over the top of the heap of wood, bracken and ferns to form an airtight layer. Fifteen centimetres from the ground leave a gap called the 'flipe'. This will allow air to enter the clamp from underneath.*

3 Start the burn: *Set up windbreaks or twisted branches called 'withy screens' to ensure the wind doesn't affect the fire. Remove the motty peg and drop in some blazing coals. When the fire gets going, pack the hole with charcoal and seal off with turfs in a 'collar'. This is called 'capping off'. NB: Cap off about six hours after the fire has been lit, when the temperature reaches 270°C. Make holes in the top of the clamp. Watch the smoke – it turns from white to brown, and then to blue. This is the crucial time. When the roast drives the water out of the wood, the sammel is prone to crack. If this happens, too much air will enter and the clamp will burn up. It is constantly shrinking, so cracks will continually appear. When the smoke goes blue, fill up the holes and make others further down the clamp. Charcoal chars from the top down. When blue smoke appears from the lowest holes, all the charcoal will have been made.*

4 Extinguish the clamp: *Rake off a section of the baked sammel while your assistant tips water into the clamp. Then reseal the clamp and watch it for twenty-four hours until cool. Then rake out the charcoal.*

But if the Charcoal Burner was poorly rewarded for his lengthy shifts, at least he got some recompense for his hard labour. One worker who owed his job to the charcoal made by the Burner wasn't so lucky.

Coin Thrall

King Alfred established a system of 'burhs', or forts. Some were refurbished Roman settlements, others were brand new and constructed from timber and earth. Burhs were extremely successful as bases for beating off the Vikings. Traders felt secure to do business inside their walls – so much so, that soon they began to operate mints. In time, many of these settlements flourished and became some of England's earliest successful cities.

Coins had been made in Britain since pre-Roman times. But it was the Saxons who introduced the basic coin of the penny in AD 765. Much of the economy of the Dark Ages was done by barter and payment in kind but, as the country became more stable, coinage became more important. When Alfred the Great pinned back the Vikings into the Danelaw, coinage and trade were given an additional boost.

Mints were officially under the control of the monarch. But the King licensed them out to moniers, supplying them with dies or moulds to produce the official coinage. Moniers were rich men who could literally make a mint from creating the local coinage on the King's behalf. But the four or five workers they had under them didn't share in the profits. Occasionally the men working in the mints were paid, but usually they were slaves called thralls who had the ultimately frustrating task of spending their day awash in money while receiving not a penny in payment.

And the lack of cash wasn't compensated by job satisfaction. Theirs was an early version of the dullest sort of piecework.

The Coin Thrall's job was simply to stamp the pattern on the coins. A smith (using charcoal) heated a silver bar until it was red-hot. It was then cooled, not in water, but in a substance that will run like a golden stream through this book. It is one of the most versatile substances in the world of Worst Jobs: stale urine. The minerals in urine made it especially effective for the rapid cooling of silver.

When cold, the bar was hammered out flat. Then either blank discs were cut out with a cutter similar to a pastry cutter, or the coins were roughly hand-cut and then trimmed off.

Next came the Coin Thrall's moment of glory. He put the blank on a die fastened to a bench, then put another die on top, and bashed it with a hammer, making a pattern on both sides of the coin.

It takes forty words to describe the process in the fanciest way possible. But the job itself wasn't half so exciting. Day after day, the poor thrall would

In earlier Saxon times all the local kings had their own coins. This penny was made for Offa, King of Mercia (AD 757-96), the man responsible for Offa's Dyke.

work his way through mounds of silver blanks, creating hundreds of kilos of currency. The temptation to pilfer must have been enormous. But if he succumbed, the penalties were fierce.

If the coins were judged too small, the Coin Thrall would be suspected of clipping the coins, creating a little store of trims to melt down and sell. This counted as defacing the King's image (still an offence today). It was also theft. It was punished by castration.

Even his boss, the monier, was not safe if he decided to embezzle. If he was found to be making lightweight coins or using the wrong mixture of metal, he was mutilated. Under Alfred's grandson, Aethelstan, every burh had to have a mint, which was assigned a set number of moniers. The king instituted a system of harsh laws to control the weight and quality of coins.

Thirdly: that there be one money over all the king's dominion, and that no man mint except within port. And if the moneyer be guilty, let the hand be struck off that wrought the offence, and, be set up on the money-smithy but it be an accusation, and he is willing to clear himself; then let him go to the hot iron, and clear the hand therewith with which he is charged that fraud to have wrought. And if at that ordeal he should be guilty, let the like be done as here before ordained.

Unfortunately much of the Coin Thrall's hard work went abroad in unintentional exports. The pressure of Viking expansionism did not relent until the eleventh century, but instead of mounting a full-scale defence of the realm like King Alfred, the English King Ethelred the Unready (so called because he was poorly advised, i.e. 'unread') simply tried to buy peace by paying Danegeld, or tribute. It was a hefty form of protection money to stop the Vikings sacking his kingdom. In 991, he paid them gold weighing 10,000 kilos. But like East End heavies, when they realized Ethelred was a soft touch, the Vikings came back for more. In 1012 Ethelred coughed up a further 20,000 kilos of tribute. Imagine the effect on the economy. There have been almost as many finds of English Saxon coins in Denmark as in England.

But what of the Vikings? They may have made life miserable for everyone living within raiding distance of the coast, but they also had to do some pretty grim jobs themselves.

Olaus Magnus in 1555 shows well-clothed professional coin-makers hammering out what appear to be hot cross buns. Eight hundred years earlier our Coin Thrall would have been working in rags, straining to stamp the design on far smaller silver discs.

Viking Worst Jobs

The popular image we have of the Vikings is the one they would have wanted: leaping out of their dragon-headed ships, rushing up the beach in full battle gear and throwing themselves on their terrified enemy. Think Viking, think epic. They didn't have horns in their helmets. That's an invention of cartoonists and hen-night male strippers, but they were self-consciously heroic. Like the Saxons, they had a warrior culture in which the greatest glory was individual military prowess, and even Valhalla, their heaven, was a divine version of a warlord's victory feast. They had names like Eric Bloodaxe and Thorfinn the Mighty, and they made sure their achievements were highly exaggerated in popular poetry.

There's no doubt they were tough. They had to be. In order to raid, they had to undergo terrible hardship. They spent nights in open boats on the freezing North Sea.

Their speedy longships were 'clinker-built', that is, built around a solid keel extending from fore to aft. Overlapping planks were then fixed along this central line, either nailed or sometimes simply lashed, giving them extra flexibility, so they could ride over the waves rather than take the impact of the swell. But there was a price to pay. There were gaps in the planking, which

The elegantly curved remains of a longboat in the Viking Ship Museum, one of a number of ships sunk in a fjord circa 1100 to act as a barrier to invaders.

were probably filled with moss, animal hair and tar, but the ships were still prone to being swamped. So someone had to constantly bail out the water, whatever the weather. The fourteenth-century Icelandic tale *Grettir's Saga* refers to 'bucket or pot-bailing, a very troublesome and fatiguing process'. The crew, who are lumbered with a particularly leaky boat, are complaining of numbed, frozen fingers. The hero, Grittir, wins friends by bailing so rapidly that he needs eight men to empty the buckets which he passes up from the bottom of the boat.

Another saga, *The Seafarer*, tells of the hardship endured at sea:

> *How I have often suffered times of hardship*
> *In days of toil, and have experienced*
> *Bitter anxiety, my troubled home*
> *On many a ship has been the heaving waves,*
> *Where grim night watch has often been my lot*
> *At the ships prow as it beat past the cliffs.*
> *Oppressed by cold my feet were bound by frost*
> *In icy bonds, while worries simmered hot*
> *About my heart, and hunger from within*
> *Tore the sea-weary spirit. He knows not,*
> *Who lives most easily on land, how I*
> *Have spent my winter on the ice-cold sea,*
> *Wretched and anxious, in the paths of exile,*
> *Lacking dear friends, hung round by icicles,*
> *While hail flew past in showers.*

But sleeping out on the high seas and numbing your hands with icy water was just the start of a Viking's troubles. The hard work really began when you got within sight of land and the captain gave the order for portaging.

Portager

Portaging means carrying. When ordered to do so, every Viking became a portager, including the women we know were frequently on board. It's an almost perversely difficult job. The Vikings would, if necessary, pick up their longships, which were perfectly suited to the element of water, and push them overland.

It's not quite as mad as it sounds.

Vikings had some of the most technologically advanced ships of the age. Under sail, they could get from Denmark to England in a day and a night. But close to shore or when the wind wasn't favourable, they had to resort to back-breaking muscle power. The mast would come down and the oars were run out. Anyone who has rowed a boat in earnest knows how tough an exercise that is. Imagine pulling against the wind and tide for days on end. If there were two fjords, rivers or inlets separated by a shortish distance of land, the Vikings would often choose to take the longship overland. By deploying this technique they could also leapfrog rivers, enabling them to penetrate much further inland than their enemies suspected.

We know about portaging from illustrations such as those of the artist Olaus Magnus in his history of Scandinavia, *Historia de Gentibus Septentrionalibus*, published in 1555. Although it was tough work, they had to handle the boat delicately in order to avoid damage. Viking ship planks were split radially from long trees, but this was a tricky and time-consuming process, so repairs away from home were not a good idea. To protect the keel and stop it sinking into the earth, they pushed their boats along on wooden runners.

First the boat was beached and most of the dead weight – masts, chests, spare cordage, etc. – was taken out. Then straight wooden logs were split in half and laid flat side down at right angles to the direction the boat was to travel. The idea was that, as the ship was pushed forwards over these runners, a relay of men would run from the rear bringing the logs that had been passed to the head of the queue. And to make this process easier, they smeared lubricant on the logs. The latest theory suggests halibut oil, although in reality anything to hand would have sufficed. It is probable that rotting fish innards or small fish were also used, or even fatty lard left over from a high-calorie meal. Given the smell of two-week-old mackerel, rubbing it over pine logs can't have been one of the most gloriously epic aspects of Viking life!

Nevertheless when you're involved in the hard slog of portaging, you're more than thankful for the fish oil. The long oars that rub hands sore in a matter of minutes are slotted through holes in the sides of the ship, and used for the pushers to get a purchase. Then the team heaves forward – the crew divided between pushers, log shifters, and those guiding the ship – along the centre of the logs. The trick is timing. Once a momentum is achieved, it hurtles along. The danger is that you run off course and plough the boat into the earth, or grind to a halt when you run out of track, because the log shifters can't keep up. The whole exercise leaves you hot, exhausted, and reeking of fish, only marginally relieved by the elation as the ship finally slides into the water at your destination.

So after the more scrupulous Vikings had washed their hands, what food could they look forward to for their celebration dinner? Their options were limited. There was fresh fish, smoked fish, rock-hard salt cod, or perhaps a little delicacy that catapults any Viking job involving its consumption into the Worst Job category: fermented shark.

This is still a delicacy today in Iceland and Greenland, but has yet to make any impact on the London restaurant scene. There must once have been some anonymous person who tried the flesh of fresh Greenland shark without first fermenting it. They didn't write about the experience because it contains cyanide. In order for it to be safe to eat, the flesh has to buried in the ground (after gutting, and removing the cartilage and head), and left for six weeks in summer or three months in winter. During this time, bacteria breaks down the cyanide, and fluid drains from the shark meat. Some historians believe that in ancient times, the bacterial process was kick-started by urinating on the flesh before burial. When the fermented shark finally emerges from its grave, it is soft and smells of ammonia. It is then washed and hung in a drying shack for another two months. Then, and only then, can you hack off the brown crust that forms over it, cut the flesh into small pieces, and tuck in. By now it has the consistency of soft cheese.

Men aboard the Viking longship replica, Hugin. *With a favourable wind the feared 'Dragon Boats' with their characteristic heads could achieve speeds that match a motor boat today.*

So the Vikings ate foul food, their lives were hard and sometimes they had to get out of their ships and push them. But every other job they did was a picnic compared to the Worst Job of all.

The Worst Job of All: Guillemot Egg Collector

For the writer the very Worst Job in the millennium before the Norman invasion was the deliriously dangerous and exposed life of the Guillemot Egg Collector. For him a day at the office meant dangling a hundred metres above raging seas, clutching at bird-poo-covered ledges, while filling a basket with eggs.

Why guillemots? Was keeping chickens impossibly namby-pamby for the testosterone-loaded Vikings?

No, of course they kept chickens, but this was food for free. Guillemots were large enough to make collecting their eggs worthwhile. The Vikings brought their food with them when they were raiding, or stole it when they arrived. But they often had to winter away from home. Food was scarce, particularly in the remoter parts of Scotland and along the rocky coasts of England. The spring brought a sudden glut of available food when seabirds congregated on the cliffs to breed. The innocent guillemots bred in such numbers that the population could easily withstand the loss of a few hundred eggs. For the Vikings, it was like taking candy off a baby.

So long as you had a rope.

And that's where the Worst Job part comes. For someone not over-fond of heights, it is dizzyingly scary. It is bad enough walking backwards off a cliff with the benefits of steel clips, karabiners and high-tensile climbing rope, but in the ninth century they had to do it in their tunics with bare feet or flimsy sandals, and with a rope made from stinging nettles.

Nettles were harvested for many reasons in the Dark Ages. (Nettle harvesting in itself could qualify as a Worst Job.) The leaves were cooked and eaten, or steeped in water to soak out the formic acid, the water then being used as a simple pesticide. And the fibrous stalks could be processed in much the same way as flax (see flax-retting. page 66) to produce thread, which was woven into clothing, or twisted into strands for rope.

The job of Egg Collector was simple. To prepare himself for the action, he passed his rope through his left hand, under his groin and around his right hip, across the front of his torso and over his left shoulder. This method allows friction to act as the braking force – not very comfortable! The rope end was tied to a nearby tree or rock, and two or three mates would help lower and raise him, while another let down a basket for the eggs.

Of course, accidents happened. The rope would have got frayed on the sharp rock; knots would have come undone. But the fear of heights and the constant feeling of vulnerability are unrelated to the statistical likelihood of something going wrong. Egg collecting must have felt dangerous even when the job was going well.

It was extremely taxing. Guillemots lay eggs directly on to the cliff ledges. They are long and pointed so that they tend to roll round their own axis rather than off the ledge if jogged. But they are still vulnerable. The collector had to move very quietly and delicately through the nesting birds. Any sudden movements or slips could send a whole cloud of guillemots squawking off the cliff face, knocking eggs as they went. Moving without disturbing them required great strength, clutching on to the rope to stop it cutting into the groin. The cliff face was exposed to the weather, which was frequently foul, and the tens of thousands of seabirds would leave footholds slippery with guano. Losing his footing would have meant scuffed knees and legs for the Egg Collector, or being left dangling on the end of the line like a conker. In addition, although guillemots are docile enough, other seabirds such as herring gulls and skuas can be more aggressive, buzzing anyone who comes too near their nest sites.

The guillemot: about the same size as a wood pigeon, it provides a tasty meal. Puffins and guillemots are still eaten in the Faroe Islands and Iceland, where they are called Black Birds.

Left: I'd never abseiled before I went over this 100-metre cliff looking for eggs (hens' eggs, not protected guillemots' eggs). I lost my leather Saxon shoes and ended up with lacerated knees and toes. A high price to pay for an omelette.

Opposite: The practice of collecting guillemot eggs went on in Yorkshire until the nineteenth century. The men who did it were known as 'climmers'. This picture of climmers on Flamborough Head is provided by the RSPB, who run the site as a nature reserve.

Given the risky nature of this Worst Job, you'd think it would have disappeared as soon as there was enough of a food supply to make it redundant. Not a bit of it. In some parts of Britain the practice continued until the nineteenth century. Fortunately, today the guillemot is a listed species throughout the British Isles. The job is now extinct, and the guillemot can nest in peace.

In 1066, the age of Viking raids came to an abrupt end. Harald Hardrada, one of the most feared warriors in Europe, led a massive fleet up the River Ouse to Yorkshire. This serious invasion attempt was repelled by King Harold II of England at the Battle of Stamford Bridge. His victory was so comprehensive that the Vikings sailed home, swearing not to return. They kept their promise and England was never again plagued by raiding Norsemen. In other circumstances this triumph would have put Harold on the highest military pedestal. But the victory was overshadowed by his defeat three weeks later at the Battle of Hastings. The death of Harold, the last Anglo-Saxon king, marked the end of one era and the beginning of another. With William the Conqueror came a new people (ironically descended from the Vikings), and a new set of Worst Jobs.

CHAPTER TWO

Middle Ages
Worst Jobs

Historical terms are seldom as tidy as we'd like them to be, and the 'Middle Ages' is perhaps the least precise of them all. It was coined centuries ago to denote the transition period between the amorphous 'ancient period' and 'the modern era', which begins with the Tudors. As such, it's virtually useless. One day no doubt it will be so distant that we'll stop calling it 'Middle' and find another name, but for now it's all we've got.

The problem is, it's almost impossible to pinpoint when the Middle Ages began. The Saxon period ended neatly with the Norman invasion of 1066 and the complete ethnic replacement of the English aristocracy. But the seeds of the social change that were to grow into what historians call the medieval period were sown well before William the Conqueror loaded up his boats for his hopeful English expedition.

Nevertheless, whenever it started, the Middle Ages is the period when Worst Jobs really began to come into their own. As towns coalesced round Saxon and Celtic settlements, and evolved their own complex economic structure, individuals started to specialize. Tasks previously performed as part of everyday life became distinct 'jobs'. The newly specialized workers soon formed themselves into guilds to set rules and standards for their job. This didn't necessarily stop their jobs being horrible. But it did keep the riff-raff out.

Getting a prescription thirteenth-century style. A physician dictates the recipe while his assistant makes up the remedy.

If anything defines the Middle Ages it is the slow breaking down of the feudal system that William the Conqueror and his Norman warriors rigorously imposed. This system, in which loyalty and service were given in return for land, had the King at its head. The great barons fought for him in exchange for their territory and titles, and at the bottom of the heap were the serfs who were 'un-free', virtually owned by their lords and masters. If you were part of the new class of free, skilled yeoman, it is perhaps understandable that you didn't want to be confused with the scummy lower classes who ploughed the fields.

Compared with later periods, the pace of change in medieval times was slow: evolution, rather than revolution. It's sometimes tempting to think of the entire 400 years as one long, grim Worst Job, with imagery supplied from Monty Python's *Holy Grail*. But it wouldn't have appeared like that to the workers. They undoubtedly saw themselves as living in modern times. At key moments, even the lowest-paid labourers would have been staggered by the cutting-edge technology changing their lives. Newly invented harnesses enabled them to use horses instead of oxen for ploughing. Windmills made grinding corn much less arduous. And in the thirteenth century, water-wheels powered the first industrial machinery to make the Worst Job of fulling more bearable.

And the medieval landscape changed too. High, defensive walls were erected around cities such as London and York. Vast new castles, monasteries and cathedrals were built using imported technologies. Likewise, stone manor houses and parish churches sprang up in villages across the country. For a couple of centuries much of Britain was a building site.

But for most of us it's not stones and mortar that sum up the Middle Ages, it's the iconic image of the knight in shining armour. Perhaps this is the result of an overdose of poorly-researched films and TV series about King Arthur, Ivanhoe and the like, because the reality is that plate armour was only developed half-way through the period.

Nevertheless, virtually all the main political landmarks along the medieval timeline are battles. There's the Battle of Hastings. Then the Crusades, the misjudged and brutal international Christian campaign to recapture Jerusalem that lasts over a century; then the English against the Scots at Stirling Bridge and Bannockburn; the English with their devastating longbowmen against the French at Crécy and Agincourt; and finally the battle at which the era ended: Bosworth, where Richard III became the last English monarch to die in battle.

The battles were real enough, but the image of the gentle knight is largely a fiction. The ideal values of chivalry were promoted from the twelfth century onwards in manuals for servants and in literature, especially the stories of King Arthur and the Knights of the Round Table. But these were stories as remote from the realities of medieval warfare as Biggles is from the horrors of the trenches. In reality, chivalry was often honoured more in the breach than the observance. It's true that the armour shone, at least at the beginning of a battle. But this wasn't down to the Good Knight, with his rag and tin of Brasso. It was the unenviable task of the Arming Squire.

THE BEST & WORST OF TIMES

1066 At the Battle of Stamford Bridge King Harold ensures that there will never be another Viking invasion of Britain. Three weeks later he is defeated at the Battle of Hastings by the Normans, who are descended from the Vikings!

1067 The Domesday Book is drawn up. It creates an accurate picture of the entire property and people the Normans have conquered.

1093 Building of Durham Cathedral begins.

1129 King Henry I institutes the Great Roll, his financial accounts, ensuring tedium for generations of Pipe Roll Transcribers (see page 67).

Arming Squire

The Arming Squire was the gentleman's gentleman in the Age of Chivalry. He was a young, unpaid apprentice on the lowest rung of the knightly ladder. His potential reward was to end up as a knight himself. This was just about the best job of the age, paying dividends in cash and glory, and all with comparatively little risk. The clanking aristocrats were pretty safe inside their plate metal. But what was life like for the boys who served them in the thirteenth to fifteenth centuries?

Shakespeare's Henry V *has formed our image of the Battle of Agincourt, including foot soldiers Nym and Bardolph. The reality was much grimmer and more crowded, with non-combatants doing the worst jobs.*

The short answer is crap. Literally. Thanks to film and television you never think of a battle lasting more than a few minutes. But in reality it could go on for hours. The fighting happened in brief intense spells of almost total confusion and terror, interspersed with brief refreshment breaks – a glass of wine or a sip of water. There certainly wasn't time to have a quick toilet break. A suit of armour had no fly buttons or quick-release trousers. If a knight wanted to relieve himself, he had to live with the result until the fighting was over.

So, throughout the day the knight would get very messy indeed. Outside, he would be splattered with mud and the blood of horses and men, and as for the inside… most battles in the Middle Ages were fought in summer. Even when standing still, a knight would have sweated buckets. Imagine how much would have poured off him during the height of battle. And that was just the top half. The bottom half would have been even worse, particularly if the knight had been very afraid. It would have been hell in there.

The worst part of the Arming Squire's job was to meet his master as he came back from battle and deal with this double layer of muck. Once the stinking armour had been stripped off and the knight served with a refreshing glass of wine, the Arming Squire had to get the armour clean and ready for the following day. He couldn't use water. That was too precious. Instead, he rubbed it down with an abrasive. The most efficient and least messy method was to put the pieces of armour in a barrel of sand, then roll it around. But in battle conditions, barrels and sand were likely to be in short supply, in which case the squire would scour the metal with a mixture of sand, vinegar and a little urine.

But tending to the armour was only part of the job. The Arming Squire was at the constant beck and call of his master. He had to dress him, lead his horse to battle, and wait on him at table using the appropriate etiquette. (An important part of this task was learning to carve his meat in the correct manner.) At night, he slept on the floor or by the door near his master's bed, ready for further instructions. He seldom took part in battle. He simply waited until his master returned, presumably with bated breath, because poor maintenance of the armour could mean the difference between life and death.

Getting a Knight Dressed

There were twenty-four separate pieces of armour in a knight's kit, weighing a massive 28 kilos. Underneath was a padded doublet lined with satin, and a pair of under-trousers called hose. Extra strips of blanket would be wrapped around his knees to protect them from rubbing against the metal. The first pieces of armour to be put on were the sabotons, *which were shoes made of chain mail. Next were* greaves *which went around the shins. The pieces for the upper legs, called* cuisses, *were buckled on to the leg with leather straps. A mail skirt was tied to the* points, *which were laces that hung down from the doublet. Then a padded backpiece and breastplate were added, along with the* vanbraces *and* gauntlets *that protected the knight's arms and hands. The most important piece of armour, the helm or helmet, was put on last.*

A mixture of sand, vinegar and urine – the Arming Squire's friend.

But there was plenty of arduous work to do before a squire got anywhere near the battlefield – 90 per cent of his time was spent travelling, actually finding the enemy and surviving. A foreign campaign meant two or three months on the road, with a couple of set battles and a bit of a skirmish if you were lucky.

Throughout this period of travelling and waiting, the knight would sit around entertaining his friends or reading the latest instalments of the stories of Lancelot and Guinevere. But the Arming Squire had no time for pot-boilers. He was hard at work. He had to oversee the raising and striking of camp. And knights didn't expect to rough it. They wanted the same quality of life they got at home. In Henry V's case this included bringing his own musicians. The squire had to ensure four-star comfort for his master. He was not only a non-commissioned officer; he was a roadie, a maître d' and a lavatory attendant.

Knights did not travel light. The 'Hastings' document from the mid-fifteenth century gives a list of 'What an Appellant shall bring to the field':

A tent must be put in the field
Also a chair
Also a basin
Also five loaves of bread
Also a gallon of wine
Also a messe of meat or fish
Also a board and a pair of trestles to sit his meat and drink on
Also a broad cloth
Also a knife to cut the meat
Also a cup to drink from
Also a glass with drink made
Also a dozen tresses of arming points
Also a hammer of pincers and a bichorn
Also a dozen arming points [rivets]
Also a spear, long sword, short sword and dagger
Also a kerchief to hele [cover] the visor of his bascinet
Also a pennant to bear in his hand during his avowing

To see what this meant in practice, let's take the most famous battle of the Middle Ages, the Battle of Agincourt. What would the Arming Squires have been doing in between all the 'Oh for a muse of fire'ing and 'Once more unto the breach'ing?

Before they got to the battlefield, the Arming Squires, along with the rest of the foot soldiers, tramped 260 miles in seventeen days, all the time protecting their cargo of armour, furniture, weapons and cutlery.

Henry V didn't intend to fight the Battle of Agincourt. He'd been sacking towns in northern France, but the campaigning season was coming to a close. On 8 October the knights and squires received the order to leave the town of Harfleur with eight days' rations because an epidemic of dysentery had broken out there. The plan was to escape from the disease, and head back to England via Calais.

But the French had other ideas. They lay in wait at the crossing point of the River Somme, so the English were forced to head up river looking for another way across. They trudged along in almost constant heavy rain. Every night the Arming Squires had to supervise the setting up of soggy tents and then attend to the rapidly rusting armour. Many had to nurse their masters through bouts of the dysentery that had travelled with the army from Harfleur. The army grew ever weaker, not only from disease but from the lack of food and clean water. Far more English died on the road to Agincourt than in the battle itself.

When they finally did find a way over the Somme, they discovered the French had blocked the road to Calais between the villages of Tremancourt and Agincourt. So Agincourt, the scene of one of the greatest victories in English history, was a decision forced on Henry.

The rains that had plagued the English now worked to their advantage. It made the ground in front of their position a quagmire, which trapped the French cavalry under a hail of English arrows. The French knights were protected by plate armour, but their horses weren't. Wounded steeds threw their riders into the mud, then careered through the close-packed ranks of French foot soldiers as they tried to shake off the hail of English arrows.

A squire's safety wasn't guaranteed simply because he didn't fight. He was part of an enormous retinue of non-combatants known as 'the baggage train', which included armourers and their assistants, bowyers, fletchers, cooks and the like, everything to keep the troops moving and fighting. This huge army within an army was highly vulnerable. According to Shakespeare's *Henry V*, at Agincourt the French slaughtered the baggage train. This was an attack so contrary to the rules of war that Henry fell into a rage and ordered his French prisoners to be killed. But perhaps Shakespeare's account should be taken with a pinch of salt. According to the rules of chivalry, captured knights were usually kept alive and ransomed back to their families. But at Agincourt, Henry had a logistical problem. The French prisoners overwhelmingly outnumbered their English captors, so he gave the barbaric order for them to be executed. The story of the attack on the baggage train could be a complete fiction to justify this act of carnage.

Occasionally a squire would be required to take the field at his lord's side. But he wouldn't have been as well protected as his master, so there was the risk of serious injury. And that meant almost certain death. There were no doctors

THE BEST & WORST OF TIMES

1150–80 Geoffrey of Monmouth and others produce the Arthurian Romances. They tell us a lot about medieval ideals, but little about medieval reality.

1150–80 Big advances in agriculture, including the invention of windmills and the horse harness.

1170 Murder of Thomas à Becket, making the new Canterbury Cathedral an international centre of pilgrimage.

1189 King Richard the Lionheart abandons his twin kingdoms of France and England to lead the Third Crusade.

on the battlefield, no St John's Ambulance running around with stretchers. The archers who won the day at Agincourt had one final job to do once the fighting had stopped. They prowled through the blood-soaked battlefield looking for those who were seriously injured. Any who were found were put out of their misery with a dagger plunged into the slot in their visor, or thrust up into their belly via the vulnerable genital region where there was thick padding but no chain mail or plate armour.

Being an Arming Squire was tough, tiring and messy. He could easily end up with his innards hanging out on the battlefield. But if all a lad wanted in life was blood, guts and the tang of human excreta he didn't have to travel halfway across Europe. He could simply get involved in the murky world of medieval medicine.

Barber Surgeon

Who would you run to if your hand got badly mangled? A) An astrologer; B) A doctor in Accident and Emergency; or C) The hairdresser? In the Middle Ages it wouldn't have been such an absurd choice, because the job of the Barber Surgeon combined all three skills.

This picture of noble physicians by Olaus Magnus tactfully omits the messier aspects of surgery.

All the major professions and trades were overseen by guilds, which set standards for qualifying members. Members of the Barber Surgeons' Guild were licensed to handle blades. They were qualified to shave off your beard, cut your hair or amputate your leg. The red-and-white striped pole, a common

sight outside barbers' shops until recently, was originally a graphic logo representing the Barber Surgeon's trade: the white symbolized bandages and the red symbolized blood from therapeutic bleeding.

Fees for consultations and surgery were high, so customers were few and far between. Consequently their hairdressing skills were particularly useful as they provided a steady income in lean times, along with the occasional bit of dentistry. On the down side, there was the risk of being sued, and the problem of collecting your fee. Many practitioners took bonds or security from their clients in case the operation went wrong and the patient refused to pay. But this was a risky business. For instance, in 1320, a patient called Alice Stockynge recovered £30 in damages, after a surgeon took 20 shillings' worth of belongings from her home because his bill hadn't been paid.

The most extreme part of the job was emergency surgery. Shattered limbs and gangrenous wounds needed to be amputated. There was no anaesthetic, so the Barber Surgeon cut through flesh and muscle, rolled the flesh up over the bone like the sleeve of a jumper, sawed through the bone of arm or leg and sewed up the skin, all to the accompaniment of screams of terror and a writhing body racked with pain. Speed was of the essence. Tools like the curved knife that sliced round a limb without repositioning the blade were invaluable.

But a Barber Surgeon also needed astrological skills. Medieval medicine was based on a 1,500-year-old pseudo science, derived not from anatomical study but from ancient mystical notions about the nature of the world. It was heavily influenced by the Greek writer Hippocrates, who said that the world was composed entirely of the four elements of earth, air, fire and water. Likewise, all human characters exhibited varying amounts of these qualities or 'humours'. A healthy person was one in whom all the four humours were correctly balanced.

Fifteen hundred years after the time of Hippocrates, there had been no essential change in this system of diagnosis. By looking at the patient's shape and complexion, a Surgeon could judge which of the four humours predominated in their character: sanguine, phlegmatic, choleric or melancholic. Then by analysing a sample of the patient's urine and comparing it with a chart, he could begin to see which humoral imbalance needed rectifying.

The author contemplates a clyster: long, cold and medically questionable but, in the right hands, possibly quite interesting.

That's when the Barber Surgeon's job got really unpleasant. In the Middle Ages there was no litmus paper or laboratory testing. A Barber Surgeon's examination of the patient involved taking a urine sample in a curvy flask appropriately called a Jordan. Then with the aid of a chart he'd make his diagnosis by examining, sniffing and actually tasting the urine.

Once the patient's symptoms had been identified, a cure was instigated. If a humour was in short supply or there was too much of it (a plethora), diet, exercise, purgatives, diuretics, emetics, blood-letting, or any combination of the above were prescribed.

*The Physician in Chaucer's Canterbury Tales **fits our medical picture exactly. He knows all about the stars and the humours. Chaucer also slyly points out that his fine red (sangwyn) clothes are gained from pestilence, but that the gold he earns is the best remedy of all.***

The clyster (see picture opposite) was used to administer enemas to get rid of bile. The long metal pipe had holes in one end. It had to be greased with lard and inserted at least 6 inches into the rectum until it was past the sphincter muscles. The recipe for the enema itself included a mixture of herbs, water, mallows, green camomile, wheat bran, salt, honey, assorted herbs and soap. A pig's bladder was filled with this concoction. It was then attached to the end of the clyster and squeezed hard to force the liquid through the holes and into the patient. This whole exercise may sound crude and outlandish but it gave the patients a rudimentary colonic irrigation, so may well have provided them with some benefit.

With us ther was a DOCTOUR OF PHISIK;
In al this world ne was ther noon hym lik,
To speke of phisik and of surgerye,
For he was grounded in astronomye.
He kepte his pacient a ful greet deel
In houres by his magyk natureel.
Wel koude he fortunen the ascendent
Of his ymages for his pacient.
He knew the cause of everich maladye
Were it of hoot, or coold, or moyste, or drye,
And where they engendred, and of what humour.
He was a verray, parfit praktisour:
The cause yknowe, and of his harm the roote,
Anon he yaf the sike man his boote.
Ful redy hadde he his apothecaries
To sende hym drogges and his letuaries…

Of his diete mesurable was he,
For it was of no superfluitee,
But of greet norissyng and digestible.
His studie was but litel on the Bible.
In sangwyn and in pers he clad was al,
Lyned with taffata and with sendal.
And yet he was but esy of dispence;
He kepte that he wan in pestilence.
For gold in phisik is a cordial,
Therefore he lovede gold in special.

The Canterbury Tales, General Prologue, 411–444

The clyster was also used to 'feed' weak patients. It was thought the stomach was a sort of furnace that sometimes grew so hot that feeble patients couldn't digest food properly. In such cases, food was pumped up the backside. This must have been deeply distressing for the patient, and sadly had no medical value whatsoever.

Just some of the barbaric-looking instruments in the Barber Surgeon's kit.

The most common and messy cure was blood-letting. Today the idea of taking an already enfeebled person and robbing them of a pint or so of blood seems absurd, but this was standard practice right up to the beginning of the nineteenth century.

The procedure was used for anything from headaches and eczema to 'evil humours' and general cleansing of the liver. For bleeding, a Barber Surgeon used his phleem. This was U-shaped, with a half-inch pointed blade like a thorn, which was pressed into the flesh, then removed and the other end inserted in order to keep the wound open and the blood flowing. Interestingly, the phleem was inserted at the same points as those used for acupuncture today.

In 1454 King Henry VI was treated for mental illness by three physicians and two surgeons, who prescribed the use of a variety of treatments for their psychologically distressed patients.

> *Pull their hair and nose, and squeeze the toes and fingers tightly, and cause pigs to squeal in their ears; give [them] a sharp clyster at the beginning… And open the vein of the head, or nose, or forehead, and draw blood from the nose with the bristles of a boar.*

Their specific treatment for King Henry was to:

> *Put a feather, or a straw, in his nose to compel him to sneeze, and do not ever desist from hindering him from sleeping; and let human hair and other evil smelling things be burnt under his nose. Apply, moreover, the cupping horn between the shoulders and let a feather be put down his throat, to cause vomiting, and shave the back of the head, and rub oil of roses and vinegar and smallage [wild celery] juice thereon.*

But the most popular form of bleeding was the administration of leeches. These voracious little worms were used widely in medieval medicine and surgery, so much so that 'leche' became another name for a surgeon. According to the eminent French surgeon Guy de Chauliac, in his *Chirurgia magna*, leeches were considered the best means of cleansing blood 'bytwene the depenesse of the body and the skyn'.

In 1454 King Henry VI was subjected to a variety of treatments, administered by physicians and surgeons, for mental illness.

THE BEST & **WORST** OF TIMES

1215 King John signs the Magna Carta. This is the beginning of the assertion of 'human rights' (though for the next few hundred years only the nobility are included).

1225 Foundations are laid for Salisbury Cathedral, the last of the great Gothic cathedrals.

1280s–90s English King Edward I attempts to conquer Scotland and Wales and unite the countries of Britain.

This may seem like a crude and primitive cure, but curiously it is the only part of medieval medicine still practised today. Leeches and their anti-coagulant saliva are employed to prevent clotting in severed limbs before they are stitched back on to their owners. The enthusiastic blood-suckers are also attached to re-grafted body-parts, for instance the end of sewn-on fingers, to encourage blood flow. Additionally they are used in the treatment of polycythemia, in which the blood cells become thick and sluggish.

It was the apothecary who supplied the Barber Surgeon with his leeches, but where did the apothecary get them from?

Leech Collector

One of the worst hazards of summer holidays has to be all those foreign bugs flying round your room keeping you awake all night. Who wants to be bitten or stung? Well, some people in the Middle Ages made a career out of it. All day, every day, they searched out thirsty leeches and encouraged them to bloat their little bodies with the blood from their feet and legs. Not as heroic as Buffy the Vampire Slayer, but no less unpleasant.

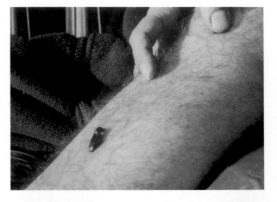

Leech Collectors operated nationwide. Many people think of leeches as exotic jungle-dwellers, but the medicinal leech, or *Hirudo medicinalis*, used to live in marshy areas right across Britain. The boggy parts of the Lake District and the Somerset Levels were particularly favoured hunting grounds. But leeches were so widely collected that they nearly became extinct. Today Romney March in Kent is one of the few places you can go to do a bit of authentic medieval leech hunting.

It's a pretty simple skill. Leech Collectors simply waded bare-legged into the shallow waters among the reeds, then jiggled around. The leeches sensed the motion and assumed it was being caused by a tasty sheep or cow come for a drink. If you were a lucky Leech Collector, they latched on to you.

Leeches leave a small incision mark in the shape of a 'Mercedes-Benz' sign, and can consume blood for twenty minutes or more, drinking five times their bodyweight before dropping off. A single bite may not be too bad; simply a tiny prick of pain. But quantity was what the collector was after, and he or she had to suffer countless sore patches. Although this was far from being the least pleasant aspect

of the Leech Collector's trade. Each wound can ooze up to 150 ml of blood in the ten hours following the bite, because leech saliva contains the anticoagulant hirudin. While drinking their dose of blood, leeches can infect their host with the bacterium *Acomones hydrophila*, which they carry in their gut, and which can cause diarrhoea and infect wounds.

We can only make informed guesses about the Leech Collectors' lives. We know the work was seasonal; leeches become semi-dormant in the colder months. But the few specific records come from a later time. Leech harvesters in the Lake District are referred to by the artist George Walker in his 1814 book, *The Costume of Yorkshire* as being mainly Scottish women, who rolled up their skirts and waded in the water. And an old, male leech collector in the Lake District is actually the subject of a superb Wordsworth poem, 'Resolution and Independence', published in 1807 (see below). But we know that not all

Romney Marsh in Kent, home to some of the last native leeches. And (top) the little charmer him- or herself (they are hermaphrodites). I'm hunting for leeches in waders (bottom) but in the Middle Ages everyone would have been bare-legged and would have emerged with a crop of leeches all over their legs, that were hastily transferred into a pail of water.

Leech Collectors were specialists. Thatchers coming to the same marshes to gather reeds for roofing all those medieval thatched cottages would often run a sideline in the leeches they picked up during the course of their work.

Resolution and Independence (extracts)

XI
Himself he propped, limbs, body, and pale face,
Upon a long grey staff of shaven wood:
And, still as I drew near with gentle pace,
Upon the margin of that moorish flood
Motionless as a cloud the old Man stood,
That heareth not the loud winds when they call;
And moveth all together, if it move at all.

XV
He told, that to these waters he had come
To gather leeches, being old and poor:
Employment hazardous and wearisome!
And he had many hardships to endure:
From pond to pond he roamed, from moor to moor;
Housing, with God's good help, by choice or chance;
And in this way he gained an honest maintenance.

XVIII
He with a smile did then his words repeat;
And said that, gathering leeches, far and wide
He travelled; stirring thus about his feet
The waters of the pools where they abide.
'Once I could meet with them on every side;
But they have dwindled long by slow decay;
Yet still I persevere, and find them where I may.'

William Wordsworth, 1802

THE BEST & WORST OF TIMES

1280s–90s The new, expensive must-have accessory for the state-of-the-art knight is plate armour. He also needs an Arming Squire to get him in and out of it.

1292 In a move which demonstrates the dark side of the religious zeal that built the cathedrals, all Jews are forcibly expelled from England.

1296 Battle of Stirling Bridge. William Wallace fights the English annexation of Scotland.

Wordsworth's Leech-gatherer (or collector) is an old Scottish man. The poet admires him for his innate nobility but his frailty and poverty show what a difficult job it was. The poem was composed in 1802. Already by that time leeches were hard to find – the victims of their own popularity!

If the collectors laboured at their trade day after day, they would have had permanently open wounds dripping blood down their legs, and dizziness from the consequent blood loss. They would also have been subject to skin infections and violent stomach upsets.

And the irony is that although Leech Collectors provided the basis for the whole medieval medical world, if they got sick they wouldn't have got the benefit of the Barber Surgeon's services because they wouldn't have been able to afford a consultation. Like other poor villagers, they had to rely on a less reputable medical practitioner.

Wise Woman

Many villages had a Wise Woman, completely untrained in the 'science' of Hippocrates, but with a firm grasp of folk remedies. Her services were sorely needed. Peasant life was hard. Stiff arms, sore backs, hernias, piles, and a host of unnamed cramps and agues were a fact of working life.

But additionally people became increasingly worried about their health to the point of hypochondria. The understandable reason for this

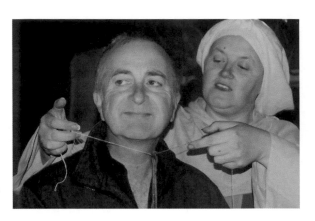

Worms again. This time threaded into a living necklace and worn to cure a sore throat. Entertainment value:10/10; medicinal value: 0/10.

deep anxiety was the Black Death. It arrived in Britain in 1348 and reduced the population by between a third and a half. Nobody ever forgot the advent of what seemed like a dreadful punishment from God. And it kept coming back in waves over the succeeding centuries. So, everyone was on their guard, watching over themselves for signs of some new disease.

There was little money in the job of Wise Woman. She was as badly off as her patients and would often work for payment in kind: a cheese here, a mended roof there. In return she would offer 'cures' of varying degrees of weirdness for anything from a sore throat to breast cancer. In later centuries it would have been these old women who were prime candidates for the role of 'Searcher of the Dead' (see page 119).

It wasn't just poverty that made being a Wise Woman a bad job. It was the ingredients and the risk.

Being poor, she couldn't get potions from the apothecary. She sourced her cures from natural ingredients available for free in the surrounding countryside. This would be more palatable to a modern sensibility if she'd stuck with herbs and similar remedies that still crop up today: balsam for coughs, St John's Wort and so on. But no, playing a leading role among the cures were eels, worms, bits of dead animals and a magic ingredient not normally associated with the doctor's surgery: dung. Lots of dung. For the following cures the Wise Woman would have had to spend half her working life following different brands of livestock around with a basket and shovel.

For a bleeding wound, the application of hot, fresh pig's dung
For jaundice, sheep's dung and beer, left overnight and then drunk

> *To prevent marking in smallpox, sheep's dung and wine, left overnight*
> *then drunk*
> *For gout, a plaster made from pigeon dung*
> *For canker in a woman's breast and baldness, goose dung*
> *To help hearing, a grey eel left to decay in horse dung and inserted into the ears*
> *For cramps, an eel tied around the affected area*
> *For toothache, a bruised cat's ear put on the tooth for three days*

But not all such alleged cures were as unscientific as these. The remedy for nosebleeds was inserting stinging nettles into the nostrils. This may seem barbarous, but it makes sense when you know that nettle stings have astringent properties. Likewise, the medieval pick-me-up of worm stew would have been highly effective. The peasant diet was largely meat-free. Except on high days and holidays the poor ate a pottage of oats flavoured with leeks, onions or peas, with barley bread and perhaps a little cheese. Worms cost nothing and added a touch of meat protein to the diet.

Recipe for Worm Stew

One pudding basin fresshe wormes
Three hunks stale bread, cubed
Mixed woodland herbs
A little butter
Water
Honey and salt to taste

Remove the gut and earth from your worms by inserting your thumbnail into their bodies and running it down their length. Chop the worms finely. Bring to the boil in a cauldron with enough water to cover. Add the bread, herbs and some butter and leave to simmer until the broth turns a browny-grey colour. Season with salt and add sugar if required. NB Many soils contain toxins, so make sure you know where your worms come from and clean them thoroughly (that's assuming you're daft enough to try it).

But where did the risk come in? Well, to the Church, many of the Wise Woman's wackier cures smacked of superstition. To cure warts, you cut the head off an eel and rubbed the blood on them, then buried the eel's head. As the head rotted, your warts supposedly disappeared. Similarly a string of worms tied round your neck allegedly dried up a sore throat; as the worms died, your throat got better.

In the early parts of the Middle Ages, churchmen turned a blind eye to this kind of mixture of luck and sympathetic magic. But as the centuries rolled on, the ecclesiastical authorities took full control of the education system. What had once been traditional came to be viewed as witchcraft. In 1484, right at the end of the medieval period, the Pope declared witchcraft a heresy. What was the difference between witchcraft and the work of the Wise Woman? Many accused women didn't live long enough to answer that conundrum.

This illustration gives a clear idea of the complexity of a building site as the work progressed from the east end of the church to the west. You can see the treadmills perched precariously at the highest points of the building.

Master Mason

Medieval religion could be brutal, but it did produce the greatest and most lasting legacy of the Middle Ages in Britain: its Gothic cathedrals. And along with them came more jobs for our pantheon of awfulness.

These cathedrals built in the Middle Ages expressed confidence and stability. Vast armies of workers were mobilized on a scale that hadn't been seen since the building of Hadrian's Wall in ancient Roman times. Erecting a cathedral in a town was a symbol of local pride, but it was also a huge economic boost. As with a new car plant or mobile-phone factory today, building a big ecclesiastical complex affected the economy of a whole region.

In the very early days of cathedral building, churches were designed by enthusiastic amateurs: abbots and bishops with enough learning to have researched the classic principles of architecture and engineering. These men built and financed their own projects. However, as time went on and architecture became more complex, the role of project manager and designer was handed over to named professionals who toured Europe as freelance architects.

They were known as Master Masons. Surely one of the best jobs in medieval Christendom? At one level, yes. They were not only artists, they were also the managing directors of their project. They had to organize a vast logistical operation that spanned not only the building site but quarries where stone was cut, forests where roof beams were felled, and the transport system over which the raw materials were moved, sometimes for hundreds of miles. The expenses sheet of Autun Cathedral in France (see below) shows just how many different facets there were to the job (and how many people benefited from the trickle-down effect of a cathedral being built in their town).

Master Masons supervised a bewildering number of other craftsmen: stone cutters, who made the shaped stones and statues; wallers and fixers, who laid the cut stone blocks; mortarers; glaziers; carpenters, who made the scaffolding and built the skeleton of the roof; roofers, who laid the lead and tiles; smiths and ironworkers; carters, who arranged the transport of stone and wood from the quarries; woodsmen; and painters and apprentices, besides hundreds of labourers who fetched, carried and supplied brute force wherever

THE BEST & WORST OF TIMES

1297 First recorded appearance of fulling mills (see page 70).

1314 Battle of Bannockburn. Robert the Bruce makes Scotland an independent kingdom once more.

1337 Start of Hundred Years War with France.

needed – all these men working their medieval socks off to put the Master Mason's vision into effect.

Except that the Master was vulnerable. He too was an employee of the donor, the rich aristocrat or churchman financing the building of the cathedral. If the money wasn't forthcoming, all the Master's dreams could turn, literally, to rubble. This often happened when a donor died. It could be years before another benefactor was found. Even Salisbury Cathedral, the quickest build of the Middle Ages, took thirty years to finish. Any delay in funding could set a project back by decades. Master Masons would often have to live with the frustration of never seeing their grand designs completed.

Expenses for Autun Cathedral

In the quarries, for the extraction of stones destined for the maintenance of the church of Saint-Lazare: 8 livres, 10 sous, 4 deniers

Ditto for lime, for the entire year: 9 livres, 8 sous

For fine timber destined for the arches of the church of Saint-Lazare, for the carpenters and the labourers: 17 livres, 2 sous, 7 deniers

For the forge of Autun, for the year: 42 livres, 10 sous, 6 deniers

For the carpenters who fitted the boards on the roof of the church of Saint-Lazare: 10 livres, 8 sous

Costs relating to the stones known as 'gargoyles': 4 livres, 10 sous, 9 deniers

For Renaud, the innkeeper, for the renting of the house where the above-named master is presently living, for two terms of this year: 3 livres

For the clothes of the said master, the coming term of the birth of Saint John the Baptist not included: 10 livres

For Benoit the saddler, for the year, for the saddles, collars, floor-fastenings, and other leather items relating to the cart: 2 livres, 10 sous

For the hay, for the harnesses of the said cart: 19 livres, 17 sous, 4 deniers

For oats: 25 livres, 3 sous, 9 deniers

For horseshoes for the horses: 4 livres, 6 sous

For the iron and nails used to strengthen the carts and to repair old ones: 6 livres, 9 sous, 1 denier

For the cartwright, for the new carts and the repair of the old ones: 2 livres, 14 sous, 9 deniers

For melted tallow, oil, vinegar, and thirty pounds of candles, for the year: 2 livres, 7 sous

**Ledger of the Workshop Committee,
Autun Cathedral, 1294–5 (extracts)**

Nor were they immune to accidents. When you are working 30 or 40 metres above the ground supported by hand-tied wooden scaffolding, no job is entirely safe. Most accidents went unrecorded, but we know William of Sens, the twelfth-century Master Mason at Canterbury Cathedral, fell from the scaffolding and suffered such severe injuries that he was forced to retire.

Nevertheless, in spite of stress, potential artistic frustration and the danger of falling to your death, it would be hard to claim the boss's job as the least attractive on a medieval building site. It was the poorly paid jobs that were the worst. Hot contenders for the worst building job are two essential support services without which the stones and the mortar could never have been put together: the Lime Burner and the Treadmill Operator.

This miniature shows stone-cutters at the quarry and masons on the building site. In the foreground a mortarer is mixing lime mortar made from slaked lime from the lime burner.

Lime Burner

Calcium oxide, or lime as it's better known, is one of the world's most versatile materials. It was the primary ingredient for disinfectant whitewash and, in the latter part of the Middle Ages, began to be used to improve the structure of the soil and neutralize its acidity, increasing crop yields. But its main use was in making mortar for building. Lime mortar, which is a mixture of lime, sand and water, still has advantages over modern cements as it allows a building to breathe and, as it isn't as strong as the stone itself, prevents it from flaking.

But to produce lime for mortar you needed a Lime Burner. Lime burning involved heating chalk or limestone (or sometimes oyster shells), thus driving off the carbon dioxide and turning the residue into lumps of 'quicklime'. This was then added to water to create 'slaked lime', a powder suitable for fertilizer and for mortar. It may sound simple, but every stage was fraught with danger. This is dramatically demonstrated by the words used to describe the substances involved: 'quicklime' means lime that is alive, and 'slaked-lime' is lime so dry that its thirst has to be quenched.

Lime Burners usually worked on the edge of a forest close to the building site, to be able to access a steady supply of wood for the lime kilns in which the limestone burnt. Once the kilns had reached the correct temperature – around 1,100°C – they had to be operated twenty-four hours a day by a two-man team of 'Quarryman' and 'Burner'. The Quarryman worked the day shift, while the Burner stayed up all night to remove the quicklime and top up the kiln with coal and limestone.

The carbon dioxide this process produced could paralyse and kill. It was not uncommon for befuddled Lime Burners to fall into their kilns and be burnt to death. Even if they kept themselves safe it was extremely uncomfortable, hot work. Building took place only in the summer, because frost could crack the stone and the mortar. It's little wonder Lime Burners often received part of their payment in beer.

The quicklime that came out of the kiln was an extremely unstable, caustic substance that could spontaneously combust. It reacted violently with any form of water (including the moisture on skin) and, as the Burner raked it out, the pungent dust would irritate the eyes and nose. This could cause blindness, and terrible burns.

To stabilize this material, the Lime Burner had to 'slake' it. This, too, was dangerous. Slaking is another extreme reaction, which produces calcium hydroxide, heat and steam. The Lime Burners had to plunge a block of quicklime into water. As soon as it was immersed, there was an explosive reaction. Tiny pieces of lime flew around like grapeshot. But once it had cracked and flaked, the lime could then be crushed into powder.

So Lime Burners suffered from stifling heat; they'd be up all night in danger of dying of carbon monoxide poisoning or nodding off and falling in the kiln.

1346 Tales of Robin Hood in circulation. Archery becomes a popular sport for the masses.

1346 Battle of Crécy. English archers rout the French, but then have to put their own injured out of their misery.

1348 Black Death comes to Britain, bemusing the medical profession and decimating the population.

They could be cut and blinded, and as a matter of course their hands and lips would be cracked, as the caustic quicklime burned into the moisture in their skin and mucous membranes.

Treadmill Operator

Treadmill Operators did just that. They trod round and round in a mill. This may have been less dangerous than lime-burning, but it was oh so tedious.

The need for this boring job came about because of a revolution in medieval cathedral building brought about by the invention of sophisticated cranes. Once machines had been invented that were strong enough to winch heavy stone and timber into place, the scaffolding could be much lighter, and buildings could be put up with a speed and efficiency never before contemplated. Previously there would have been a solid wall of timber to support the great weight of stones waiting to be put into place, but now architects could design spiral staircases and walkways for the masons in the fabric of the cathedral itself, and could fix their lightweight scaffolding poles into holes in the stonework. This scaffolding could then be easily dismantled and set up elsewhere on the building or taken away to the next job.

Pictures of cranes appear in almost every late-medieval illustration of the building process. Small cranes were worked by turning a wheel from the outside. Larger cranes, which could pivot on their axis as well as lift up and down, had to be winched into place in parts by smaller cranes or windlasses and then constructed high up on the cathedral.

This treadmill in Normandy (above and below) had been constructed using existing medieval models and illustrations from manuscripts. There are original examples you can still see, such as the one at Salisbury Cathedral.

These machines were powered by two men walking inside a treadmill. They were literally at the centre of a revolution in architecture, even if all they were doing all day was walking!

It's said that blind people from the local community were often chosen for this particular Worst Job. The crane was constructed at the highest point the building had reached. It would have had a commanding view of the town and surrounding countryside. No local would ever have been so high or seen so far in their lives. Just to look out would have been both thrilling and unnerving. But the Treadmill Operators in their wooden cage were suspended above a vertiginous drop. They walked on nothing more than a series of wooden slats with small gaps between them. Consequently they were constantly confronted by the plunging void below.

The theory was that the visually impaired could avoid the vertigo that must have affected those with better vision.

Throughout the entire working day the Treadmill Operators walked up and down, from dawn till dusk, come rain come shine, for little more than living expenses. But the worst part of their job was not the boredom.

Once the treadmill was moving, it was extremely difficult to control. It worked like the lowest gear of a mountain bike. The wheel went round two or three times to power one rotation of the axle holding the rope. It would have been quite easy to build up the momentum. The hard part was stopping. It was very dangerous for the operators to put any part of their body outside the cage because the movement of the massive wheel would slice off protruding hands, arms or legs against the fixed stanchions of the crane.

So they were stuck in a moving cage. And if it had been badly assembled, or the timber was faulty, or it had been damaged by rain or frost, it would have been a terrifyingly dangerous cage. Imagine how a blind Treadmill Operator would have felt if this primitive technology started to fall apart 50 metres above all-too-solid earth. And such an occurrence was not uncommon.

So was the Treadmill Operator's job the Worst Job in the Middle Ages? There are plenty of other candidates for that dubious distinction. Flax Retting, for instance.

Flax Retter

There were two essential clothing materials in the Middle Ages: wool and linen. The production of each gave rise to Worst Jobs. Behind the linen of fine shirts, Crusader flags and cathedral altar cloths lay the essential but mind-numbingly dull task of the Flax Retter, a job so slow that, by contrast, watching a slow-motion film of Dulux Weathershield hardening would seem positively racy.

The blue-flowered flax that still coats the countryside in late May today is an exceptionally versatile plant. When crushed, its seeds produce linseed oil. And its fibrous stems can be treated to form linen fibres. Flax retting is the painstakingly slow process by which the bundles of fibres in the stem are separated from the core and each other by controlled rotting.

'Slow rotting' is not a phrase you want to read in a job description, yet the task was even worse than these words suggest.

Once the flax had been harvested at the right degree of ripeness, and the seeds removed for oil, the Flax Retter would get his or her hands on the stems. Retting (the word is related to rotting) breaks down the pectins and gum that bind the fibres together. The process required some skill, since if the plant rots too much or unevenly then the interior material is damaged. But it was the level of watchfulness required that made it such a tedious task.

THE BEST & WORST OF TIMES

1381 Yeomen in London, Essex, Kent and south-east England lead the Peasants' Revolt. The Revolt fails, but the Black Death has created such a desperate shortage of workers that the survivors can work where they please. Thus the demand for an end to serfdom is brought about by economic muscle.

1381 *Piers Plowman* by William Langland and *The Canterbury Tales* by Geoffrey Chaucer are written in the English vernacular. They paint a vivid picture of everyday life.

1415 According to Shakespeare's *Henry V*, the principal victims of Agincourt are the squires and the baggage train.

1415 Henry V wins the Battle of Agincourt, with minimal battlefield casualties.

You had to watch it… all the time… for weeks.

Two main methods of retting were employed in medieval England: dew-retting and water-retting. The first involved placing the flax plant in a field of short grass and leaving it there for three or four weeks. The fibres would slowly break down, but would have to be checked day-in, day-out. This slow method produced a finer product, but was expensive.

The alternative, water-retting, required more skill but took only seven to ten days. In this case the flax was carefully bundled (to ensure even rotting) and placed underwater. It worked quickest in still water, as the sun's heat could be retained to expedite the process.

Both methods had their drawbacks. Dew-retting was a real pain. It involved a month of constant observation. And even if you could stand the tedium of staring at what was effectively a compost heap for most of the summer, you could still lose your whole crop if the weather changed, as this could make the rotting uneven.

On the other hand, water-retting, while the speedier and more commercial method, was really quite vile. The reaction of water on flax produces a substance called butyric acid. And this causes the most gut-wrenching stink, particularly if still water like a pond or tank is used. For the Flax Retter who tried to avoid the stench by using running water, there was an even less desirable outcome. It may have been quick and odour-free, but the rot polluted the water supply, so Flax Retters were often ostracized by their neighbours.

The poor Flax Retter was in a no-win situation. His choice was between constant monitoring of a field of dead plants, creating a great compost-like stench or being the most unpopular man in the village.

Flax Retters never became fully extinct (flax is still processed today, only it takes about thirty-six hours rather than many months), but their job was made far less important by the introduction of a new plant. In the fourteenth century a new, lighter fibre was introduced from the Arabic world. It was qutn – or cotton as it became better known.

But as far as tedium is concerned, the job that gets the highest accolade, the *sine qua non* of dreariness, is a post a million miles away from the bucolic niff of retting. And it was at the very centre of government.

Pipe Roll Transcriber

Would you take a well-paid job that involved writing out Inland Revenue accounts in longhand without a mistake? This was the unenviable task of the Pipe Roll Transcriber.

In the twelfth century, medieval society was growing increasingly more sophisticated. The wool industry was making individuals and institutions rich, and the King's tax affairs were becoming correspondingly complex. In 1129 Henry I instituted the Great Roll, a system whereby all the debts owed to the King from the various shires were recorded once a year. Any not paid were carried forward to the next year. The various Sheriffs came to the Treasury with their tax payments, and a running tally was painstakingly written down and then copied out by the Chancellor's scribe or Transcriber.

The Chancellor of the Exchequer gets his name from the chequered tablecloth resembling a chess board that was used to keep a temporary account of transactions in the Treasury. It acted like a sort of abacus. Counters on the columns represented the pounds, shillings and pence owed and being paid in. Most of our information about the Chancellor's Scribe and the taxation system comes in a book written in 1176–8, not long after the pipe rolls had been instituted. The *Dialogus de Scaccario* by Richard Fitznigel of Bath, the King's Treasurer, is written as a dialogue between a disciple and his master who tells him in great detail about the business of government. This is how Fitznigel describes the exchequer:

> *The exchequer is a quadrangular surface about ten feet in length, five in breadth, placed before those* [who] *sit around it in the manner of a table, and all around it it has an edge about the height of one's four fingers, lest any thing placed upon it should fall off. There is placed over the top of the exchequer, moreover, a cloth bought at the Easter term, not an ordinary one but a black one marked with stripes, the stripes being distant from each other the space of a foot or the breadth of a hand. In the spaces, moreover, are counters placed according to their values; about these we shall speak below. Although, moreover, such a surface is called exchequer, nevertheless this name is so changed about that the court itself which sits when the exchequer does is called exchequer; so that if at any time through a decree any thing is established by common counsel, it is said to have been done at the exchequer of this or that year…*

By 1300 these documents were being referred to as 'pipe rolls'. The term comes from the distinctive way in which the membranes were sewn together. When rolled up, they looked rather like pieces of piping, with perhaps the hint that they helped make money flow into the Treasury like a pipe. The rolls were quite wide and, as the years went by, gradually grew to about 6 feet long. In addition, more and more rolls were produced each year because so many debts to the Crown were never discharged, and simply kept appearing on the following year's pipe rolls.

Because the information contained in them was so important, Transcribers wrote on vellum. The use of this material helped to avoid fraud, because it was difficult to erase anything written on it. But of course this also meant that mistakes couldn't be rubbed out. Consequently, if errors were made, they were

THE BEST & WORST OF TIMES

1431 The French fight back; Joan of Arc is burnt at the stake.

1455 The beginning of the Wars of the Roses – a struggle for the English crown between the Houses of Lancaster and York.

1475 Michelangelo is born in Italy.

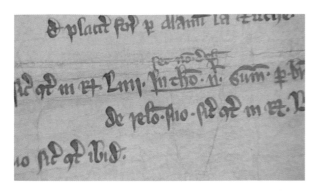

Pipe rolls from the National Archives in Kew, Surrey. No columns of figures, just text written in the approved formal handwriting of the day. Mistakes were marked by underlining (top) and the correction added above.

indicated either with a line under the offending word or by a small dot next to the erroneous letter.

Pipe Roll Transcribing was a job that craftily combined maximum stress with minimum interest. The Chancellor's scribe worked in tandem with another poor soul, the Treasurer's scribe, who prepared the vellum and took immediate dictation. Then once he'd written the amounts as they came in, the Transcriber had to copy them out word for word. Quickly.

So, for instance, the Sheriff of Sussex might turn up with his deputation. On the chequerboard table would be the debt he owed to the King: £642 14s 9d. He then paid into the Treasury his levies of £619 7s 3d. The beads would be entered, and the sum outstanding would be £23 7s 6d. All these amounts would be entered into the pipe roll and then copied out by the Transcriber. Gripping stuff.

But for the scribe it was high-pressure work. He had to be fast and accurate. There was no room for error. He sat in a draughty stone chamber with cold hands, and the knowledge that today would be exactly the same as every other tedious day. As he laboured, he was constantly scrutinized by the Chancellor's Clerk peering over his shoulder on the look-out for mistakes. It would have required phenomenal concentration to get everything right, because the material was so boring. In later centuries, court stenographers and audio typists would transcribe material that made sense. Pipe roll transcription was more akin to copying out the telephone book. Fitznigel's phrase below sums up the essence of the job: 'diligent and at the same time laborious discretion'.

> *The care, the labour, the zeal of the remaining scribe sitting at his side consists chiefly in this, namely, that he shall take down from the other roll word for word; as we said before, the same order being observed. Likewise it pertains to him to write the writs of the king concerning outlays of the treasury, but only for those payments which, in the judgment of the barons, while the exchequer is in session, ought to be made by the treasurer and chamberlains: likewise he writes the writs of the king concerning the computing or remitting of those things which the barons have decreed should be computed or remitted at the exchequer. It is his duty also, when the accounts of the sheriff have been gone through, and the dues of the king for which the summonses are made, estimated, to write out the latter, with diligent and at the same time laborious*

discretion, to be sent throughout the whole kingdom: for by them, and on account of them, the exchequer of the following term is called together.

And it robbed the Chancellor's scribe of all personality. Elsewhere in the Middle Ages official documents carry traces of the scribes who wrote them: doodles, scribbles, facetious comments about how boring the job was. But the rules stated that the Transcriber 'must be careful not to write anything of his own in the roll'. He was not even allowed the individuality of his own handwriting. All scribes had to learn a uniform hand so that their work was indistinguishable from that of others. Because the accounts had to be written under pressure, a speedier modern joined-up script was used, rather than the more angular early-medieval writing employed in the *Anglo-Saxon Chronicles*.

Rolled up you can see how the interleaved sheets form a 'pipe'.

On the up-side though, they earned good money. In 1136 Transcribers were paid 5d a day; even knights of the court received only 8d a day. They also got long holidays between the court's sessions.

When the pipe roll system was finally dispensed with after the reforms of 1832, there were still debts on the rolls dating back to the thirteenth century. Partly from a need to house the 624 rolls somewhere other than the Exchequer, the Public Record Office (now the National Archive) was established. The rolls provide historians with a fascinating resource, enabling them to track down the minutiae of court life through the various payments and debts.

The length of the rolls grew as the English economy expanded, driven by the wool industry. Its power and influence were dramatically symbolized by the image of the Lord Chancellor sitting in state on a sack of wool. By 1300 there were 15 million sheep in England – three times the human population.

If your surname is Fuller, Tucker or even Walker, one of your distant ancestors worked in the wool industry, and spent every day trudging, up to their knees, in stale human urine (hence the name Walker).

Surely that must qualify as the very Worst Job of the Middle Ages?

The Worst Job of All: Fuller

When sheep were sheared, the wool was carded, spun into yarn and then woven. To ease the weaving process, the natural grease was left in the wool. But the resulting cloth was coarse and widely meshed. So a Fuller was employed to 'full' or pound and clean off the grease and other impurities. The washing made the fabric softer, shrank it to close the holes and make it thicker, while the trampling meshed the scales of the wool fibres together to make a consolidated surface that was less likely to fray.

The solution in which the loosely woven cloth was soaked needed to be alkaline in order to break down the grease, and the cheapest form of alkaline solution available was stale urine. A Fuller had to obtain gallons of the stuff. It was usually collected from farms and private houses, but an enterprising Fuller in Winchester set up a series of public toilets that he regularly plundered.

Fulling wasn't all bad. Fullers owned their own materials, and they didn't starve. They were essential to the major industry of the day and earned a rate comparable to similar labourers such as thatchers.

That said, to modern sensibilities not only was the job revolting, it was also mind-bogglingly monotonous. It could take seven or eight hours of tramping up and down on the spot to produce a finished piece of thick cloth. And, like Flax Retters, Fullers didn't dare let their minds wander. They had to be vigilant to ensure the whole cloth received equal, consistent treatment, and skilled enough to know when it had been trodden sufficiently. Lack of attention could lead to holes in the fabric, ruining a whole bolt of material.

A fifteenth-century scene of sheep-shearing. Is the figure in red just hanging around or waiting to get into a smelly fulling tub?

After the process was completed, the cloth was rinsed in clean water and hung out on a tenterframe. These frames were usually mounted on hillsides, where sun and wind would dry the soggy material. Carrying a large, heavy, wet cloth up a hill and hanging it out was tough work. It was then heaved on to the tenterframe and hooked by its edges on to both rails. Finally the lower rail was adjusted to draw the cloth tight and even. It is from this process of creating tension that we get the saying 'on tenterhooks'.

It's little wonder that fulling was one of the first industries to be mechanized. In the thirteenth century the harnessing of water-power facilitated the invention of 'fulling stocks'. Big oak hammers were attached to waterwheels to pound the material, creating a very similar action to the stamping of feet. They were so shaped that each time the hammers hit the cloth downwards they also cause it to rotate. This small movement ensured that the cloth was uniformly pummelled, thus minimizing the possibility of damage. But mass-production couldn't get rid of the smell of urine. In some cases a mixture of mined clay, silica and aluminium oxide (fuller's earth) was employed, but wee was still being used in the late seventeenth century, as this description of fulling mills on the Isle of Wight by Celia Fiennes in 1698 illustrates:

Nothing can prepare you for the raw-meat smell of stale urine. The ammonia it gives off is so strong that it makes you want to vomit every time you breathe in. But I proved beyond doubt that the process worked. Even after a few minutes the grease was clearly oozing out of the cloth and into the urine.

> *... they bring them all just from the loome and soe they are put into the fulling-mills, but first they will clean and scour their roomes with them – which by the way gives noe pleasing perfume to a roome, the oyle and grease, and I should think it would rather foull a roome than cleanse it because of the oyle – but I perceive its otherwise esteemed by them, which will send to their acquaintances that are tuckers the dayes the serges comes in for a rowle to clean their house, this I was an eye witness of; then they lay them in soack in vrine then they soape them and soe put them into the fulling-mills and soe worke them in the mills drye till they are thick enough, then they turne water into them and so scower them; the mill does draw out and gather in the serges, its a pretty divertion to see it, a sort of huge notch'd timbers like great teeth, one would thinke it should injure the serges but it does not, the mills draws in with such a great violence that if one stands neere it, and it catch a bitt of your garments it would be ready to draw in the person even in a trice.*

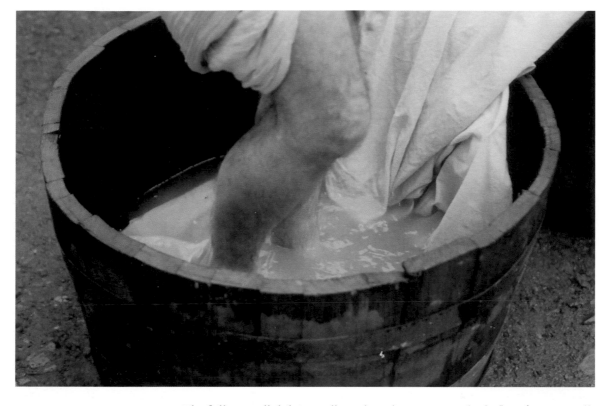

The fulling-mill didn't totally replace the ancient method of production. Mills were prohibited in London between 1298 and 1417, in order to protect the old methods. And fulling by foot was retained for centuries in places such as Florence, as the Florentines maintained that only this process could produce a sufficiently high-grade heavy, woollen cloth.

It may seem a relatively easy job if you hold your nose. But I promise you, after even half an hour of traditional fulling, you'll never look at your pullover in the same way again.

The fulling process is used in William Langland's fourteenth-century poem *The Vision of Piers Plowman* as a metaphor of baptism. It's clear that a hundred years after the invention of fulling stocks, both mechanized fulling and foot power still existed side by side.

> *Clooth that cometh fro the wevyng is noght comly to were*
> *Til it be fulled under foot or in fullyng stokkes,*
> *Wasshen wel with water and with taseles cracched [scratched],*
> *Ytouked and yteynted and under taillours hande.*

CHAPTER THREE

Tudor Worst Jobs

A Tudor kitchen. This time with women acting as the turnbroaches, loading and basting the chickens on the spits.

It's amazing how well we seem to know the Tudors. They come bursting out of the death throes of medieval history, like characters from an epic movie. Henry VIII and his six wives, Thomas More, Bloody Mary, Mary Queen of Scots, Queen Elizabeth, Francis Drake, Walter Raleigh – they are modern, intelligent, passionate and nationalistic.

If we think this is a true picture, then the Tudor spin-machine succeeded. From the very moment that Henry Tudor defeated Richard III on the battlefield at Bosworth, he and his descendants tried to draw a clear line between the 'bad old days' and the new up-beat Tudor age. They were lucky that the century-and-a-bit of their rule encompassed a unique confluence of economic expansion and culture that allowed them to achieve this propaganda coup. But the net result was a rose-tinted 'Ye-Olde-Merrie-England' version of the Tudor Renaissance.

The English Reformation brought money flowing into the royal coffers that had previously belonged to the monasteries. Military victories and English naval prowess further increased trade and power. And this wealth was used for patronage. Humanist ideas flooded in from the Continent. The painter Hans Holbein arrived to paint unforgettable images of the great Tudor political players. Composers like Tallis, Byrd and John Dowland created a distinctive 'English' sound in music. Writers like Spenser and, above all, Shakespeare took the English language to new heights while subtly praising their patrons and denigrating past monarchs.

But much of this apparent Tudor revolution is illusory. The reality of life in the sixteenth century escapes us. For the majority of the population, there was far greater continuity with the medieval past than the Tudors would care to admit. The English Renaissance centred on the court and urban environment.

But only 6 per cent of the population were in the towns, half of them Londoners. The rest lived as they'd always done: on the land. Their lives were affected less by the flowering of English literature, more by the frequent outbreaks of plague and the two major famines in the 1550s and 1590s.

If they'd been asked, many of them might well have chosen a return to the bad old days before Henry VII. He may have removed the instability of the Wars of the Roses, but his son, Henry VIII, brought an even greater terror to the country. The man who wrote anti-Protestant tracts on the Mass, and was given the title 'Defender of the Faith' by the Pope, broke from the Catholic Church in 1534 in order to legitimize his marriage to Anne Boleyn. Not only was the rest of the Tudor era characterized by insecurity, repression and persecution as successive regimes violently imposed their own religious ethos, but the destruction of the monastic orders also removed at a stroke the medieval social security system. The greatest impact of the Reformation for most people was the huge increase in unemployed beggars and vagrants.

So what work was available on the Tudor job market?

Executioner

The Tudors' iron grip on power is summed up by the twin symbols of the Tower of London and the grim, hooded axe-man. There had been executions throughout the Middle Ages, but it is with the Tudors that the axe becomes an icon of state control. Any headless ghost worth their salt, from the lady of the Bloody Tower to Hogwarts' Nearly Headless Nick, will be attired in a Tudor ruff. Some of the most famous names of the period – Thomas More, Anne Boleyn and Mary Queen of Scots – were beheaded.

The sheer horribleness of being an executioner, the pariah status that accompanied the post, the gruesome mess and the psychological damage of ending the lives of your fellow human beings all contribute to making this a Worst Job. But swinging the axe was only a minor part of the job of being an executioner. There were 70,000 executions in the Tudor period, and only a tiny proportion of these were beheadings. A swift death with the blade was a privilege reserved for the nobility. There were 289 burnings of Protestants in the reign of Queen Mary, and the odd hanging, drawing and quartering for traitors. The rest were straightforward hangings. And while we're exploding myths, they didn't usually execute people in the Tower of London. There have only ever been seven executions inside the Tower, starting with William, Lord Hastings in 1483 and ending with Robert Deveraux, Earl of Essex on 25 February 1601. Other executions either took place outside the Tower on Tower Hill or at Tyburn.

The Tyburn connection accounts for the nickname 'Jack Ketch' that public executioners acquired from the sixteenth century onwards. The land around

Tyburn had been owned by a family called Jacquette for the best part of 300 years, and Jack Ketch is a corruption of that name. Today the place where the gallows stood is marked by a brass circle laid into the pavement. It's on a pedestrian traffic island in the middle of the Edgware Road at the junction with Marble Arch.

Hanging was a grisly job. In the early part of our period, the victim was dragged to the gallows on a hurdle behind a horse. The Executioner's assistant was on top of the gallows. The victim was stripped and made to climb the ladder. Then the assistant dropped a rope around their neck. Finally the Executioner would pull the ladder away.

This was superseded by a superior method that could dispatch several people at one time. The victims were put on a cart with nooses round their necks. The ropes were all tied to the horizontal bar of the gallows and the horse was slapped to make it pull the cart away.

Both methods were slow and painful. The nooses weren't tied in a way that would break the neck as in modern judicial hangings. This was death by strangulation that could last for half an hour, with eyes bulging, legs kicking, and the humiliating loss of bladder and bowel control. Afterwards the Executioner had the perks of the victims' clothes to sell, and he also sold pieces of the noose, which were thought to bring good luck. It was indeed money for old rope, one of several phrases associated with Jack Ketch's job that have become part of our language.

Five criminals are subject to execution by hanging.

The victims all had hangers-on. To ease the hanged man's suffering, friends would grab hold of his legs and hang on, hoping to break his neck or speed strangulation. But the hangers-on could make life very risky for the Executioner. If a popular local figure was going to swing, the atmosphere could be ugly, and there was the danger of reprisals. The best example of this comes from a slightly later period. George 'Cornet' Joyce, the man who executed King Charles I, was so terrified when Charles II was restored to the throne that he started a new life in Ashby-de-la-Zouch – as a woman called Jane Joyce! But his new identity failed to fool his enemies, who found and killed him.

The Executioners' ceremonial hood would have done little to provide anonymity. Everyone knew who they were. Some even achieved a certain sort of fame. They were often condemned criminals themselves who took the job to save their own necks. John Crossland was granted a pardon on the understanding that he executed his father and brother who had also

been sentenced to death. Now his tormented ghost is said to wander by Derby Cathedral. Thomas Derrick was an Elizabethan hangman. He'd been convicted of rape, but was pardoned by the Earl of Essex (who ironically was executed himself for treason in 1601– by Derrick). During his career Derrick was responsible for hanging 3,000 convicts. He was so prolific that his name became another synonym for the job itself, and has passed into modern usage as a name for the gallows-like crane that is used to hoist goods on board ship.

Practical research has shown that the ceremonial full hood with tiny eye slits was totally inappropriate for a job that required hand–eye co-ordination and dexterity. The uniform probably consisted of a workaday leather jerkin, and breeches tied with a rope belt. The Executioner also discarded his ceremonial hood in favour of a less constricting one with large eye holes or even a simple mask, so that he could see what he was doing. This face-wear wasn't disguise. It conveyed the symbolic message that this was the faceless representative of Crown justice. In those days, the word 'executioner' didn't mean killer. What Jack Ketch was 'executing' was the sentence of the court.

> '*Derick, thou know'st at Coles I saved Thy life lost for a rape there done.*'
> **Anon, *Ballad of the Death of the Earl of Essex*, c. 1600**
>
> '*I would there were a Derick to hang him up too.*'
> **Thomas Dekker, *Seven Sinnes*, 1606**
>
> '*Would Derrick had been his fortune seven years ago…*
> **Thomas Middleton, *The Puritan Wife*, or *The Widow of Watling Street*, 1607**
>
> '*He rides circuit with the devil, and Derrick must be his host, and Tyborne the inn at which he will light.*'
> **Dekker, *The Bellman of London*, 1608**
>
> '*Deric…is with us abusively used for a Hang-man; because one of that name was not long since a famed executioner at Tiburn.*'
> **Thomas Blount, *Glossographia*, 1656**

Hangings were riotous and risky, but beheading meant killing someone with your own hands. Aristocrats were permitted this mode of execution because it reflected the noble ideal of being killed by cold steel in battle. Beheadings were rare, and therefore a popular spectacle. The Executioner would have had little opportunity for a dress rehearsal, and would have been under a lot of pressure from the crowd to put on a good show.

1517 Germany: Martin Luther pins to the door of Wittenberg Cathedral his '95 Theses', challenging the very basis of medieval Catholicism. This act sparks the Reformation, which will tear Europe and Britain apart for 200 years.

1520 France: Henry VIII meets Francis I of France at the international summit known as the 'The Field of the Cloth of Gold'. The event itself is a stunning success, but the ensuing peace is short-lived.

1521 The Pope names Henry VIII Defender of the Faith for his spirited attack on the ideas of the religious reformers.

It's the Tudors who've given us our abiding image of the Tower of London as an instrument of state repression. But still only a handful of people were executed within its walls.

The victims also expected a professional job. They wanted a swift killer blow, not someone hacking away at their neck for several minutes trying to deliver the *coup de grâce*. It took several swings of the axe before Mary Queen of Scots was properly executed, and even then the Executioner had to use the slitting knife that he carried on his belt to sever the last sinews. It's not difficult to understand why he expected a generous tip of seven to ten shillings to encourage him to make a clean cut. In an age when a labourer earned seven pounds a year, this was big money. But the tip could be even bigger. Record Office accounts inform us that 100 crowns in French money was paid by Sir William, Constable of the Tower, to Anne Boleyn's Calais executioner. And if he messed the job up there was no money-back guarantee.

The shape of the axe made it ceremonially impressive rather than practically useful. The edge might not be sharp enough for the job, in which case death resulted from smashed vertebrae rather than a clean slice. The scene would have been horrific. Arterial blood spurting from the semi-severed neck would drench the Executioner and the surrounding platform. Even when the head was off, the heart, which beats for several minutes after death, would be pumping gore. Although usually the victim would have been unconscious after the first blow, the stories of lips moving after death and other nervous reactions are probably true.

This is an extract from an eyewitness account of Mary Queen of Scots' execution by Robert Wyngfielde. It spares no details. There was a fear that Mary would be turned into a martyr figure, so her clothes weren't given to the Executioner. Instead they were destroyed.

Her prayers being ended, the executioners, kneeling, desired her Grace to forgive them her death: who answered, 'I forgive you with all my heart, for now, I hope, you shall make an end of all my troubles.'

Then, groping for the block, she laid down her head, putting her chin over the block with both her hands, which, holding there still, had been cut off had they not been espied. Then lying upon the block most quietly, and stretching out her arms cried, In manus tuas, Domine [Into your hands, O Lord] etc., three or four times. Then, lying very still upon the block, one of the executioners holding her slightly with one of his hands, she endured two strokes of the other executioner with an axe, she making very small noise or none at all, and not stirring any part of her from the place where she lay: and so the executioner cut off her head, saving one little gristle, which being cut asunder, he lifted up her head to the view of all the assembly and bade 'God save the Queen'. Then, her dress of lawn [her wig] falling from off her head, it appeared as grey as one of threescore and ten years old, polled very short, her face in a moment being so much altered from the form she had when she was alive, as few could remember her by her dead face. Her lips stirred up and down a quarter of an hour after her head was cut off.

Then one of the executioners, pulling off her garters, espied her little dog which was crept under her clothes, which could not be gotten forth but by force, yet afterward would not depart from the dead corpse, but came and lay between her head and her shoulders, which being imbrued with her blood was carried away and washed, as all things else were that had any blood was either burned or washed clean, and the executioners sent away with money for their fees, not having any one thing that belonged unto her.

Even after the body had been cleared away, the Executioner's ghoulish job was not over. Heads of traitors were displayed on London Bridge, the only thoroughfare between the City and Southwark. However, to prevent them being pecked clean too quickly by the waiting carrion, the Executioner had the job of parboiling the heads in a large kettle with cumin seed and salt to deter the birds. Bishop John Fisher was executed along with Sir Thomas More at Tower Hill in 1535. Dr Thomas Bailey, writing about the event some thirty years later, remarks that the deceased's parboiled head looked more healthy after fourteen days' exposure than it had in life. This is the stuff of nightmares. No wonder executioners frequently ended their own lives.

THE BEST & WORST OF TIMES

1526 The over-ambitious Cardinal Wolsey draws up the Eltham Ordinances. These lay out proper court etiquette but also isolate the King from Wolsey's political enemies. Wolsey hands Henry VIII Hampton Court to try to stave off political disgrace. He fails.

1526 Painter Hans Holbein flees religious chaos in Switzerland. His flattering but realistic Renaissance art gives us a lasting image of Henry VIII and senior court figures.

1533 Henry marries Anne Boleyn four months before his self-declared annulment from his first wife Catherine of Aragon.

The execution of Mary Queen of Scots in Fotheringay Castle. It's said that Queen Elizabeth bitterly regretted signing her death warrant 'til her dying day.

Spit Boy

In 1526 Cardinal Wolsey gave Henry VIII the great Tudor building of Hampton Court. The King had been offended by Wolsey's overweening behaviour, and the Cardinal was trying to appease him. The palace is a lasting reminder of the complex politics of the Tudor court. Ranks and hierarchy were paramount.

At Hampton Court Palace there were 1,200 courtiers in winter, 800 in summer, and upwards of a thousand servants. They all needed feeding. When he took over, Henry had the kitchens expanded. There were fifty rooms for food preparation: 36,000 square feet devoted to Henry's stomach. In the mornings, in preparation for the main meal of the day served at the early hour of 11am, every inch was heaving with activity. Hierarchy was everything here too. Ranks of kitchen staff were marked by different colour liveries. Two hundred or more

people chopped, stewed, shouted and swore at each other. How different from a top-class hotel kitchen today!

At the very bottom of the food chain were the Spit Boys, sometimes known as Turn-Broaches or Galipines. As opposed to the vegetable pottage and dairy products on which ordinary people survived, 70 per cent of the aristocratic Tudor diet was meat. Most of it was roasted. The Spit Boys turned the great iron spits for hours on end in front of the six huge open fires.

This was supremely monotonous work and very arduous, straining the muscles of the back and arms. It was too tough for a youngster. Experimental archaeologists working in the Hampton Court kitchens have demonstrated that 'boy' must have been a derogatory rather than a descriptive term. The spits were 2 centimetres thick and nearly 3 metres long. It took a hundred great joints of beef, each weighing 6 kilos, to satisfy the appetites of Henry VIII and his courtiers: over half a ton of flesh. This was man's work.

It was incredibly hot. The Spit Boys were the same distance from the blazing fire as the meat they were roasting. They operated the spit from a small brick alcove, and so were sheltered from the direct heat. Nevertheless the ambient temperature was suffocating.

You can get some idea of how tough the Spit Boys' life must have been from the Eltham Ordinances (see box on page 84). These rules controlling court etiquette made provision for the master cook to provide clothing for the Spit Boys, and forbade them to work naked or in filthy rags as they had previously done. They were also forbidden from urinating in the fireplace. As they had to get up at four in the morning to stoke the fires and then worked solidly for the next six hours, this ordinance could have been a problem (although, given the heat of the fires, most of their bodily moisture may have been sweated off). One suspects that these strictures were less about improving the conditions of the staff, and more about increasing the sense of order and grandeur in the court.

But Spit Boys weren't badly paid. Kitchen staff at Hampton Court got sixpence a day when on duty and fourpence when sick – so even when they were laid up they were getting four times the pay of a field labourer.

A revision of the ordinances, probably from 1591, gives us a sense of the huge range of meats that would have been included in the Spit Boys' annual 'turnover': 1,240 oxen, 8,200 sheep, 2,330 deer, 760 calves, 1,870 pigs and 53 wild boar went through the royal accounts in one year. And that's just the everyday stuff. Dishes in Tudor times also included a vast range of birds including swan, goose, stork, pheasants, herons, bitterns, shovellers, partridges, quails, cocks, plovers, gulls, pigeons and larks.

Lent and Fridays were traditional days of religious 'fasting'. This didn't mean eating nothing. It simply meant no meat. A Tudor meal fit for a king involved two courses or removes. Each course comprised a set number of dishes. So a Friday meal of fish and vegetables for Henry VIII might start with

The meeting of Francis I and Henry VIII at the Field of the Cloth of Gold in 1520 was one of the most spectacular displays of political one-upmanship in history. And in the white tents in the background, the Spit Boys are preparing some suitably over-the-top meal for their indulgent monarchs.

THE BEST & WORST OF TIMES

1534 Henry's Catholic fervour is forgotten, as he wrangles with the Pope over his divorce. The Act of Supremacy is passed, making Henry, not the Pope, head of the Church in England.

1535 Henry's ex-Chancellor Thomas More is beheaded for opposing Henry's break with Rome.

1536 Anne Boleyn is beheaded by the executioner's sword for alleged adultery. Henry Norreys, the King's Groom of the Stool, is accused of being her lover and is executed.

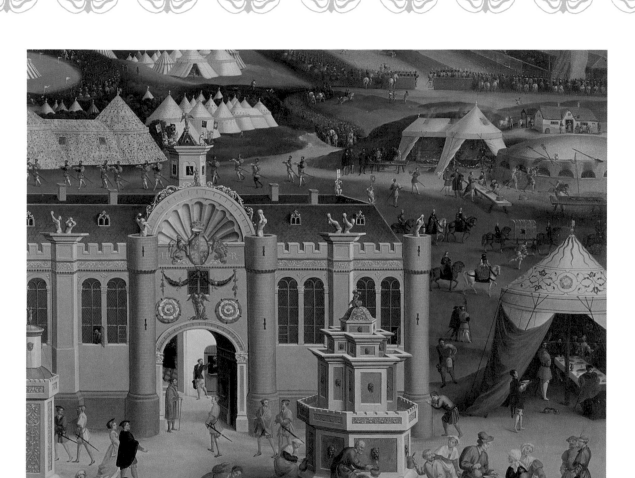

fifteen separate dishes for him to sample, including soup, eels, lampreys, pike, Thames salmon, whiting, haddock, mullet or bass, sea-bream or sole, conger, carp, trout, crabs, lobster and porpoise or seal (which was counted as fish in those days). Then there'd be a second course of nine dishes that to us sounds like more of the same. There might be another soup, sturgeon, bream, tench, perch, eels, lampreys, salmon roes, crayfish, shrimps, tart, fritters, fruit, baked pippins, oranges, butter and eggs.

The Eltham Ordinances

The Tudor age was obsessed with order in all things. There was a proliferation of rules and regulations. In 1526 Cardinal Wolsey revised earlier rules governing the royal household. These were known as the Eltham Ordinances, and continued to be revised throughout the Tudor period. They cover every aspect of court administration, particularly the catering, which was a major expenditure.

The first duty in a court of 1500 was to root out gatecrashers: '… *once or twice in the week, view all the Offices and Chambers of the Household to see if there be any Strangers eating in the said Offices or Chamber at the Meale times, or at any other time, contrary to the King's Ordinance'*.

And you could only control what you spent on food if you stopped courtiers having midnight feasts: '… *sundry noblemen, gentlemen and others, doe much delight and use to dyne in corners and secret places, not repairing to the King's chamber nor hall.'*

The status-obsessed Tudors had to make sure that each class of courtier got appropriate food. Only the King and his closest Privy Councillors were served with the whole menu. Simple yeomen such as the *'Wardrober of the Bedds, Groome Porter, Yeomen and Officers of the House'* had to get by on beef, veal *'or other rost'*, and *'pig, goose or cony* [rabbit]*'*, washed down with ale.

It was no coincidence that the Eltham Ordinances appeared in the same year that Wolsey handed over Hampton Court Palace to Henry VIII. The Archbishop's revision of court etiquette was another nail in his political coffin. He had been struggling to eliminate those he thought were influencing the King. In the Ordinances, he went too far. He halved the number of 'Gentlemen of the Privy Chamber', getting rid of enemies such as William Compton, the Groom of the Stool (see below). But the King resented this interference. The gift of his Thames-side mansion was Wolsey's futile attempt to appease the angry monarch.

Groom of the Stool

What goes in must come out. Henry VIII partook freely of those twenty-odd dishes twice a day. His high-meat, high-fat, low-veg diet turned him from one of the most eligible princes in Christendom – six-foot-two, broad-shouldered, dashing and fond of the ladies – into the massive piggy-eyed king of Holbein's portraits. In his latter days he had a 54-inch waist, and probably suffered from

1536 The Dissolution of the Monasteries begins. Henry VIII gets a huge financial boost from all the land and property he appropriates. But the traditional system of almsgiving in which monks look after the poor is disrupted. Consequently vagrants and beggars (including strolling players) become a serious problem. A law is passed that people caught outside their parish without work shall be whipped through the streets. For a second offence the vagabond is to lose part of an ear.

1540 The state continues its clamp-down on leisure: the English are now banned from playing football (a version with goalposts a mile apart!).

both gout and syphilis. At 24 stone, he was so heavy that he had to be winched into the saddle. His increased size dates from a jousting accident in 1536. He suffered a thigh wound which not only prevented him from taking exercise but which gradually became ulcerated, so he also had suppurating sores on his upper thighs. Dealing with this mass of blubber, and monitoring the by-products of Henry's disastrous diet, was the poor soul who had to wipe his bottom: the Groom of the Stool.

Yes, he really did wipe the King's bottom. The Tudors believed their sovereign was a divinely appointed being, ordained and anointed by God. Everything had to be done for him. And where we might want some privacy on the toilet, the King's bathroom life was lived under the public gaze.

The Groom of the Stole (as it was usually written) was actually an extremely prestigious position at court. Only a top aristocrat was thought worthy enough to touch the royal behind. The Groom had the privilege of being alone with the King in his most private moments. He had keys to the royal apartments and helped his master to dress. The post was extremely well paid and was a stepping-stone to high office.

But being that close to the King had its dangers, too. When Henry was looking around for a way to get rid of Anne Boleyn, he picked on his Groom of the Stool. Sir Henry Norreys was executed in 1536 for allegedly committing adultery with her.

*State-of-the-art Tudor plumbing. Built to last; built, in fact, like a brick ****house.*

MARCI 16
ITE IN MVDVM VNIVIRSV ETPREDICATE
EVANGELIVM OMNI CREATVRE

Henry VIII. No portraits exist from the point of view of the Groom of the Stool.

Other than the political risks, the job was simply unpleasant. The mechanics and tools of the trade were simple. First you needed a piece of furniture for the King to sit on. This was a padded box or 'close stool' with a hole in the top, and a bucket or basin hidden underneath. It is this stool that gave its name to the things the King dropped into the bucket. The close stool was ornate, but lightweight. His Majesty could not be expected to rush upstairs if the call took him, so it had to be sufficiently portable for the groom to go and fetch it.

The other accoutrements are laid down in The Babees Boke of Nurture, a fifteenth-century text: 'Look there be blanket, cotton, or linen to wipe the nether end, and ever he clepith [whenever he calls], wait ready and entende [attend], basin and ewer, and on your shoulder a towel.' While common folk might use moss to wipe their bottoms, only the best was good enough for the King. He'd have diaper cloth. Diaper was double-woven into a diamond pattern. It was thick and absorbent – hence the American name for a nappy.

The royal turd wasn't discarded when it landed in the bucket. It still had a tale to tell. The King's stools were examined with interest for signs of his well-being. When the royal digestive tract got blocked because of his appalling diet, the Groom was expected to administer an enema. Sir Thomas Heneage became the Groom of the Stool after the demise of Henry Norreys. In September 1539 he reported to Thomas Cromwell, the King's Secretary, with obvious satisfaction that their master had had 'a very fair siege' after he had administered a laxative and an enema.

Once it had been properly scrutinized, the royal stool was free to begin its voyage to the Thames via a state-of-the-art sewage system.

In the 1480s, as part of a revival of interest in the classical world, a book on Roman plumbing, *De Aquae urbis Romae* by the Roman author Sextus Julius Frontinus, was rediscovered. When Hampton Court was built, it was equipped with the very latest plumbing system informed by this classical knowledge. There are two miles of culverts and pipes still in existence which once took the court waste down to the river. Inevitably these pipes sometimes got blocked. When this happened a man was called in for whom grooming the stool must have seemed an unobtainable life of luxury.

THE BEST & **WORST** OF TIMES

1545 Henry's flagship, the *Mary Rose*, sinks near Portsmouth.

1548 Edward VI becomes King at the age of nine. Tutored by a strict Protestant, he turns his father's pragmatic break from Rome into an ideological reality.

1548 Introduction of the *Book of Common Prayer* – still the basis for Church of England liturgy. The book sets out twenty-seven holy days when working people can refrain from 'lawful bodily labour'. Apart from these days and Sundays, people work long hours every day.

Gong Scourer

Gong (or gung) is dung, human excrement. And the Gong Scourer did exactly what his name suggests. He was the Dyno-Rod man and cesspit cleaner of his day. He was also known as the Gong Farmer or Fermour, a name derived from the French word meaning 'to cart away'.

His working life was spent up to his knees, waist, even neck in human ordure. He usually worked as part of a team, often having a couple of young boys on hand with buckets. A boy would have been useful for chipping out a blockage in a confined space.

For this disgusting work the Gong Scourers at Hampton Court were well rewarded. Normally they received sixpence a day. Queen Elizabeth's Gong Scourer, a man called Sampson, asked for his wages to be part-paid in brandy. But the Hampton Court sewage men had it comparatively easy compared with their counterparts in the City of London.

The culverts at Hampton Court Palace. They are cleaned up today, but 400 years ago they meant a nightmarish journey in the dark for a young Gong Scourer's assistant with only a single wick for illumination.

During the sixteenth century, London's population grew by 400 per cent. One of the biggest headaches facing the city was sewage arrangements. We tend to imagine human excrement and waste being tipped out of upstairs windows on to unsuspecting passers-by in the filthy streets below. While this was often the case, it was not the whole picture.

The city fathers tried to provide access to one privy for every twenty households. Most of these public loos were lean-to structures with wooden seats. They were built over watercourses such as the River Fleet, which flowed through the City of London into the Thames. In addition, many of the bigger houses had privies with private cesspits. Again, not much more than a row of seats over a tank, but there was a clear sense that owners had responsibility for their own waste. When a neighbour's cesspit was built too close to another person's house and leaked into the cellar, it could lead to a court case.

The strict rules that governed the Gong Farmers show how seriously the City authorities tried to control the management of the waste and the odours they thought harboured disease. Gong Farmers were only allowed to live in certain areas of the city, and had to work a perpetual night shift, from nine at night till five in the morning. There were no street lights, so they had to work with only the assistance of smoky tallow candles made from animal fat.

The Gong Farmer would transport a big vat or 'pipe' through the streets on a horse-drawn cart. When he and his team arrived at the cesspit, they would prise up the boards of the privy seat. With a particularly large or difficult privy they might break open the walls and empty it from the side.

They would then remove the effluent. This consisted of two layers. At the top was liquid, which could be bucketed out. This was easy to get at, because the Gong Farmer was only called in when the owner's cesspit was full. But underneath there was solid, thick sludge that had to be dug out. Bad enough in the cooler months, but imagine working in the depths of the privy itself in the sweaty heat of a summer night. It must have been like one of the circles of hell. All manner of awfulness could be found, including the small rotting corpses of unwanted babies, which were often disposed of down the privy.

The job was horrifically smelly and dangerous. Indeed, when tobacco became available, many Gong Farmers took up the habit, using it to counteract the

THE BEST & WORST OF TIMES

1550s First famine of the Tudor period.

1553 Edward VI dies at the age of sixteen. His death ushers in a period of instability as Mary I becomes Queen. She reinstitutes Catholicism with a wave of persecution.

1555 Leading Protestant Churchmen Latimer and Ridley are burnt at Oxford.

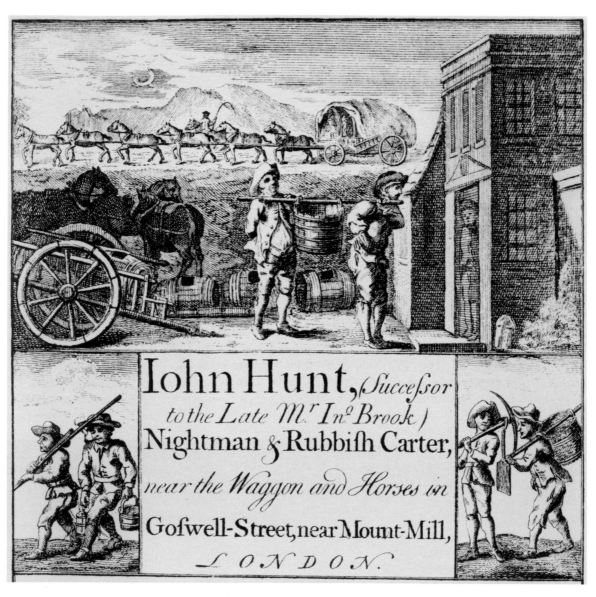

Iohn Hunt, (Successor to the Late Mr Ino Brook) Nightman & Rubbish Carter, near the Waggon and Horses in Gofwell-Street, near Mount-Mill, LONDON.

Nightmen or Gong Farmers at work. The barrels with the opening in the background are the 'pipes' that transgressing Gong Farmers could be forced to sit in as punishment.

noxious fumes. There are coroners' reports of Gong Farmers who were asphyxiated, almost certainly due to hydrogen sulphide poisoning.

Like their counterparts at court, the Scourers were well paid. Accounts of some of the big city houses show ten shillings being paid for the clearing of a communal privy, though this would have been split between several workers and included the cost of a horse and cart.

But the penalties for transgressing the strict city ordinances were harsh. One Gong Farmer poured effluent down a drain instead of carting it outside the city. He was put in his 'pipe', which was filled with filth up to his neck, and

he was then left in Golden Lane in London with a sign hung around his neck stating his crime.

But this treatment was a mere slap on the wrist compared with the punishments meted out to working women who overstepped the mark.

Fishwife

Fish'wife – a woman who carries fish about for sale; a coarse, loud-mouthed woman (*Chambers Dictionary*).

The attitude of Tudor men towards the vast army of women workers is epitomized by their treatment of fishermen's wives.

For most women there was only one career option, and that was marriage. They were not expected to have an independent job except as an adjunct to their husbands, e.g. the baker's wife.

Fishwives became the exception to this rule by nature of their work. They helped their husbands by gutting, smoking and selling fish. But when their men were away at sea, they were self-employed, and had a great deal of freedom. They needed a big voice and personality to call their wares. It was no use being a shrinking violet in a Tudor market. So fishwives were loud. But they didn't get to eat much of their fish. White fish was an expensive food earmarked for the gentry. Fishwives had to make do with the working-man's seafood – oysters!

Tudor fishwives from a detail of a 1582 map. Loud, foul-mouthed and independent, today they'd be ideal Big Brother *contestants; in the sixteenth century they were a threat to the social order.*

THE BEST & WORST OF TIMES

1558 England loses Calais – the last remnant of French land won by Henry V. Mary dies and Elizabeth I becomes Queen.

1563 In October, the new queen buys 120,000 pins from her pinmaker.

1570 Francis Drake sets off on his first voyage to the Indies. His attacks on Spanish ships stuff Elizabeth's coffers with Catholic gold.

1584 Sir Walter Raleigh sails for the New World.

These were tough women. They drank, they smoked, they swore. This behaviour brought them into direct opposition with prevailing Tudor morality. They became an archetype for the sort of woman by whom men felt threatened. Their job title became the object of a reactionary backlash. We still use it today as a pejorative term.

The Protestant Reformation was spreading through the country, causing both social disruption and political pressure. In all areas of life those in charge were desperate to reassert order. The proliferation of books of behaviour – which included instruction manuals on how women should behave (see below) – were indicative of a desire to clamp down on private life and bring it under strict control.

The Good Wife

John Fitzherbert's *A Book of Husbandry* is an improving manual like the Babees Boke (see page 87). Anyone following these instructions for the aspiring perfect wife wouldn't have much time for scolding.

When thou art up and ready
Then first sweep the house.
Dress up thy dishboard and set up all things in good order within thy house
Milk thy kine
Feed thy calves
Sile [strain] up thy milk
Take up thy children and array them.
And provide for thy husband's breakfast, dinner, supper and for thy
children and servants and take thy part with them.
And to ordain corn and malt to the mill,
To bake and brew withal when need is
Thou must make butter and cheese when thou may
Serve thy swine both morning and evening
And give thy pullen [chicken] meat in the morning
And when time of the year cometh, thou must take heed how thy hen,
ducks and geese do lay and to gather up their eggs and when thy was
broody to set them theras no beasts, swine or other vermin hurt them.

John Fitzherbert, *A Book of Husbandry*, 1525

Women who broke the social rules were known as 'scolds'. In Tudor times, 'scold' was a word used to describe offensive behaviour, second only in its opprobrium to the word 'whore'. You could even be declared a scold by a court

of law. The modern legal equivalent would be a charge of harassment, involving persistent verbal abuse, threats or physical violence.

The women who were brought up in front of a magistrate for being scolds were usually married, and came from the broad, lower-middling ranks to which the bulk of the population belonged. These were the wives of butchers, bakers, weavers and of course fish-sellers. But there were also a few well-heeled scolds, including merchants' wives and even the occasional gentlewoman.

Three Scolds

Although some of the biggest name players of the day, like Mary Tudor, Elizabeth I and Mary Queen of Scots, were women, it's unusual for ordinary women to make it into the history books. Ironically, the ones we know most about tend to be those who became infamous for making a nuisance of themselves.

Like Catherine Barnaby in London, who was declared a scold because she accused one of her neighbours of murdering her own child and keeping company with 'none but thieves, rogues and peddlers'. She didn't mince her words. 'Thou … art a drunken quean [a brawling woman] and a coppernosed quean and thou goest a drinking from house to house every day.'

Agnes Davis and Margaret Davis (no relation) were involved in long-standing quarrels and eventually both were accused of being common scolds. Agnes was given remission but Margaret was ducked. In revenge, her supporters raided Agnes's house on Christmas night, ate two mince pies and urinated in her pottage pot. Then they tied her to a ducking stool and ducked her seven times.

Being led by the bridle yanks painfully at your mouth and makes you dribble uncontrollably.

Queen Elizabeth was the most independent of women who avoided marriage like the plague. Yet ironically in her reign there was a sharp rise in prosecutions of unruly women. And the punishment meted out to convicted scolds became more severe. Previously they might only have been fined. Now they had to face one of two humiliating punishments: the scold's bridle or the ducking stool.

The scold's bridle was most common in northern and eastern towns. There are records of its use in Bridgnorth, Chester, Preston, Manchester and

In order to experience a ducking, I was tied to a chair, in the bitter December wind, with half-a-dozen burly blokes getting up a hearty momentum at the other end of the ducking stool. I had the backup of a diver on standby. Nevertheless I was only too aware that I was not only going to get wet and extremely cold but was in danger of half drowning if something went wrong. With an uncaring mob and no safety checks, it's no wonder that women died on the stool.

Newcastle. The bridle or branks (see picture opposite) is a metal mask like a facial chastity belt that was locked round the offender's head. A metal tab was placed in the mouth, pressing down on the tongue (the offending organ of the scold). A rope was then tied to the nose of the bridle to lead the scold through the streets. The punishment was symbolic of taming a wild and unruly beast.

Elsewhere a ducking stool was used. This had been a community punishment for both men and women since the eleventh century, but in Tudor times it became used exclusively for women. In symbolic terms the ducking stool was seen to be particularly appropriate for cooling the immoderate heat of the female tongue.

Legal handbooks, such as John Kitchen's *Le Court Leete*, said it was the duty of every manor and similar jurisdiction to provide and maintain a ducking stool. The chairs were made of wood, and were often very ornate. They could be a seesaw shape or suspended on ropes. Some of them had wheels, so the scold could be paraded through the town.

In some places it was considered effective simply to show the scold the punishment she might undergo. And towns such as Dorchester in Dorset

applied some humanity by ordering duckings only when the weather was warm. But in other places you could expect no mercy. A ducking was a fun day out for the community. Sometimes high spirits and over-enthusiasm led to women being drowned.

One French commentator, Henri Misson, described the process as 'rather amusing', but he was of course talking from the spectator's point of view. Both the branks and the ducking stool were bitterly humiliating. This was community justice and one of the worst aspects was that the jeering crowd were your neighbours, people you'd have to live with afterwards.

Yet for some of these tough-as-nails women, even such deterrents proved ineffective. Women were known to go down into the water still pouring invective on their persecutors. The antiquary John Stow quotes the case of a woman who hooted at the Bishop of London. She was set on the ducking stool. Far from being repentant, 'she sat there for one hour greatly rejoicing in her lewd behaviour'.

In this atmosphere it may seem amazing that high culture should flourish, but the Elizabethan period was the golden age of English literature. Poets like Edmund Spenser and Sir Philip Sydney were practising their craft, as were playwrights Shakespeare, Marlowe, Kyd and Webster. The theatres of the Rose and Globe were right at the heart of this dramatic renaissance; and supporting them was another Worst Job: boy actor.

The disadvantages of this particular job are particularly clear to me. I began my career as a child actor in the original cast of Oliver! *Of course the life was exciting, but I worked late nights and was always tired. I would have been mortified if I'd had to wear a dress like young Tudor actors!*

Boy Actor

You'd have thought that actors taking part in works of art such as *Hamlet* would be seen in a very different light from bear baiters, clowns and street musicians. Not a bit of it. All these entertainment trades were lumped together as morally dubious, and banished to the ghetto of Southwark, safely across the Thames from respectable London. During an outbreak of plague the preacher at St Paul's told his congregation, 'The cause of plagues is sin, if you look to it well: and the cause of sin are plays: therefore the cause of plagues are plays.'

Southwark was a grim place where a boy apprentice might be mugged by cutpurses on his way to work, but out of London the players could find things even tougher. Under an Act of 1530 designed to discourage vagrants, players performing without a licence could be whipped twice in a market town,

A visit to Shakespeare's (reconstructed) Globe today is a high-end cultural treat. For the Tudors the original Globe was no more special than the nearby bear-baiting pits.

and then could lose part of their ears or be put in the pillory if they were caught again.

It was because the theatre was so disreputable that boy actors were necessary. Women were not allowed to appear in plays. The female roles had to be played by boys, and the older 'dame' parts by adult men in drag.

Shakespeare seems to have enjoyed playing with the sexual ambiguity of his female leads. In *Twelfth Night*, Viola is a part for an adolescent boy, playing a girl, disguised as a boy!

Boy actors earned only their keep. Exhaustion must have been commonplace and, on stage, a poor performance could be met by verbal abuse and even missiles hurled from the groundlings in the pit of the theatre.

Every actor ran the risk of being caught in a fire – illumination in early theatres could be deadly. But the whole business of playing a woman was fraught with discomfort and even danger. The white stage make-up was deadly lead-based stuff that eventually caused lumps of flesh to drop off, and the dresses and ruffs themselves were supremely uncomfortable.

The corset can't have been much fun to wear. It was pulled tight round the stomach and constricted the diaphragm. But the real torture came from the pins. Hundreds of them. Undergarments were stitched, but most dresses were simply pinned together. This method made it much easier than today's practice of

Nathan Field, an Elizabethan actor. Patronage was essential for Tudor actors. An Act of 1572 ruled that 'all common players … not belonging to any baron of this realm or [to] any other person of greater degree … shall be adjudged and deemed rogues, vagabonds and sturdy beggars'. Periodically the Queen's Council would forbid plays in the London suburbs because of plague epidemics, which made actors' jobs even less stable.

altering a garment to fit different people, and it preserved the cloth. Even that icon of the Tudor period, the ruff, was shaped with a heated iron from a single length of starched cloth and then pinned in place with up to 200 pins. A playwright called Tomkis, noting how it took five hours' pinning to attire a boy actor like a woman, said: 'A ship is sooner rigged than a gentlewoman made ready.' Can you imagine adolescent boys keeping still for long enough to avoid being pricked by those myriads of pins? It must have been like wearing a particularly large hedgehog inside out (which, of course, all women of the age knew from daily experience. No wonder Queen Elizabeth looks so stiff in all her portraits!).

Nor were the boys allowed to muck about and get their stage clothes dirty or torn. Their dresses weren't just stage props – they were the real thing, complete with jewels and expensive material. In a society that had lost the colourful festivals and dramatic liturgy provided by the Roman Catholic

THE BEST & WORST OF TIMES

1587 After being undermined by Elizabeth's Protestant ministers, Mary Queen of Scots is executed at Fotheringay Castle.

1588 Spanish Armada is defeated by British ships and British weather. The last major threat to the Protestant Tudor Queen is removed.

religion, the theatre was one of the few places where ordinary people could still get a taste of pageantry. A stage dress would have been jealously guarded and passed on in actors' wills to their apprentices. This was an important perk of the trade. A costume was often the most valuable thing that an actor owned.

But however bad the life of a boy actor must have been, it was nothing compared to the lot of those who made his pins.

Pinner

Pin making was a major part of the economy in Tudor times. Both men and women needed pins to keep their rich clothes from falling apart. Pins were often given as presents. Today the phrase 'pin money' means a bit of extra cash, but when it was coined it referred to the essential money you needed for keeping your clothes on your body. In October 1563 alone, Queen Elizabeth bought 121,000 pins from her pin maker Robert Careles. In 1587 almost three million pins were imported into London.

Bodger Hodgson, who supplies authentic Tudor props to Shakespeare's Globe, reconstructs a pinner's garret.

But there was also a large pinning industry based in the capital. Maybe as many as 3,000 people were Pin Makers. Proportionately, that's as many people as work in London Transport today. But we know virtually nothing about those people and their trade. They were too lowly and their trade too common for anyone to bother writing about them.

Most of our information about the trade has been provided by archaeologists. In particular they have helped establish how the pins were made. A cow's foot-bone had horizontal grooves carved into it. Copper wire was drawn through these grooves, then cut to an appropriate length, and held in place while the end was filed to a sharp point. Another short piece of wire was wound round the top of the pin and fixed to it by 'crimping' the head on to the shaft using a stamp. The better pins were frequently 'tinned' with a thin layer of chemically deposited tin.

The size of the grooves seems to indicate that Pinners used child labour. The most fiddly parts of the job could only have been done by little fingers. Pinning is one of the earliest trades in which various workers performed different parts of the job. By the eighteenth century this process was sufficiently well organized for the economist Adam Smith to use it, in his book *The Wealth of Nations*, as an example of his theory of the 'division of labour'.

There was a high-end and a low-end of the pinning market. We know for instance that there were at least twenty-seven different kinds of pins and some were quite beautiful. The better quality ones were made by craftsmen of the Pinners' Guild, but most of the work was organized in people's homes. They often lived close to places where they could obtain the raw materials for their bone tools, like the butchers' market at Smithfield. The workforce usually comprised a Master Pinner supervising family members and apprentices. They would labour in a garret, if possible with a south-facing window, in order to provide enough light for the fiddly operations. It would have been an incredibly dull job, with the inherent health hazard of breathing in shards and dust from the raw materials.

To make matters worse, Henry VIII, in an effort to block cheap imports, instituted a law saying that all pin heads had to be soldered. This added another element to the production line and another danger. The solder was either a tin-rich flux (borax) or a mix of 4 per cent silver and 96 per cent tin. This silver solder gave off cadmium fumes and could cause lung cancer.

Pinners tended to earn practically starvation wages. In Elizabethan times a penny bought a loaf of bread, or a play ticket, or a wherry across the Thames. To make one shilling (i.e. twelve pennies) you had to make 1,000 brass pins. Experiments with Tudor technology have found that this would take about fifty hours. Even if experienced Tudor Pinners were able to work at double this rate, they would hardly have been able to afford much more than the basics of life. No wonder this job was mostly the preserve of the very young, the old, and the destitute. Yet despite the hazards, the boredom and the low pay, pinning has not been given the five star award for the Worst Job of the era. That honour has been reserved – purely on account of the gut-wrenching stink it produced – for the manufacturer of the colour blue.

THE BEST & WORST OF TIMES

1590s Second great famine of the Tudor period.

1592 First recorded performance of Shakespeare's first play, *Henry VI Part 1*, at the Rose Theatre – taken off after nineteen performances because of an outbreak of plague; a blow for the boy actor who would have been taking the starring role of the child king, Henry VI.

1593 Christopher Marlowe, playwright, who may also have been a spy for Elizabeth's secret service, is stabbed to death in a pub brawl.

1596 Publication of Spenser's *Faerie Queen*, celebrating Elizabeth I.

The Worst Job of All: Woad Dyer

Before the importation of indigo from the East began at the end of the sixteenth century, the only source for the rich blue we can still see in Tudor tapestries and textiles was the indigo extracted from the plant woad.

Woad, *Isatis tinctoria*, is related to the cabbage. It's a robust plant that produces yellow flowers on a metre-high stem. It was brought to Britain from southern Europe by the Celts, who called it glasto. The ancient settlement of Glastonbury means 'a place where woad grows'.

But the process by which the blue dye was extracted was so foul that it forced Woad Dyers, an outcast group like the Gong Farmers, to live on the fringes of society.

The problem was the smell. It is difficult to describe the stench on paper. Put it like this. How far away from a bad smell would you consider a safe

distance? Queen Elizabeth not only ordered Woad Dyers to stop work completely before she travelled through a town. She also decreed that they shouldn't come within five miles of where she was staying. Woad dying was that smelly.

But Woad Dyers were by no means the lowest of the low. They were highly skilled craftsmen, the forerunners of the chemical industry. They spent their lives working on a precise chemical process.

The woad was fermented and dried into woad balls. This part of the job was called couching and caused particularly noxious fumes to be given off. It took about 50 kilos of leaves to produce just under 5 kilos of pigment. Most of the woad used in Tudor England was imported in this form from south-west

The alchemy of woad. These two pictures are taken within ten seconds of each other, the blue dye instantly activating on contact with air.

Without the hideous stench of woad, the exuberant beauty of such tapestries as this sixteenth-century French one would have been impossible. The rich background blue from woad also survives the centuries far better than the red and green dyes that fade more easily.

France, where, it was said, you could get rich by sitting still and watching your woad grow.

But the smell got worse because, to extract the dye, the balls had to be crushed and further fermented in an alkaline solution.

Yes, alkaline, just like the Fuller. And the Woad Dyers did indeed sometimes use urine, although lime or wood ash and boiling water were just as good. The dried, couched woad was put into a vat with the solvent and kept at 50°C for three days. At this stage the craft of the Dyers was in maintaining alkalinity without special equipment to test the pH value of the solution. They did this by using a combination of their senses.

They could feel its texture: the mixture was slippery like water with bath oil in it. But they also employed taste and smell. Presumably this nauseous activity was all part of a day's work but, to our senses, cooked woad smells and tastes like rotting boiled cabbage mixed with sewage. This is not merely our modern imagination at work. Chemical analysis shows that the brew contains elements of the same gases that are given off by raw human waste.

Once the mixture was ready, the wool was dyed before it was woven to ensure that the colouring agent was evenly distributed; in other words it was literally 'dyed in the wool'. The wool was placed in the vat overnight in a trammel, a sort of metal colander, to protect it from the woad sludge at the bottom of the vat.

When the cover was taken off, the wool wasn't blue, just greeny-white. But the alchemy occurred when the wool was taken out of the vat. The indigo only works on exposure to oxygen. The effect is almost instantaneous. As the unpromising light-green wool is removed and brought into contact with the air, it turns magically to the deepest shade of blue.

Woad Dyers may have been more successful than medieval alchemists, but they were still despised. There are a number of records dealing with the anti-social behaviour of Dyers. They were sometimes caught disposing of their dangerous and environmentally unfriendly chemicals by pouring them into the street or the nearest water course. Understandably, this caused protests.

Dyers tended to be secretive and inbred. Even if they changed their clothes and had a thorough wash they still stood out in a crowd. Their hands and fingernails were permanently blue, and it was even reported that some had blue sweat. They usually married other Dyers, who presumably didn't mind people who looked like a human Stilton.

Woad Dyers disappeared with the introduction of indigo from the tropics, but their skills underpin modern dyeing techniques. Today, with a resurgent interest in natural dyes, woad is back, and is being grown once more in the south of England and East Anglia. But if someone sets up a woad shop next door to you, you should either complain to the local authority or have your nose surgically removed.

THE BEST & WORST OF TIMES

1597 The tomato is introduced to England. Along with the newly introduced potato, the foundations are now laid for chips, tomato ketchup and obesity.

1601 Elizabethan Poor Law introduced. Parishes are made responsible for dealing with the poor, replacing the work done by the demolished monastery system. Workhouses now have to be provided for the old and ill who can't work. Those who refuse to contribute money to help the poor can now be sent to prison. This system remains in place until 1834 (when it is toughened up!).

1603 Death of Elizabeth I – end of the Tudor period. James, son of Mary Queen of Scots, becomes King of Scotland and England. The rift between the two countries begins to close.

CHAPTER FOUR

Stuart Worst Jobs

I n 1603 the childless Queen Elizabeth died and was succeeded by the son of her great rival, Mary Queen of Scots. James VI of Scotland became James I of England, thus uniting the two kingdoms in one person. The Act of Union formalized the new country of Britain.

James Stuart's reign ushered in a turbulent century of religious, political and social upheaval. The great questions of whether the monarchy should be Catholic or Protestant, and whether the King should reign supreme or with the assent of Parliament, were to lead to the Gunpowder Plot, the Civil War, the execution of Charles I, and the 'Glorious Revolution' of 1688. But, as usual, the ship of state wasn't sailing by itself. All these momentous political events needed an army of menials willing to spread the halibut and push it over the logs (for an explanation of this metaphor, see the Viking Portager, page 37).

By 1700 the population of Britain was about 7.5 million. Over a third were labourers surviving on an average wage of a shilling a day. Twenty per cent of people relied, at least occasionally, on the parish handouts established by the Elizabethan Poor Laws. To vote, you had to be a yeoman with at least forty shillings' worth of land. The political turmoil that divided the country was being orchestrated by an elite group that the common people had never met or even heard of.

Nevertheless, many of the poor were deeply embroiled in the great events of the age. There was one job in particular without which Guy Fawkes, and Cavaliers and Roundheads alike, would not have been able to function at all. If it hadn't been for the Saltpetre Man there would have been no gunpowder, or 'black powder' as the Stuarts called it, to fire muskets or attempt to blow up the King and his Parliament.

Although the sedan chair was fashionable it also had a racy reputation. This engraving, The Covent Garden Frolick *by Louis Boitard, shows an exhausted Betty Careless, a woman of dubious reputation, being carted home in a sedan with a lover still sprawling on the roof. Not only are the Sedan Chair carriers excluded from the fun, they're having to carry an extra non-paying passenger. No wonder they look fed up.*

Guy Fawkes' target, James I.

Saltpetre Man

Gunpowder is a simple but lethal concoction of three chemicals: 10 per cent carbon, 15 per cent sulphur and 75 per cent potassium nitrate or saltpetre. The nitrates in saltpetre produce oxygen, which expands on burning, creating an explosive reaction with the carbon. You need 25 g of gunpowder to fire a single musket ball, and 400 g of it to launch a cannonball. Consequently, in times of war vast quantities of saltpetre were required. And it was all garnered by Saltpetre Men.

The Saltpetre Man was a strange combination of milkman, bailiff, farm labourer and Gong Scourer. His job was simple. The main sources of nitrates in Stuart times were our old friends urine and faeces, which had been left in the earth long enough to break down into calcium and sodium nitrates. First, the

Saltpetre Man had to find some urine-soaked dungy earth, then he had to dig out the choicest bits using good old-fashioned hard labour. His stamping ground was the latrine, the pigpen, the manure heap, the dovecote – anywhere a good helping of guano had had a chance to soak into the soil. Gong Scourers (see page 87) simply got rid of waste. Saltpetre Men turned it into a commodity.

Shifting tons of chemical-rich earth could be a hernia-inducing task. The milkman side of the job was intended to circumvent some of this hard work. In 1625 Sir John Brooke and Thomas Russell devised a way to extract nitrates directly from urine. Householders in London and Westminster were encouraged to put out their pisspots for door-to-door collection once a day in summer, and once every two days in winter. The Saltpetre Men then went round the streets decanting the precious liquid into barrels. Smelly and sticky it may have been, but it avoided hours of shovel-wielding. Sadly, the revolutionary urine churn was abandoned two years later as the technique was found to be inefficient, and the Saltpetre Men returned to the tried and trusted methods of yore.

If you've got the impression that Saltpetre Men were innocent sons of the soil, forget it. Gunpowder was too vital a commodity to be left to enthusiastic amateurs. Demand had to be met; the defence of the realm was paramount. The nation needed saltpetre and wasn't too concerned where it came from. Saltpetre Men had a special licence from the King to go into anyone's home and dig. They used and abused their position and were hated for it. The precursor of *The Times* newspaper called them 'rabble'. Individual Saltpetre Men became infamous. They acquired nicknames such as 'Rough Ralph' and 'Welsh Will', with bully-boy reputations to match.

So not only did they have to spend their days in shit-rich earth, but they must have needed a morality by-pass and skin as thick as a VAT inspector as they burst into homes to dig up hen houses and privies. In 1638 Saltpetre Men even tried to get permission to enter churches in their search for nitrate-rich material because 'women pee in their seats which causes excellent saltpetre'. Perhaps the alleged incontinence was due to the length of seventeenth-century church services.

People tried to avoid having to let the Saltpetre Men in – for example, they gravelled or paved the areas round their latrines so there was no earth to be plundered. Sometimes they'd be ordered to remove the paving and reinstate the earth floor to allow a build-up of saltpetre. Sir Henry Sambourne was arrested in 1634 for refusing to let Saltpetre Men into his dovecote, and wasn't released till he'd paid a fine.

To add insult to injury, once they had removed all they wanted, they expected the householder to supply transport for it at reduced rates. And they got special rates on road tolls. Eventually, in response to public outrage, they were obliged to ask consent before they entered a property, and had to make good after they had extracted the necessary soil. A law was also passed exempting the premises of 'persons of quality'.

THE BEST & WORST OF TIMES

1603 James VI of Scotland, from the Stuart family, accedes to the throne of England as James I. The Act of Union is passed, creating the kingdom of Britain.

1605 The Gunpowder Plot. Guy Fawkes and his fellow conspirators are foiled. Their (French) gunpowder was damp anyway – they should have used their local Saltpetre Man!

1607 British settlers establish the colony of Jamestown in America.

Given the amount of power Saltpetre Men wielded, you might have expected the job to be compensated by a big fat pay packet. After all, there was a lot of money in saltpetre.

But, as usual, the people who did the grafting didn't see much of it. The money was pocketed by gang masters who could afford the initial outlay. Producers were contracted to deliver an agreed amount of saltpetre at fixed rates. To make a big profit, they paid their labourers as little as possible. The men who had to force their way into people's homes, putting up with complaints and insults while emptying the earth under the latrine, didn't earn much more than a farm worker. They couldn't even make a bit on the side by missing out a house accidentally on purpose. It was deemed an offence to bribe a Saltpetre Man.

If you were wondering how they knew which bits of soil were rich in saltpetre, the answer is – they tasted it. Thoroughly urine-soaked earth contained white deposits. These crystals contained sodium and tasted salty and quite sharp. They also reacted with water in an endothermic (heat-absorbing) reaction, which meant that when a Saltpetre Man put a drop on his tongue, it turned to scum and felt cold.

But the job didn't simply comprise of tasting and digging. Gunpowder manufacture is an Arabic invention, described in a thirteenth-century book by Hassan Al-Rammah. Once extracted, the urine-rich soil had to be mixed with ashes at a refinery. This mixture was then dissolved in water, boiled up in an evil-smelling soup, and allowed to crystallize. The crystals were then mixed with glue or blood. The scum that rose to the top of the brew contained any remaining organic residue. Once this was removed, the mixture was re-crystallized and washed.

Finally, the refined saltpetre was delivered to the State's licensed gunpowder-maker, who during this period was John Evelyn in Surrey. It was Evelyn who mixed in the other ingredients (keeping them damp to avoid sparks and accidents), using rollers powered by horses. The resulting powder was then ground and dried before it could be used to kill, maim and blow up the enemy's defences.

Saltpetre absorbs moisture from the air so, when left, gunpowder will go damp or 'decayed'. This was the state the Gunpowder Plot powder was in. Guy Fawkes was brought into the plot because he was an explosives expert but, given how secret the plan needed to be, he couldn't just go and buy fresh powder over the counter. He did a dodgy deal and bought French gunpowder that was decayed. He had thirty-six barrelsful. Each would have held 100 lb of the stuff. If his 3,600 lb of gunpowder had been fresh, it would have been enough to lay waste an area of Westminster with a radius of over 500 yards. But the most famous gunpowder in history was totally useless.

Despite this debacle, the rest of the Stuart period was punctuated with bangs big and small. The most beneficial of these were the gunpowder explosions

Robert
Winter

Christopher
Wright

Iohn
Wright

Thomas
Percy

Guido
Fawkes

Robert
Catesby

Thomas
Winter

The Gunpowder plotters. Just think, if they hadn't got the foreigner Guido Fawkes in as a gunpowder expert, we might have ended up with fireworks on November 5th celebrating 'Robert Catesby Night'.

THE BEST & WORST OF TIMES

1616 William Shakespeare dies.

1620 Voyage of the *Mayflower*.

1625 Death of James I. Charles I becomes the second Stuart king.

used to halt the progress of the Great Fire of London. On 5 September 1666, Samuel Pepys, the head of the Admiralty, obtained the King's permission to use his sailors to bring in gunpowder to blow up rows of houses, thus creating a fire-break to stop the fire spreading. John Evelyn, the grandson of the famous gunpowder maker, noted in his diary that this tactic had been proposed when the fire first started, and most of the city might have been saved were it not for the rich men who originally vetoed the creation of fire-breaks, fearing their property would have to be sacrificed in the process.

Most of the uses of black powder were not so beneficial. In the Civil War, Oliver Cromwell developed the habit of 'slighting' the castles of aristocrats who had stood out against him. Today, slighting means making someone feel a bit miffed by ignoring them, but in the seventeenth century it involved taking a building back to ground zero. By completely blowing up one side of a castle (as happened at Tutbury in Derbyshire and Ashby-de-la-Zouch in Leicestershire) and leaving it exposed to the elements, Cromwell reduced his opponents' strongholds to rubble.

This kind of draconian action vividly demonstrates the bitterness felt on both sides during the English Civil War. From 1642 to 1646 a series of bloody battles and desperate sieges were fought out across England. Gunpowder featured heavily in the struggle. It fired muskets, cannons and an unusual weapon that provided the riskiest job of all: the petard.

Petardier's Assistant

A petard was a directional explosive device used in siege warfare. It comprised a wooden back plate, a small bell-shaped metal container with a hole in the end for a fuse, and 6 lb of gunpowder packed into the bell. This bomb was designed to break open the gates of a besieged castle or city. It did so by blowing doors off their hinges, punching a hole in them or destroying any bar or lock keeping them in place. It was invented by the Huguenots at the end of the sixteenth century.

During the Civil War, the petard was the province of the Petardier, whose name sounds similar to his close cousin, the bombardier. Both were engineers specializing in the use of gunpowder. Besides making petards, the Petardier also carried out undermining operations to create explosions under the walls of a castle. They were skilled officers and were rewarded as such. In 1627 a Chief Petardier got six shillings and eightpence a day and two assistants to help him. Apart from the occupational risks of working with gunpowder, there was nothing very dangerous about his job. He was indispensable and couldn't be put at risk. It was his assistants who drew the short straw.

The petard was simply a warhead. The Petardier's Assistant was the human guided missile who had to deliver the payload. His unenviable task was to approach the gates while constantly under fire, ram home the petard while being pelted from above by defenders with missiles, then light the fuse and scarper.

A Petardier's Assistant had two options: either go in heavily armoured and slow, or run like a seventeenth-century Jonny Wilkinson carrying a 20-lb rugby ball. Nobody cared much about the Assistant, but it was important not to waste the petard. So he usually went in at dawn or dusk, and had covering fire from flanking infantrymen.

Nevertheless, the attrition rate was enormous. It wasn't just the defenders who might kill him – he could also be blown to smithereens by his own bomb. Petards were unpredictable, and the following bears witness to this:

> ... *Let it work; For 'tis the sport to have the engineer*
> *Hoist with his own petar: and it shall go hard*
> *But I will delve one yard below their mines,*
> *And blow them at the moon.*

Hamlet, Act III Scene IV

The phrase 'hoist with his own petar(d)', a metaphor similar to shooting oneself in the foot, was coined by Shakespeare just a year before James I came to the throne. However, a host of alternative imagery is provided by the fact that the petar(d) gets its name from the Latin verb *pedere*, 'to fart'; presumably a reference to the muffled explosion the device produced when heard from the lines.

THE BEST & WORST OF TIMES

1634 Public-hire sedan chairs introduced to England by Sir Saunders Duncombe.

1642 Battles of Edgehill, Marston Moor, Naseby etc., provide plenty of business opportunities for Saltpetre Men. Petardier's Assistants are working flat out during the sieges.

1642 Civil War between Charles I's Cavaliers and Parliament's Roundheads.

In a modern-day experiment conducted with a petard of the right weight, flankers for covering fire and paintballs instead of muskets, the defenders on the castle walls dropped the would-be Petardier before he'd got within 50 metres of the gate.

Once he'd got to the gate, the Petardier's Assistant had to secure the petard. A contemporary instruction manual tells him what to do: 'A strong hooke is to be scrued into the substance you intend to ruine; and upon the hooke hangs the wringle [ring] of the Petard, and likewise to be shored up with a strong forked Rest to stay the Reverse of it…' Then he had to light the fuse. He did this with a piece of cord soaked in saltpetre called a 'slow match', a device just like the little red taper you get for lighting fireworks today. It would be burning at both ends, in case one end went out during the frenzied journey through enemy lines. By now the Petardier's Assistant would have been quaking with terror in case the petard went off unexpectedly and he became an unwilling suicide bomber.

Indeed, this was such a high-risk job that Assistants often prepared with the help of a little medication. When George Cranage blew down the door of Oswestry Castle with his petard, he had to be 'well lined with sacke' before he would attempt it. (Sack was a sort of sherry.)

The manual gives the seventeenth-century equivalent of the instruction 'light the blue touchpaper and retire to a safe distance': 'the Petardire must be careful to avoyd the danger of her Reverse by retyring in side line from it'. In other words, don't run away in a straight line. Forces are equal and opposite. When the petard went off, the explosion might inadvertently fire the contraption backwards. If the retreating Petardier's Assistant hadn't followed the instructions, he could find himself speeding back to the lines rather quicker than he'd intended, with a metal bell up his backside.

The Civil War ended when Oxford fell, though not because of the work of a Petardier. King Charles I surrendered. You could argue that one of the Worst Jobs of the period was his, because three years later he was tried by Parliament and beheaded. As he went to meet his fate at the hands of our old friend and executioner 'Cornet' Joyce (see Tudors, page 77), he was stripped of all royal dignity. Part of his humiliation was to be deprived of his carriage on the way to Whitehall. Instead, he was carried there by two practitioners of our next Worst Job.

Sedan Chair Bearer

Sedan chairs were the black cabs of the seventeenth and eighteenth centuries. But whereas we have cabbies, they had Sedan Chair Bearers. Unfortunately for the latter, though, they were not there simply to steer their vehicles and bore their customers with their political opinions. They also had to be the engines and wheels. Their job was simple but backbreaking: a pair of Bearers carried their passenger in a wooden box supported by two long poles. The weight was taken on the Bearers' shoulders by leather straps that were hooked on to the poles.

Anyone who has ever given another adult a piggyback will know just how heavy a human being can be after a relatively short distance. Most of us could only stagger if carrying this kind of weight, but Sedan Chair Bearers weren't allowed to walk slowly. Their pace was supposed to be a trot.

We may think of sedan chairs as part of the Georgian scene, but they were actually a Continental innovation brought over to England in the reign of the Stuart king, Charles I. He gave a royal warrant to a gentleman called Sir Saunders Duncombe entitling him to manufacture sedan chairs and rent them out in London and Westminster.

Sedan chairs were immediately popular. In the crowded streets of London they were far more practical than coaches. They could reverse and turn round easily, take short cuts, and drop their customers right at the door. They were also less likely to get caught in traffic jams.

Gentlemen started going to coffee and chocolate houses in them. If you had a romantic assignation and you didn't want your husband or wife to know, you could draw the curtains and the chair would get you to your secret tryst anonymously in all your finery. Given their obvious major advantages, sedan chairs soon spread to every major town in the country. Their presence in a town was a matter of pride – they were proof of 'culture', of the new world of evening entertainments, masquerades, concerts and intelligent rich patrons.

As the craze spread, so did ownership. The first fleets of chairs were carried by hired men. Later, Bearers bought their own chairs, and would either hire a

THE BEST & WORST OF TIMES

1646 Royalists sign articles of surrender after the siege of Oxford is ended.

1649 Charles I is carried to execution by Sedan Chair Bearers.

1649 Charles I is beheaded and the Commonwealth begins.

This scene from William Hogarth's The Rake's Progress *shows a sedan chair being dismantled like a flat-pack assembly model. The chairs couldn't be too solid or they'd be impossible to lift.*

second man or go into partnership. Like taxi driving today, chair bearing was a job that was open to immigrants. So there were numbers of Welsh, Scottish and especially Irish carriers. There is a record of a female Sedan Chair Bearer, too.

The similarities with taxis don't stop there. The very rich might have their own private chair, but otherwise you could book one in advance, pick one up on a rank, or hail one on the street. Instead of a yellow light, like cabs use today, Bearers would carry their chair the wrong way round to indicate that they were for hire.

The front man would negotiate the fare but, once the passenger was in, the Bearers earned every penny of it. They had to be super strong and super fit. The sedan chair itself weighed around 30 kilos empty. Add an average 80-kilo man to that and that's 55 kilos per Bearer to carry at a trot for up to a mile. Obviously sedans were intended for short journeys, but there are records of longer ones – in 1728 a woman went from London to Bath in one, and another used to make an annual trip from London to Switzerland using a relay team of Bearers.

But there was a fundamental unfairness built into the fare system, because everyone paid the same no matter how much they weighed! The difference between carrying Nell Gwyn and Samuel Pepys (they both used chairs) would have been very noticeable. In later years, Dr Johnson published a letter in the *Rambler*, supposedly written by a Chair Bearer:

It is common for men of the most unwieldy corpulence to crowd themselves into a chair, and demand to be carried for a shilling as far as an airy young lady whom we scarcely feel upon our poles. Surely we ought to be paid like all other mortals in proportion to our labour. Engines should be fixed in proper places to weigh chairs as they weigh wagons; and those whom ease and plenty have made unable to carry themselves, should give part of their superfluities to those who carry them.

But the misery of sedan-chair bearing wasn't restricted to the problems of weight. Bearers were essentially street traders, out in all seasons. Indeed, inclement weather was the best time for trade; who wants to walk when it's teeming with rain? So soaking clothes, with no modern way of drying them out overnight, were common. In icy weather, householders were encouraged to throw ashes on to the streets to give the Bearers a better foothold.

John Evelyn, the diarist, wrote sneeringly that the chair was 'held a conveyance for voluptuous persons and women of pleasure to their leu'd Rendivozes incognito'. And a song from 1695 called 'The Jolly Chairman' also expresses the range of clientele the chairmen could expect.

We carry the lazy, proud, Gout and the Pox,
and live by the carrying of Jack in a Box.

The chairs were not only heavy, they were awkward. The poles were deliberately long so that the Bearer behind could see where he was going. But still the front man had to keep shouting directions to the back one.

According to the seventeenth-century version of the highway code, sedan chairs had priority over pedestrians. 'Have a care!' or 'By your leave, sir!' apparently rang through the streets to clear people out of the way. There were no raised pavements in those days. Rails separated the notional road from the pavement, and pedestrians were frequently knocked down. A French visitor César de Saussure describes this in his diary: 'I received a tremendous push which hurled me four feet further on, and I should undoubtedly have fallen on my back had it not been for the wall of a house which broke my fall, much to the injury of my arm.' Other pedestrians, crushed against buildings by pavement-hogging chairs, were known to succumb to pavement-rage and punch in the glass of the chair.

At night a boy with a lamp would light the way, but sedan chairs were still

This is Charles I's death warrant. He liked the idea of sedan chairs because he thought too many coaches caused traffic jams. Little did he know when he gave permission for them to be introduced into London that he would be bundled into one to go to his death. After Charles II's restoration in 1660, Sir Purbeck Temple, testifying against the people who'd signed the death warrant, alleged that 'the people cried out: "What, do you carry the King in a common Cedan, as they carry such as have the Plague?"'

THE BEST & WORST OF TIMES

1650 First coffee house is opened by Puritans.

1651–2 The second English Civil War in support of Charles II. More work for Saltpetre Men.

1653 Oliver Cromwell becomes Lord Protector.

vulnerable to chair-jacking. This was usually more a problem for the customer than the Bearers. If stopped, they would stand meekly back and let the robber fleece the person in the box. The greatest danger as far as the Bearers were concerned was that the chair would be damaged!

By the beginning of the eighteenth century sedans were so popular that the trade had to be controlled. There were fines, suspensions and even imprisonment for Sedan Chair Bearers who used foul language, charged excessive fares, indulged in violent or disorderly behaviour, obstruction or drunkenness, or who kept their chair in poor condition.

Sedan chair bearing was a tough Worst Job, but there was another, equally knackering, career that didn't even offer the human interest and entrepreneurial opportunities the Chair Bearers enjoyed.

Water Carrier

Water carrying was an essential occupation. As towns grew, the supply of pure(ish) water became a big problem. Most of it wasn't for drinking; beer and wine were infinitely preferable to sour, brackish or polluted water. But it was still needed for cooking, washing and giving to the kids. Men with barrels of water suspended from a yoke over their shoulders were a part of Stuart life.

Our best information about them comes from London, which had been organizing water delivery since the Middle Ages. In 1496 the Waterbearers' Company was incorporated in the City of London. Its members walked the streets with tall conical containers on their backs. At that time they could get water for washing from the rivers, or fill their containers with drinking water from springs, wells or the newly erected conduits.

But by Stuart times the population of the city had grown to 500,000 people. The lack of available water was developing into a crisis. Although a few select houses had piped water connected to a main water-pipe, the vast majority of Londoners had no personal water supply. For the poor there were still the traditional wells and springs but they were now contaminated with typhoid and cholera from faecal waste.

The problem was solved by a daring piece of business enterprise. In 1609 Hugh Myddelton financed the construction of a new river to bring water to the

The triumphant opening of Sir Hugh Myddleton's New River in 1613 with local grandees overseeing the events.

capital from Hertfordshire. Myddelton was no engineer, but a goldsmith with an eye for the main chance. He arranged for an artificial channel to be cut from the springs at Amwell and Chadwell right into Clerkenwell.

It was a massive undertaking to construct a smooth slope over 40 miles long. Myddelton nearly went broke, but succeeded in getting King James to take a half share in the scheme. The cutting was finished in 1613.

From Clerkenwell, the water from the New River head was distributed across London though a system of wooden and lead pipes to the wealthy, and to everyone else via 4,000 Water Carriers carting it on their shoulders.

Water is heavy. Every litre weighs a kilo. Each Carrier had two 15-litre barrels slung on his back. If you have ever watched television's *Strongest Man in the World* competition, with large contestants grunting up and down a course carrying barrels, you will have some idea of the toughness of everyday life for the water carrier. Hugh Myddelton was made a baronet and his statue is on Islington Green. There are no memorials to the people who carried the water.

Would you trust this mountebank?

Toad Eater

Myddelton was not alone. The world of the Stuarts was full of enterprise and invention. This was the time when the Royal Society was established. In Cambridge, Isaac Newton defined the laws of gravity. In business, the English East India Company laid the economic foundations of what was to become a world-wide empire. But this explosion of new commerce wasn't limited to the rich and educated. Patent recipes, remedies and products were everywhere. They all had to be marketed, and an early form of commercial gives us perhaps the oddest Worst Job in the book: the Toad Eater.

Compared with the simple hard-working life of the Water Carrier, Toad Eaters were lazy charlatans. They worked the markets as assistants to quack doctors who wanted to sell their own patent brands of medicine. No one in the seventeenth century would have argued at the Toad Eater's inclusion in a canon of Worst Jobs. They did the unthinkable: they put toads in their mouths and swallowed them. Everyone knew this was crazy, tantamount to suicide.

Toads are gentle creatures. They live most of their lives in damp shady habitats. Unlike frogs, which escape predators by hopping or swimming away, toads simply sit still and, when disturbed, exude a milky white toxin from their paratoid glands behind their ears. This causes most potential predators to give them a wide berth.

It was widely believed that this foul-tasting substance was potent enough to kill a man. The quack or mountebank (so called because he would get up on a bench to call his wares), would attract attention by demonstrating an amazing escape from death. His associate, the Toad Eater, would eat a toad and then, as an antidote to its poison, would swallow a dose of whatever patent medicine was on sale. When he survived unscathed, the hope was that bottles of the remedy would fly from the shelves.

Was this show business rather than a pharmaceutical breakthrough? Perhaps the Toad Eater swallowed the toad and then regurgitated it, though this seems unlikely. Toad milk is not really deadly but it can make you pretty ill, and even temporarily ingesting it would make you very queasy. So the probability is that the Toad Eater palmed the frothy little amphibian. This sort of marketing was not uncommon. The equivalent French expression is *un avaleur de couleuvres* (literally 'a swallower of grass snakes').

Even at the time nobody was sure if the toads really were swallowed. Most people knew someone who'd met a bloke who had a brother who had actually seen it happen, but there are no first-hand accounts. It's possible, of course, that Toad Eaters really did perform the dreadful deed. But there is no definitive proof either way. Nevertheless, let's give these bravura performers the benefit of the doubt and designate the consumption of toads as a particularly nasty Worst Job.

The memory of Toad Eaters, or Toadies as they became known, still survives in our language. Someone who was actually prepared to swallow a poisonous creature because their boss told them to must be the worst kind of sycophant, or so the logic went. So a toady today is a creep, even if letting your boss win at golf isn't as bad as tickling your tonsils with a toxic amphibian. Which brings us to another unpleasant task whose job has entered our lexicon.

Toad Eaters made it into literature. A Rabbie Burns poem written eighty years after the Stuart dynasty ended already uses the term in its metaphorical sense. Here it is addressed to a name-dropping social crawler.

The Toadeater

Of Lordly acquaintance you boast,
And the Dukes that you dined wi' yestreen,
Yet an insect's an insect at most,
Tho' it crawl on the curl of a Queen!

Robert Burns, 1791

Nit Picker

Every person of status in Stuart times had to deal with nits. Luxuriant wigs on both men and women are an emblem of the era. They were made of human hair and were prone to the same parasite that appears in regular hair and skin: *Pediculus humanus capitis*, the head louse.

Most of us have come under scrutiny for head lice during our school days, or know children who've had them. It's not very savoury going through hair with a nit-comb trying to remove the sticky lice eggs or nits that cling to hair follicles. So who would choose to do it for a living? The answer, of course, is Nit Pickers.

Today, nit picking is a synonym for being ultra-fussy or pedantic. Three centuries ago it was a career option. In smaller houses the maid might delouse and pick nits out of the family's wigs. But a fully professional service was available for the well-to-do.

The Stuart fashion for men was to have their own hair cropped, but on to the back of their heads was pinned a large periwig made from human hair sewn

Samuel Pepys sporting his itchy finery.

on to a mesh. There were often nits attached to this wig hair, and when the lice hatched they'd crawl through the mesh and on to their victim's head, in order to feed by sucking blood from the back of the neck and behind the ears.

Lice aren't life threatening but cause considerable discomfort. Scratching leads to dermatitis and secondary infection. Prevention was difficult. Some people attempted to make a hard flour-and-water casing round the wig's mesh to prevent the lice getting through. But wearing a hard hat of dried dough was almost as uncomfortable as having nits.

So periodically, Nit Pickers, usually women, went from door to door offering their services and were invited in to clean the wigs.

The other option was to send the infested wig back to the wig maker and get a clean new one. Consequently wig makers often had supplies of lousy second-hand wigs. Samuel Pepys was incandescent when his wig maker sent him a 'new' wig crawling with parasites.

For poor people unable to afford the fashionable accessory of a custom-made wig, there was 'the dip' at Holborn – possibly the origin of the term 'lucky dip'. For a flat-rate contribution of threepence, people could dip their hands into a box full of wigs. The lucky part was getting one that wasn't infested!

The women who went nit picking had a flesh-creeping job, but the lice they had to deal with were relatively harmless. Had the people of the Stuart era known it, the parasite they really had to worry about was a flea, carried into the country on the back of black rats; a flea that, in turn, was the carrier of microscopic weapons of mass destruction. In laboratory experiments, mice keel over after being infected with just three bacilli of *Yersinia pestis*. Each flea delivers 24,000 bacilli with every bite, administering an almost certain fatal dose of bubonic plague.

Worst Jobs in the Plague

The Great Plague struck Britain in 1665. It was a particularly virulent form of the disease, combining *bubonic plague*, characterized by suppurating sores known as buboes, *septicaemic plague* that went straight into the bloodstream and *pneumonic plague*, which attacked the lungs. Many parts of Britain were affected, but London was by far the hardest hit. In just a few months, the population was reduced by a third.

The plague first appeared in St Giles, in the shadow of the city wall where the poor lived in dirty overcrowded hovels amid piles of rubbish. On 12 April 1665 Margaret Porteous became the first official victim. Two months later, 6,000 people were dead; by August, 31,000. Monthly rolls were kept detailing the way people died but, as Samuel Pepys points out, many of the poor never appeared in the official figures.

Samuel Pepys himself makes a connection between lousy wigs and the plague. In these diary entries he notes the scale of London's problem and then wonders about its knock-on effects on the wig industry.

31 August 1665

Thus this month ends, with great sadness upon the public through the greatness of the plague, everywhere through the kingdom almost. Every day sadder and sadder news of its encrease. In the City died this week 7,496; and of them 6,102 of the plague. But it is feared that the true number of the dead this week is near 10,000 – partly from the poor that cannot be taken notice of through the greatness of the number, and partly from the Quakers and others that will not have any bell ring for them.

Lord's Day, 3 September 1665

Up, and put on my coloured silk suit, very fine, and my new periwigg, bought a good while since, but darst not wear it because the plague was in Westminster when I bought it. And it is a wonder what will be the fashion after the plague is done as to periwiggs, for nobody will dare to buy any haire for fear of the infection – that it had been cut off of the heads of people dead of the plague.

THE BEST & WORST OF TIMES

1665 Plague creates jobs for Searchers of the Dead, Plague Buriers, and Cat and Dog Killers.

1665 Great Plague sweeps England. Kills 60,000 in London from July to October.

1666 Great Fire of London helps to end the plague, but ruins St Paul's Cathedral.

Once labelled as a plague victim by the Searcher of the Dead, a corpse had to remain indoors until the middle of the night when the Plague Buriers did their rounds.

The mountebanks and Toad Eaters had a field day. People resorted to anything to protect themselves against the fearsome disease. Tobacco was highly recommended as a way of warding off infection. In an inversion of natural law, any boy at Eton caught not smoking was liable to be punished.

The year 1665 bit deep into the popular psyche. We still use the phrase 'avoid it like the plague', and it's said that the children's game 'Ring-a-ring o' roses' is a macabre reference to the symptoms of the disease and its outcome. In Stuart times they all fell down.

Well, not quite all. There were still enough living souls to tend to the dying and do a whole host of other plague-related jobs.

Searchers of the Dead

Seeking the dead wasn't difficult. They were everywhere. The Searchers' grim job was to enter the houses where a death had occurred and carry out a perfunctory and amateur autopsy. If they diagnosed death by plague, the house was boarded up and its inhabitants quarantined.

A generall Bill for this present year,

ending the 19 of December 1665. according to the Report made to the KINGS most Excellent Majesty.

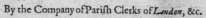

By the Company of Parish Clerks of London, &c.

Parish	Buried	Pla.	Parish	Buried	Pla.	Parish	Buried	Pla.	Parish	Burie	Pla.
St A'lbans Woodstreet	200	121	St Clements Eastcheap	38	20	St Margaret Moses	38	25	St Michael Cornhill	104	52
St Alhallowes Barking	514	330	St Dionis Back-church	78	27	St Margaret Newfishst	114	66	St Michael Crookedla.	179	133
St Alhallowes Breadst	35	16	St Dunstans East	265	150	St Margaret Pattons	49	24	St Michael Queenhit	203	122
St Alhallowes Great	455	426	St Edmunds Lumbard	70	36	St Mary Abchurch	99	54	St Michael Quene	44	18
St Alhallowes Honila	10	5	St Ethelborough	195	106	St Mary Aldermanbury	181	109	St Michael Royall	152	116
St Alhallowes Lesse	239	175	St Faiths	104	70	St Mary Aldermary	105	75	St Michael Woodstreet	122	62
St Alhall. Lumbardstr.	90	52	St Fosters	144	105	St Mary le Bow	64	36	St Mildred Breadstreet	59	26
St Alhallowes Staining	185	112	St Gabriel Fen-church	69	39	St Mary Bothaw	55	30	St Mildred Poultrey	68	46
St Alhallowes the Wall	500	356	St George Botolphlane	41	27	St Mary Colechurch	17	6	St Nicholas Acons	46	28
St Alphage	271	115	St Gregories by Pauls	375	232	St Mary Hill	94	64	St Nicholas Coleabby	125	91
St Andrew Hubbard	71	15	St Hellens	108	75	St Mary Mounthaw	56	37	St Nicholas Olaues	90	62
St Andrew Vndershaft	274	189	St James Dukes place	262	190	St Mary Summerset	342	262	St Olaues Hartstreet	237	160
St Andrew Wardrobe	476	305	St James Garlickhithe	189	118	St Mary Staynings	47	27	St Olaues Iewry	54	32
St Anne Aldersgate	282	197	St John Baptist	138	83	St Mary Woolchurch	65	33	St Olaues Siluerstreet	250	132
St Anne Blacke-Friers	652	467	St John Euangelist	9		St Mary Woolnoth	75	38	St Pancras Soperlane	30	15
St Antholins Parish	58	33	St John Zacharie	85	54	St Martins Iremonger	21	11	St Peters Cheape	61	35
St Austins Parish	43	20	St Katherine Coleman	299	213	St Martins Ludgate	196	128	St Peters Cornehill	136	76
St Barthol. Exchange	73	51	St Katherine Creechu.	335	231	St Martins Orgars	110	71	St Peters Pauls Wharfe	114	86
St Bennet Fynch	47	22	St Lawrence Iewry	94	48	St Martins Outwitch	60	34	St Peters Poore	79	47
St Benn. Grace-church	57	41	St Lawrence Pountney	214	140	St Martins Vintrey	417	349	St Stevens Colmanst	560	391
St Bennet Pauls Wharf	355	172	St Leonard Eastcheap	42	27	St Matthew Fridayst.	24	6	St Stevens Walbrooke	34	17
St Bennet Sherehog	11	1	St Leonard Fosterlane	335	255	St Maudlins Milkstreet	44	22	St Swithins	93	56
St Botolph Billingsgate	83	50	St Magnus Parish	103	60	St Maudlins Oldfishst.	176	121	St Thomas Apostle	163	110
Christs Church	653	467	St Margaret Lothbury	100	66	St Michael Bassishaw	253	164	Trinitie Parish	115	79
St Christophers	60	47									

Buried in the 97 Parishes within the walls, —— 15207   Whereof, of the Plague —— 9887

Parish	Buried	Pla.	Parish	Buried	Pla.	Parish	Buried	Pla.	Parish	Buried	Pla.
St Andrew Holborne	3958	3103	Bridewell Precinct	130	179	St Dunstans West	958	665	St Saviours Southwark	4235	3446
St Bartholmew Grea	493	344	St Botolph Aldersga.	997	755	St George Southwark	1613	1260	St Sepulchres Parish	4509	2746
St Bartholmew Lesse	193	139	St Botolph Algate	4926	4051	St Giles Cripplegate	8069	4838	St Thomas Southwark	475	371
St Bridget	2111	1427	St Botolph Bishopsg	3464	2500	St Olaues Southwark	4793	2785	Trinity Minories	168	123
									At the Pesthouse	159	156

Buried in the 16 Parishes without the walls —— 41351   Whereof, of the Plague —— 28888

Parish	Buried	Pla.	Parish	Buried	Pla.	Parish	Buried	Pla.	Parish	Buried	Pla.
St Giles in the Fields	4457	3216	St Katherines Tower	956	601	St Magdalen Bermon.	1943	1362	St Mary Whitechappel	4766	3855
Hackney Parish	232	132	Lambeth Parish	798	537	St Mary Newington	1272	1004	Redriffe Parish	304	210
St James Clarkenwel	1863	1377	St Leonard Shordisch	2669	1949	St Mary Islington	696	593	Stepney Parish	8598	5583

Buried in the 12 out-Parishes, in Middlesex and Surrey — 28554   Whereof, of the Plague — 21420

Parish	Buried	Pla.	Parish	Buried	Pla.
St Clement Danes	1969	1319	St Mary Sauoy	303	198
St Paul Covent Garden	408	261	St Margaret Westminst.	4710	3742
St Martins in the Fields	4804	2883	whereof at the Pesthouse		156

Buried in the 5 Parishes in the City and Liberties of Westminster — 12194   Whereof, of the Plague — 8403

The Total of all the Christnings —— 9967
The Total of all the Burials this year —— 97306
Whereof, of the Plague —— 68596

The Diseases and Casualties this year.

Casualty	Number	Casualty	Number	Casualty	Number
Abortive and Stilborne	617	Executed	21	Palsie	30
Aged	1545	Flox and Small Pox	655	Plague	68596
Ague and Feaver	5257	Found dead in streets, fields, &c.	20	Planet	6
Appoplex and Suddenly	116	French Pox	86	Plurisie	15
Bedrid	10	Frighted	23	Poysoned	1
Blasted	5	Gout and Sciatica	27	Quinsie	35
Bleeding	16	Grief	46	Rickets	557
Bloody Flux, Scowring & Flux	185	Griping in the Guts	1288	Rising of the Lights	397
Burnt and Scalded	8	Hangd & made away themselves	7	Rupture	34
Calenture	3	Headmouldshot & Mouldfallen	14	Scurvy	105
Cancer, Gangrene and Fistula	56	Jaundies	110	Shingles and Swine pox	2
Canker, and Thrush	111	Impostume	227	Sores, Ulcers, broken and bruised Limbs	82
Childbed	625	Kild by severall accidents	46	Spleen	14
Chrisomes and Infants	1258	Kings Evill	86	Spotted Feaver and Purples	1929
Cold and Cough	68	Leprosie	2	Stopping of the stomack	332
Collick and Winde	134	Lethargy	14	Stone and Strangury	98
Consumption and Tissick	4808	Livergrown	20	Surfet	1251
Convulsion and Mother	2036	Meagrom and Headach	12	Teeth and Worms	2614
Distracted	5	Measles	7	Vomiting	51
Dropsie and Timpany	1478	Murthered and Shot	9	Wenn	1
Drowned	50	Overlaid & Starved	45		

Christned	Males	5114	Buried	Males	48569	Of the Plague	68596
	Females	4853		Females	48737		
	In all	9967		In all	97306		

Increased in the Burials in the 130 Parishes and at the Pest-house this year —— 79009
Increased of the Plague in the 130 Parishes and at the Pest-house this year —— 68590

A copy of a bill of mortality showing the causes of death in London parishes in 1665. Plague accounts for an astonishing number, but you might suspect that some of the high number dying of 'Ague and Feaver' might also have been victims, either diagnosed as such or with relatives who slipped the Searcher of the Dead something for turning a blind eye.

But why would anyone choose a task so grim?

The answer is that choice didn't come in to it. Most were women who were old enough to have picked up some amateur medical knowledge, but poor enough to be driven to do a job that everyone believed dramatically increased their chances of becoming plague victims themselves. Many were destitute and dependent on the parish. They were paid for doing their work but, if they refused, there was the threat that the parish alms would be withdrawn, leaving them penniless.

Their job wasn't created by the 1665 outbreak. There had been incidences of plague every fifteen years or so throughout the Tudor and Stuart period, and we know that four women Searchers from Stepney were paid fourpence per corpse during a plague outbreak in 1625.

But rates of pay plummeted in the Great Plague. There were so many dead and dying that even rich parishes had to reduce their rates. Searchers of the Dead now were paid around tuppence for each body they examined.

By the time Searchers arrived at the house of someone who'd died, the rest of the inhabitants would already be trying to 'sweeten' the atmosphere with herbs, or attempting to choke out infection by burning sulphur. In this smoky atmosphere the Searchers would begin their enquiry.

First, they would question friends and neighbours about the symptoms; asking how long the person had been ill, and how they died. Then they would move on to the corpse, gingerly looking for the buboes and blackening of the skin that were the tell-tale signs of the plague. Dabbling their fingers in the feverish sweat and weeping pustules of the recently deceased must have seemed like dicing with death. But, ironically, it was when they were talking to the rest of the family that they were most at risk. It was the living who might still be in the infectious stages, not those who'd already succumbed to the disease.

The Searchers conducted their examination on the basis of what they could see. But diagnosis wasn't necessarily simple. The giant suppurating sores and the accompanying patches of blackened skin may seem pretty obvious. But victims of other dreadful illnesses like smallpox could look equally horrific. In the dim light of a London hovel, the possibility of error was substantial.

Once a person was declared dead of the plague, their home was marked and no one except a doctor or a Searcher was allowed in or out for forty days. Searchers compiled lists of causes of death along with their supervisor, the local clerk or sexton. But as they often died as well, records were none too accurate.

Searchers had to take an oath to undertake their work honestly. But despite this they were often accused of being bribed by families of plague victims. This ploy would have been in order to ensure that the cause of death was described not as the plague but as something else, like 'quinsy' or 'fright'. If they obtained a 'health certificate', the relatives would have been allowed to move to areas freer of the dreadful disease.

The Searchers' job was made harder by the fact that the Great Plague was a combination of different types of the disease. *Bubonic plague* was the

THE BEST & WORST OF TIMES

1666 Isaac Newton formulates his Laws of Gravity.

1667 John Milton's *Paradise Lost* published.

1672–4 Third Anglo-Dutch war. Even more work for Saltpetre Men.

most common. A flea bite deposits the bacilli into the body's lymphatic system. As a result, the 'buboes' appear. These are large, inflamed and painful swellings in the lymph glands of the groin, armpits or neck. If the infection spread to the blood, death was the almost inevitable consequence

In *septicaemic plague*, the bacilli enter the bloodstream directly, meaning that the patient might die without exhibiting the 'classic' symptom of buboes. Like *bubonic plague*, it is transmitted by flea bites.

Pneumonic plague causes severe pneumonia and is usually fatal. It doesn't require flea bites to spread it. The bacilli are present in water droplets spread by coughs and on clothing. So it is highly contagious, especially in crowded, poorly ventilated buildings. When the bacilli reach the lungs, severe pneumonia occurs.

Death from *pneumonic plague* takes three or four days, but it's even faster with the *septicaemic* type: twenty-four hours. In all three, internal bleeding causes large bruises to appear on the skin, hence the plague's name in the fourteenth century: the Black Death.

As you can see from the lists of the dead, the monthly mortalities were overwhelming. And all those corpses needed burying. Which leads us on to another Worst Job.

Plague Burier

The ninety-seven parishes within London's city walls, and the thirty-three without, all had to bury their own dead. The popular Monty-Python-inspired image is of a cart trundling through the streets with the driver ringing a bell and shouting 'Bring out your dead' in a wobbly voice. But in reality the job was seldom this hi-tech.

Plague Buriers were recruited from the desperately poor. They operated at night. Burials were private – no relatives were allowed for fear of infection. Few could afford the luxury of a cart. They usually hauled the hideously disfigured bodies in a canvas sling that looked like a hammock.

It was a long hot summer. The Buriers would have reeked of the smell of death and rotting corpses. Soon the graveyards were so full that mass plague-pits were dug. Mistakes could happen: there's at least one case of a comatose drunkard, a street musician, being so sozzled that he was presumed dead and carted off for burial. Presumably, because we know the story, he must have come round before he died of suffocation.

Fear was like a pall hanging over the city. The Plague Buriers smoked heavily to try to ward off infectious air, but must have thought their chances of survival were less than a Petardier's Assistant with a limp. As far as the general populace was concerned, their cheek-to-cheek association with plague victims made them virtually dead men walking. They carried red wands to warn people not

THE BEST & WORST OF TIMES

1675 Work starts on the restoration of St Paul's Cathedral under Christopher Wren.

1685 Accession of the Catholic king James II.

1685 Birth of JS Bach. Together with Vivaldi and Handel, he exploits to the full the sound of the newly invented gut violin strings.

As the bodies are bundled into a mass grave the Burier puffs frantically at his pipe for protection.

to approach them. Often they'd be forced into isolation, living in huts in the graveyard to keep them from infecting others.

In reality, they had the same chance of survival as the rest of the population. It was fleas and infected water droplets from living victims that caused the plague. Burying the dead didn't make a ha'pence-worth of difference. What makes this a Worst Job though, apart from the stench and the nastiness, was the pervasive fear they must have felt, however ill-founded, that the job was probably going to be fatal.

These excerpts from the Lord Mayor's instructions on dealing with the plague detail the Searchers' and Buriers' jobs, and the tragic attempts at human organization in the face of this natural disaster.

ORDERS CONCEIVED and PUBLISHED by the LORD MAYOR and ALDERMEN of the CITY OF LONDON, CONCERNING the INFECTION of the PLAGUE, 1665

Whereas, in the Reign of our late Sovereign, King James, of the happy memory, an Act was made for the charitable relief and ordering of persons inflected with the Plague, whereby authority was given to Justices of the Peace, Mayors, Bailiffs, and other head officers, to appoint, within their several limits, Examiners, Searchers, Watchmen, Keepers, and Buriers for the persons and places infected, and to minister unto them oaths for the performances of their offices. And the same Statute did also authorize the giving of other directions as unto them for the present necessity should seem good in their directions. It is now upon special consideration, though very expedient for preventing and assiding of infection of sickness (if it shall so please Almighty God), that the officers following be appointed and these orders herafter duly observed …

SEARCHERS

That there be a special care to appoint Women Searchers in every parish, such as are of honest reputation, and of the best sort as can be got of this kind: and these to be sworn to make due search and true report to the utmost of their knowledge, whether the persons whose bodies they are appointed to search, do die of the infection or of what other diseases, as near as they can. And that the Physicians who shall be appointed for the several parishes under their respective cares, to the end they may consider whether they are fitly qualified for that employment, and charge them, from time to time, as they shall see cause, if they appear defective in their duties.

That no Searcher, during the time of visitation, be permitted to use any public work of employment, or keep any shop, or shall be employed as a laundress, or in any other common employment whatsoever.

BURIAL OF THE DEAD

That the burial of the dead by this visitation be at most convenient hours, always either before sun rising or after sun setting, with the privity of the Churchwardens or Constables, and not otherwise, and that no neighbours nor friends be suffered to accompany the corpse to church or to enter the house visited upon pain of having his house shut up or be imprisoned.

THE BEST & WORST OF TIMES

1688 The Glorious Revolution. William III and Mary II take over the throne. James II flees.

1696 Act of Parliament establishes workhouses (see the Victorians, page 185, for the outcome).

1697 2 December: Official opening of St Paul's Cathedral.

> *And that no corpse dying or infectious shall be buried or remain in any church in time of common prayer, sermon, or lecture: and that no children be suffered at the time of burial of any corpse in any church, churchyard, or burying-place, to come near the corpse, coffin, or grave. And that all the graves shall be at least six feet deep.*
>
> *And further, all public assemblies at other burials are to be forborne during the continuance of this visitation.*
>
> **EVERY VISITED HOUSE TO BE MARKED**
> *That every house visited be marked with a Red Cross of a foot long in the middle of the door, evident to be seen, and with these mark printed words that is to say 'Lord have Mercy upon us' to be set close over the same Cross, there to continue until lawful opening of same house.*
>
> *Sir John Lawrence, Lord Mayor*
> *Sir George Waterman, Sir Charles Doe – Sheriffs*

But there's one plague job even more terrible. For a nation of animal lovers, the most unenviable task would surely have been the role of the Dog and Cat Killer.

Dog and Cat Killers

It was widely believed that feral dogs and cats spread the plague. Dogs, known as 'curs' or 'mutts', were thought to carry the disease on their coats. So councils paid up to a penny for each animal killed. Forty thousand dogs and eighty thousand cats were slaughtered. There were also some attempts to poison the rat population with arsenic and rat-bane (like the rat-catcher in Victorian times – see page 179), not to mention the slaughter of the occasional rabbit and pigeon. But by killing kittens and cats, the plague-carrying rats were now free of natural predators.

The Dog Killer was an extension of the ancient parish office of 'dog whipper', a title given to the man employed to drive dogs out of the church. (They also seem to have been given the additional task of prodding people awake during long sermons!) In Exeter Cathedral, a room was provided for the dog whipper. He was paid by the Parish Clerk and provided with the tools of the trade: a whip, gloves and tongs – to grab the dog at arm's length. At Baslow, not far from the famous plague village of Eyam in Derbyshire, they've still got a whip that was used by their dog-whipper.

During the plague it was natural for these whippers to be made responsible for rounding up dogs and exterminating them. People regarded stray dogs with the same fear and loathing now accorded to rats. As they are often seen trotting around either alone or in packs, people presumed it was they who were spreading it. As soon as there were plague deaths in a house, the household pet would be put down.

This holocaust of living things was strictly enforced and the methods employed to effect it were far from humane. Knives, sticks, traps and blocks of wood were used to exterminate the unfortunate cats and dogs. But the pseudo-science that justified this carnage made it totally ineffectual. As almost every schoolchild knows, the plague was 'cured' not by any doctor but by a baker, and a careless baker at that.

The blaze that started in Pudding Lane on 2 September 1666 became the Great Fire of London. The traditional view is that this second great natural disaster of Stuart times eradicated the first. But nobody has quite explained why. In fact the plague dribbled on for some time. The fire seems to have removed enough of the city to drive out some of the rat population and contributed to ending the epidemic.

But the Great Fire of London certainly made an end of the old St Paul's Cathedral. The building consumed was actually the fourth cathedral church on the site in a continuous line back to King Ethelbert of Kent in AD 604. All the previous buildings had burnt down too. The diarist John Evelyn wrote after the fire that 'St Paul's is now a sad ruin and that beautiful portico now rent in pieces …' Even before the fire, the architect Christopher Wren had had great plans for pulling the old cathedral down and replacing it with a classical design. The authorities had previously said no to his plans but the fire gave him his golden opportunity. He built the largest cathedral in Britain and one of the most famous landmarks in the world. And, in doing so, he created another sort of Worst Job.

Dome Painter

There were, of course, thousands of workers employed in building it, all working to Wren's designs and initially overseen by Charles II himself. The work was begun in 1675 and was completed in 1710. Wren celebrated his seventy-sixth birthday and the completion of the cathedral by having himself hauled up in a basket to the lantern surmounting the dome.

The great triumph of Wren's work was this dome. Wren's uncle was the Bishop of Ely. The cathedral there has a luminous octagonal lantern that gives a focus to the whole cathedral. Wren took his inspiration from it and translated it into classical style. The dome is over 100 metres tall, one of the highest in the world. Until recently it dominated the London skyline. Inside, it gives a massive scale to the building. If you climb the 259 stairs to the Whispering Gallery, you're only half-way to the top.

THE BEST & WORST OF TIMES
1700 Population of England and Scotland approx 7.5 million.
1702 Publication of first English daily newspaper, the *Daily Courant*.
1702 William III dies. Anne Stuart becomes Queen.

And it's the painting of the inside of the dome that is being nominated as one of the Worst Jobs of the age. It would have been bad enough just rolling emulsion on to the 1,440 square metres of wall, but this Worst Job is a sad combination of physical endurance and spiritual desolation. It is specifically the story of one man: James Thornhill.

Wren wanted an austere approach to decoration. This was, after all, a Protestant cathedral. It was only relatively recently that Puritans had gone round smashing stained glass and painting over church decorations. People suspected anything smacking of papism (it was even rumoured that Catholics had fanned the flames of the Great Fire). Wren's model of 1673–4, made before the work on the cathedral started, shows the dome interior painted to look like coppering.

But the cathedral authorities decided that they wanted something more special. In 1708 they commissioned a scheme of giant murals from the great French painter Louis Laguerre. Then, a few months later, the Whigs took parliamentary power from the Tories and now they controlled the destiny of the interior of St Paul's. They demanded a more respectable Protestant approach. Laguerre's designs were deemed far too flamboyant and colourful – and therefore associated with the baroque excesses of Rome. He was dropped from the project.

In this portrait of Sir James Thornhill there is an anxious quality about him, as though he seems doubtful of his standing among others.

There was a competition to select the most appropriate replacement. The shortlist included Sir James Thornhill and the Italian painter Pelligrini. The Dean asked Wren what he thought of the tendered designs. He said he didn't like any of them, and Thornhill's least of all. But this was a new Dean and a new Chapter. Wren was overruled.

Thornhill was given the commission. He had the double advantage of being English and a staunch Protestant. He was commissioned in June 1715. (Strictly speaking, we are now drifting into the Georgian era. But St Paul's itself is an icon of the Stuart Age and the tendering for the paintings started in Queen Anne's reign.)

Thornhill's winning designs depict eight scenes from the life of St Paul, the first post-Reformation figurative paintings. There may have been anti-Rome sentiments within government and country, but St Paul was an uncontroversial subject. He was an apostle. His theology was at the root of Protestantism and the themes were strictly biblical; far less inflammatory than the Virgin Mary or one of the more legendary saints.

Even before St Paul's was finished it was dirty, due to the London smog. Grime continued to accumulate right up to the implementation of the Clean

Air Act in 1956. Now, at a cost of £40 million, the building and Thornhill's paintings are being restored. Londoners will see Wren's building as he intended, and perhaps Thornhill's reputation will get a belated boost.

The scheme is a giant *trompe l'oeil* mural. The figures are framed by elaborate architectural arcading that supports a range of urns, scallop-shell forms and swags. It was painted in grisaille – a technique using browns, greys and ochre to drain all colouristic (and perhaps papal) association from the palette.

There are parallels with Michelangelo's life and work. The dome of St Paul's could have become Thornhill's very own Sistine Chapel. The great Renaissance artist suffered for his masterpiece, spending years with his nose to the ceiling, painting on his back. Thornhill was prepared to go through similar agonies, but on an even larger scale. On the plus side he did have the help of two or three assistants, but the work still took two years to complete.

Painting the dome was not for the faint-hearted. It is 35 metres from the church floor to its lowest point. Every day it would have taken Thornhill and his assistants the best part of an hour to get to the bit they wanted to paint. Then the hard work started.

The vast interior had to be swathed in scaffolding suspended from the ceiling. There were no rails to prevent the painters toppling off. While they could work almost upright on the lower stages, further up they would have been

St Paul's dome featuring Thornhill's giant trompe l'oeil *mural.*

forced backwards by the curvature of the dome. Behind them was a vertiginous drop to the distant marble below. The work would have involved a cocktail of acute discomfort and chronic vertigo. No one died, but there's one account of a near miss. Thornhill was walking backwards, dangerously close to the edge of the scaffold. How could his assistant attract his attention without making him jump and consequently plummet to the ground? His solution may not have got him the thanks he deserved. He simply threw a tin of paint at the wall!

The monumental task involved several stages. First, the huge area had to be prepared with two layers of base paint. Then the designs were drawn on with mathematical precision. Mapping out the gigantic figures in the right proportions was an incredible accomplishment. Close to, the work would have made little visual sense. The figures are gigantic. St Paul's feet alone are as long as a man's arm. There would have been a frustrating 'Can-you-see-what-it-is-yet?' sense to the process (and of course you couldn't step back to admire your work!).

In addition, the painters were literally working in the dark. Especially in the winter months, the upper areas of the dome are both dark and very cold. Candles don't provide much useful light for painting, especially when your palette consists only of browns, blacks and greys. It was lonely up there too. When visited by the diarist and MP Dudley Ryder, in August 1716, Thornhill complained that no one else had ever climbed the scaffold to talk to him.

But eventually the job was finished, and Thornhill was paid £6,500. He became the first British painter to be knighted and was made an MP in 1720. In many ways he'd made it.

So what was the problem?

Well there's a knife in the gut of this Worst Job. After climbing thousands of stairs and straining his eyes to complete his life's work, Thornhill found himself as fashionable as a pair of flares at a punk concert. Overnight the public's aesthetic had changed. Thornhill's paintings were criticized almost before they were finished for being too dull and austere. The Rococo style with its flamboyant swirls and decoration had become all the rage.

The inscription on Sir Christopher Wren's tomb at St Paul's says, 'Lector, si monumentum requiris, circumspice' – 'Reader, if you're looking for a memorial, look around you'. Wren is probably Britain's most famous architect. St Paul's made him so. Thornhill, who must have started with high hopes that the paintings would be his memorial too, is lost to history. The star painter of Stuart times, he's remembered, if at all, for being the father-in-law of the much more famous Georgian painter, Hogarth. His own work, poorly illuminated and very high up, is forgotten – but at least it shows not all Worst Jobs are badly paid!

Indeed this book's award for the very Worst Job in the Stuart period goes to someone who was very respectable, very cultured and, occasionally, extremely well rewarded. Not only that, but his contribution to the performing arts of this country is paramount. So what could be so bad about being a violin string maker?

THE BEST & WORST OF TIMES

1710 Parliamentary Act to grant licences to widows of coachmen and Sedan Chair Bearers.

1712 Last trial for witchcraft in England.

1714 Queen Anne dies. The Hanoverian George I becomes king. The Stuart era is over.

The Worst Job of All: Violin String Maker

During the Stuart period the music people were listening to changed dramatically. When James I came to the throne, elegant, polyphonic lutes and viols abounded. But by the end of Queen Anne Stuart's reign the big hits were new, cutting-edge masterpieces such as Bach's and Vivaldi's violin concertos and Handel's Water Music. Baroque music had arrived and the modern orchestra was born, with violins providing the bulk of the sound.

But this musical transformation was only possible because a small, dedicated group of people were prepared to freeze their socks off washing the dung out of the guts of freshly slaughtered sheep.

In the seventeenth century there was a revolution in string-making technology. Prior to that, violins had only three strings. Anyone who has ever twanged elastic bands knows that a short, thin, taut string produces a high note, and thick, long strings give a lower sound. Violin makers had found it impossible to produce a thick string to play the bottom notes that was nevertheless short and tense enough to fit on a violin.

The problem was finally solved by a new technique of twisting strands of sheep gut. It was this technique that gave rise to the modern four-string violin. It enabled Stradivarius and his fellow craftsmen in Cremona to produce their famous fiddles, and the Baroque composers to write their music.

So String Makers were revolutionary craftsmen. The twisting of the gut may not have been too difficult, but first they had to get hold of the raw materials. Today traditional String Makers buy their gut already prepared, but in Stuart times the craftsman himself had to get it from a sheep.

Yes, a sheep – not a cat. Violin strings are sometimes called 'cat-gut', but string makers have never come from the ranks of the Cat Killers. The *Encyclopaedia Britannica* suggests that the phrase 'cat gut' came about because the Italian term for violin was 'kit', so the strings were 'kit gut', mutating into 'cat gut'. Given the screeching sound of a learner sawing on the fiddle, it's not surprising that the phrase stuck.

Sheep-gut strings are made from the animal's lower intestine, which can be up to 30 metres long. String Makers often lived close to abattoirs, so they could source their raw materials. Removing the guts intact is a delicate and yet profoundly disgusting business. You need to slit the stomach gently enough not to burst the intestines. A shaky knife can fill the stomach cavity with half-digested grass and ruin the guts for string-making.

One of the things that Worst Jobs have in common is that nothing goes to waste. Once slaughtered, our forebears would use every scrap of an animal. The division of a sheep's intestine between sausage-makers and violin string makers is the perfect example.

Stradivarius gets all the attention but he never had to pull a sheep's rectum out backwards.

But emptying the guts out into a tub is the easy part. String Makers generally worked in family units, so it's likely that a son or daughter would have had the delightful task of preparing the lengths of intestine.

First, all the fatty tissue, muscle and blood vessels had to be scraped off the guts by hand. This was both revolting and painstaking, so naturally another task for an assistant. Then they had to squeeze the tubular guts free of bile and thoroughly clean them.

This could be done by running water through them. But simply pouring water through the intestine wasn't enough. The guts needed to be spotless. As in flax retting, you could just leave them in a river, but this was time-consuming. Soaking them in a solution of wood ash was more common. This took about a week, with the solution being regularly changed. This process had to be carefully monitored because if the guts were left too long they'd start to rot and become irreversibly damaged.

Once thoroughly cleaned, the wider, more expensive ends of the intestines were sent off to make sausage skins. The thin ends were divided up into strands, which were bundled together in varying thicknesses. They were then fixed at either end to little hooks, which were repeatedly turned to twist the strands together. After this, each string was dried.

Then all you needed was a violin, a bow and an appreciative audience.

CHAPTER FIVE

Georgian Worst Jobs

Jane Austen and Colin Firth have a lot to answer for. The mere mention of the Georgian age for most people conjures up a landscape of gentility dotted with country parks and neo-classical architecture. And this demure stage is filled with a cast of eligible bachelors 'in want of a wife' taking tea with respectable maidens in empire-line dresses concealing elegantly repressed passion.

The truth, of course, was very different. Behind every dazzling Georgian façade was a dark, hidden interior. The elegant life of the new squirearchy was supported by a seemingly bottomless well of human misery. Countless impoverished country dwellers gravitated to the new industrial cities seeking work in the mills and factories. Life for them was closer to the chaos of Hogarth's engraving of *Gin Lane* than Jane Austen's *Pride and Prejudice*.

Even that most innocent of beverages, tea, had a sinister side. Coffee and chocolate had been favourites in the coffee houses since the seventeenth century. Now the exotic eastern drink of tea was becoming fashionable. It was a luxury and consequently subject to heavy import duty. And where there is import duty there is the opportunity for smuggling. A staggering three-quarters of the tea drunk in Britain during the eighteenth century was smuggled into the country.

Hogarth chronicled the seamier side of Georgian life. This is a detail from his Gin Lane, *where you could get 'drunk for a penny, dead drunk for tuppence.'*

In response, the two separate services of the Customs and the Excise mounted a desperate operation to catch contraband. Ships patrolled offshore, and along the coast was the last line of the country's creaking fiscal defences, and a Georgian Worst Job. As you hear the sorry tale of the Riding Officer, try not to be prejudiced by the fact that he is not only the forerunner of the coastguard, but also of the VAT man.

Riding Officer

The Riding Officer was responsible for riding up and down the coast looking for ships 'hovering' offshore, or small boats bringing in contraband. The Landguard of Riding Officers had been established on the south coast in 1690 around Romney Marsh. However, by the Georgian era the system had spread to cover the entire country. There was a Riding Officer every ten miles along the coast. This narrowed to every four miles in areas such as East Sussex or around Robin Hood's Bay in Yorkshire where smuggling was rife.

Riding Officers received only about £40 a year, not much more than a labourer. Out of this they had to pay for their own horse. But this was not the only drawback to a career that was dangerous, uncomfortable and social suicide.

The hours and conditions were terrible. Smugglers chose the worst nights of the year, when storm-clouds gave cover, for their operations. So the Riding Officer was forced to patrol at night and when the weather was at its filthiest. But riding along the cliffs in a sodden woollen cape with rain spattering his tricorn hat was the least of a Riding Officer's worries. The trouble really started when he caught sight of the tell-tale signal light.

There is a stereotypical image of smugglers as cheery, anti-establishment fishermen out to earn a few bob to supplement their income – wrinkled salts with rosy-cheeked sweethearts helping to hide the odd bottle of gin under their skirts. Nothing could be further from the truth. In the eighteenth century, smuggling was organized crime. There could be 500 people on the beach unloading vast quantities of tea, gin or brandy. And they would be heavily armed.

The Riding Officer was issued with a pistol and cutlass, but on his own he was useless. It was like sending in a bobby on a bicycle to stop a Colombian drugs cartel. And although theoretically he could call on the local garrison of dragoons for backup, 'local' could mean forty miles away. Roads and communications were so poor that instant action was impossible. Indeed, in Yorkshire the roads were so bad that even the pay packet for the Riding Officer sometimes failed to get through. In January 1722, a customs officer in Whitby sent a plaintive message back to headquarters: 'if you have now got money I beg you'll favour me with a line that I may send for it, for our officers be in great want having rec'd no salaries since last midsummer quarter.'

If the Riding Officer did stiffen up his sinews and confront the crowd of smugglers, he was often the loser. In 1740 Thomas Carswell was shot as he tried to arrest members of the notoriously violent Hawkshurst gang who operated on the border of east Sussex and Kent. The next year at Lydd, two Officers were seized by the smugglers they were supposed to be pursuing, trussed up and taken to Boulogne. The next night they were returned and reunited with their horses which, in the meantime, had been used to transport the smugglers' wares.

Report to a Parliamentary Committee on smuggling in 1745

That about Nine Years ago, the Mob went afterwards to Passage, and took a Custom-House Officer, named May, out of his House, And cut out his tongue, and cut off his Ears, One of which he saw nailed on Cork Exchange; That they dragged him with a Rope about his Neck, through all the Kennels, gave him several Blows, and threw him into the River, and he died of this Usage, And great Rewards were offered to discover the Offenders, but to no Purpose.

The Riding Officer was also a perpetual social outcast. He would have been met by a wall of hatred and stony silence wherever he went.

In places like Rye or Robin Hood's Bay, everyone would have been in on the business of smuggling. It was the local economy. In the eighteenth century Robin Hood's Bay had one of the highest per capita incomes in the country. No one wanted that to stop.

It was notoriously difficult to get convictions in local courts as the juries were either sympathetic to smugglers or took part in the activity themselves. Even local Justices of the Peace might be in the pay of the criminals. A Riding Officer could theoretically earn a £20 bonus for the conviction of a smuggler. The catch was, he had to pay for the costs of the prosecution. With the chances of a conviction so low, it was hardly worth his while.

So the Riding Officer was wet, cold, out-gunned, poorly paid and useless. In his annual report in 1783, Sir William Musgrave, the Commissioner of Customs, said that Riding Officers were 'of very little service, 'tho' a great Burthen to the Revenue'.

With so much potential for corruption and so many miles of coastline to cover, it's no wonder that the hands-on policing of smugglers made little difference. It took the reduction of revenue duties to make any significant dent in illegal imports. Then, when import taxes (on tea at least) were phased out, smuggling all but disappeared. In 1822 the Coastguard was formed, and eventually it took over the work of the Riding Officers.

Because of the extreme hostility they faced, many Riding Officers ended up adopting an if-you-can't-beat-'em-join-'em accommodation with the smuggling community. Turning a blind eye made more money than fruitless prosecutions. The Riding Officer who is the subject of this parliamentary deposition certainly doesn't seem to have been over-zealous in keeping the Isle of Man free of contraband.

The EXAMINATION of Mr DANIEL GILL,
Riding Officer at the Port of Ramsay, the Isle of Man,
taken at Douglas the 12th of October 1791

THIS Examinant saith, That he is Riding Officer at the Port of Ramsay, and has been since 1773. He was appointed by a constitution of the Treasury, dated in that year, and had a deputation from the Commissioners of the Customs. He took the oaths of office, and gave bond and security. He received printed instructions for his conduct with his deputation.

He has forty pounds a year as Riding Officer, and takes no fees or gratuities. He always keeps a horse.

His station is from Ramsay to Laxey, which is nine miles, and from Ramsay to Kirk Michael, which is eight miles He generally rides about six or seven times a month, and these rides are in the day time. He looks upon the coast, to discover if any goods are exported or imported, or to be exported or imported, contrary to law.

He endeavours to get information as to any illicit practices, and makes seizures whenever he can. He has not, as appears by his journal, made any seizure since the 1st. of January 1789, nor can he recollect when he made the last. He does not recollect his having given any Commanders of Admiralty or Revenue cruisers, any intelligence of vessels hovering or being on the coast, or of any kind respecting illegal proceedings. He has not since the 1st of January 1789, given any of the officers of the Customs in the Isle of Man, any information of this kind, nor can he remember at present any instance of his having so done.

Brandy and gin are, he apprehends, now the principal articles respecting which smuggling is carried on.

DANIEL GILL

Jno Spranger
Wm Osgoode
Willm Roe
David Reid

THE BEST & WORST OF TIMES

1723 50 capital offences are added to the penal code.

1727 George I dies. George II becomes King.

1732 Opening of Covent Garden Opera House – a star venue for Castrati.

Bath Guide

These bucolic smugglers don't have the ruthless air of the notorious Hawkhurst Gang. Under the cover of thick fog they're not particularly bothered about the Riding Officer either.

The Riding Officer may have had to get soaked to the skin in pursuit of his trade, but he didn't have the wettest work in Georgian Britain. That dubious honour went to the Bath Guides.

They were a strange cross between lifeguards and care assistants in a nursing home for disgusting skin diseases. However, they were also essential

GEORGIAN

cogs turning the wheels of one of Georgian Britain's most important social and recreational machines: the spa town of Bath.

From the bowels of the earth below Bath spring one million litres of water per day heated to 46°C. These springs were a sacred place for the ancient Britons long before the Romans arrived and dedicated the site to Sulis Minerva.

The springs continued to be used for their soothing and healing properties throughout the medieval and Tudor periods. But it was Queen Anne's patronage that really transformed Bath's fortunes. She was a frequent visitor, and started a massive craze for taking the waters. In 1698, the population of Bath was only 1,200. The Georgian era saw it transformed into one of England's principal resorts teeming with frivolity and entertainment. By the turn of the century, its population was over 34,000. Architects such as John Wood and John Palmer oversaw the building of the elegant Palladian town that still survives largely unscathed. Queen Square, the Circus, the Guildhall, Lansdowne Crescent and the Royal Crescent turned Bath into a model eighteenth-century city.

A trip to Bath was for the Georgians what skiing at Gstaadt is today. It was a place for the smart set to take a break among their own kind. It was good for the health but also excellent for social contacts and gossip. It was a place for letting your hair down. The 1798 publication *The Comforts of Bath* depicts scenes that would not be out of place in Ibiza Uncovered.

And it was the Bath Guides who kept the whole thing running. They were responsible for helping people from their sedan chairs and down into the waters of the King's Bath.

It was damp, damp work. The Guides dressed in canvas smocks that got drenched at the beginning of every shift and stayed that way until they went home. They spent up to twelve hours a day being chafed by their soaking canvas tents as they moved about the waters serving their customers. The poet Cowper didn't have much sympathy for their sodden plight. He wrote in a letter to his brother: 'The nastiest sight, I think, that can be seen there, is the guides in the Bath; they look sodden and par-boil'd …'

As if this constant soaking wasn't bad enough, the water permanently changed the colour of their skin. The hot waters bubbling up in the springs at Bath have a high iron content. This has stained the walls orange over the years. It also stained the Guides, giving them the appearance of having carelessly applied cheap fake tan. This photograph of the King's Baths today shows the staining effect of the iron in the water; the water level in Georgian times is marked by the tide-mark half-way up the walls. Imagine your skin turning that colour. How envious David Dickinson would have been! A writer called Ned Ward described 'a Score or two of Guides, who by their Scorbutick carcasses, and Lacker'd Hides, you would think had lain pickling a Century of Years in the Stygian Lake'. And this in a day and age that prized a pure white skin as the ideal of beauty.

This photograph of King's Bath today shows the staining effects of the iron in the water. The water level in Georgian times is marked by the tide mark half-way up the walls. Imagine yourself turning that colour – how envious David Dickinson would have been!

THE BEST & **WORST** OF TIMES

1742 First performance of Handel's *Messiah* given in Dublin.

1742 England goes to war with Spain.

1744 'God Save the King' is sung for the first time.

They also had to put up with the high jinks of the customers. Many of the bathers were fit and well and, as in a public swimming pool today, the Guides had to enforce all those 'No Dive-bombing', 'No Petting' rules.

On a Lady's Going into the Bath

When Sylvia in her Bathing, her Charms does expose,
The pretty Banquet dancing under her Nose;
My heart is just ready to part from my Soul;
And leap from the Gal'ry into the Bowl;
Each day I provide too,
A bribe for her Guide too,
And give her a Crown,
To bring me the Water where she sat down;
Let crazy Physitians think Pumping a Cure,
That Virtue is doubtful, but Sylvia's is sure.
The Fidlers I hire to play something Sublime,
And all the while throbbing my Heart beats the Time;
She enters, they Flourish, and cease when she goes,
That who it is address'd to, straight ev'ry one knows;
Wou'd I were a Vermin,
Call'd one of her Chairmen,
Or Serv'd as a Guide
Tho' show'd as they do a damn'd tawny Hide,
Or else like a Pebble at bottom cou'd lye,
To Ogle her Beauties, how happy were I.

Thomas Durfey, *Pills to Purge Melancholy*, 1719

Durfey's double-entendre-rich poem shows that mixed bathing was as exciting as flirtation on the beach is today. (The poem and the other quotes from this job have all been culled from Paul Cresswell's *Bath in Quotes – A Literary View from Saxon Times Onwards*.)

Bath Guides were employed by the local authority but relied heavily on tips. In 1784, the charge for 'general bathing' was three shillings. Half of this went on a costume and towel. Plus a shilling for the guide and sixpence for other staff.

Perhaps the worst part of the whole job was dealing with the terrible afflictions of the age. The customers who needed most help were those who came to soothe their pox or running sores. The waters were thought to heal scrofula, skin complaints and the ravages of sexually transmitted diseases.

THE BEST & WORST OF TIMES

1755 Period of canal construction begins, creating the first work for Navvies (see Victorians, page 171).

1755 Publication of *The Dictionary of the English Language* by Dr Samuel Johnson.

1760 5 May: First use of the hangman's drop – a revolution for the Executioner (see Tudors, page 76). This new method is used on Earl Ferrers, the last aristocrat to be executed at Tyburn.

Ned Ward in the passage quoted below describes 'an Old Fornicator hanging by the Rings, loaded with a Rotten Humidity; Hard by him was a Buxom Dame, cleaning her Nunquam Satis from Mercurial Dregs… Another, half cover'd with Searcloth, had more Sores than Lazarus, doing Pennance for the Sins of her Youth'.

After spending all day in this steamy cocktail of dead skin, scabs, pee, make-up and medication, the guides weren't free to go home when the bathers finally departed. They had to stay behind and clean the pool of its scummy dross.

The Terrors of Bathing

I have done with the waters; therefore your advice comes a day too late … Two days ago, I went into the King's Bath, by advice of our friend Ch…, in order to clear the strainer of the skin, for the benefit of a free perspiration; and the first object that saluted my eye, was a child full of scrophulous ulcers, carried on the arms of one of the guides, under the very noses of the bathers. I was so shocked at the sight, that I retired immediately with indignation and disgust – Suppose the matter of those ulcers, floating on the water, comes in contact with my skin, when the pores are all open, I would ask you what must be the consequence? – Good Heaven, the very thought makes my blood run cold!

… But I am now as much afraid of drinking, as of bathing; for after a long conversation with the Doctor, about the construction of the Pump and the cistern, it is very far from being clear with me, that the patients in the Pump-room don't swallow the scourings of the bathers. I can't help suspecting, that there is, or may be, some regurgitation from the bath into the cistern of the pump. In that case, what a delicate beverage is every day quaffed by the drinkers; medicated with the sweat and dirt, and dandriff; and the abominable discharges of various kinds, from twenty different diseased bodies; parboiling in the kettle below.

Tobias Smollett, *The Expedition of Humphrey Clinker*, 1771

But if the Bath Guides had the wettest job in Georgian Britain, at least they had constant employment. They were professionals who could hold their heads up. There was no shame in keeping the eighteenth-century leisure industry going. The same couldn't be said of the job that made Britain's artistic reputation.

Artist's Model

The Georgian era was the golden age of British painting. It was the first time that Britain had produced home-grown talent comparable with artists on the Continent. Joshua Reynolds, Gainsborough, Hogarth, Ramsay, Blake, Turner and Constable were all products of the eighteenth and early nineteenth centuries.

But before these artists were unleashed on the world they had to be trained. Antique classical Greek forms were thought to be the highest expression of art, so artists were taught to capture their mystery through constant drawing and painting. It took many hours of long, hard concentration. But it also required a human form to concentrate on: thus the cold and cramp-inducing job of Artist's Model.

It sounds like a cushy number. It's a job defined by the fact that you don't have to think, do anything strenuous or even move. But consider the practicalities. Being an Artist's Model wasn't just a question of taking your kit off and sitting on a stool. You had to assume a suitably classical pose. And hold it. For hours. To help Models do this, they were literally strung up. Ropes

This is Old George White, the Navvy from the fever hospital, with his characteristic beard. Some of the lowliest members of Georgian society ended up immortalized in high art.

One of the classics of Georgian art: Thomas Gainsborough's portrait of Mr and Mrs Andrews cheekily highlights the gathering storm clouds of a marriage between two incompatible people. Gainsborough resented the economic imperative that forced him into portrait painting. He wanted to paint landscapes like Claude or Poussin, or, the highest ideal, classical subjects based on Artist's Models. In this painting Gainsborough not only got his own back on the unattractive sitters, but also managed to sneak in a sun-filled landscape in the background.

were slung from the ceiling, and their arms (and sometimes legs) were tied up in whatever heroic pose the class had to paint. To be tethered like this is okay for a few minutes, but to be bound for hour upon hour is excruciatingly painful, with limbs and fingers going to sleep and unused muscles screaming for a rest. It is also very chilly. The human response to cold is to huddle your arms close to your chest. This option wasn't open when you were posing as a discus-thrower. And as for your other extremities …

You had to be hard up to want to do the job. Candidates were found in obscure places. George White was a famous model. He was an old man whom Reynolds discovered in a fever hospital. He had a classically muscular physique due to his day job laying paving slabs. He had a luxuriant bushy beard, which meant he was ideal for biblical patriarchs and saints. Members of the armed forces and bare-knuckle boxers also sat. They were viewed with respect by the artists as their muscle-bound bodies fitted the classical ideal that painters sought. The artist Benjamin Robert Haydon praised his soldier model Hodgson as 'a perfect Achilles'.

But if it was ironic that dossers from the fever hospital and street fighters were employed to provide the perfect representation of Greek heroes, it was nothing compared to the gulf between Greek goddesses and the women whose poses inspired their portraits.

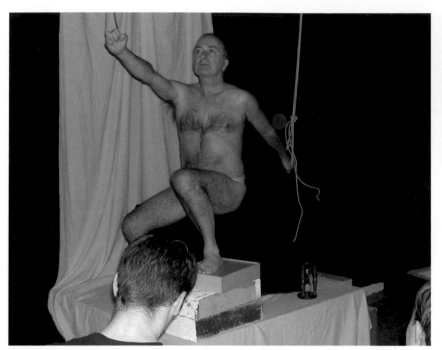

Tony posing as Apollo for art students. Where else could a television presenter be tied up naked, exposing himself to nubile young women, without fear of prosecution?

To be a female Artist's Model was deeply shameful. Posing naked in front of an exclusively male audience and then being captured on canvas was like appearing in a hard-core porn film today. Not only were you doing something disgusting, you were recorded doing it. No wonder that female models were often prostitutes. And even they found the job distasteful. James Northcote in his memoir of 1830 called one of Reynolds's models 'a battered courtesan', and said the female models 'looked upon it as an additional disgrace to what their profession imposed upon them, and as something unnatural, one even wearing a mask'.

Undoubtedly most serious students were too hard at work to see their sitters as anything other than an interesting arrangement of limbs and musculature. But it cannot be denied that there was a seedy element to some of the classes attended by women models. There were plenty of incidents of unauthorized people sneaking in, including underage students. Even the Prince of Wales used to pay an entrance fee to sit in on life classes at the Royal Academy when he felt like looking at a naked woman.

Their shame was reflected in the women's rate of pay. Male models at the Royal Academy earned five shillings a week, plus an extra shilling for each sitting. But their female counterparts received half a guinea per sitting (another parallel to the porn-film industry, where women are still paid more).

But at least in the great artistic academies such as the Royal Academy, the hours of work were regulated. Classes began at 6 pm in winter and 4 pm in summer, with the models working two-hour sessions. However, once trained,

artists still needed models for their private commissions. From them, models could expect a much harder time. In preparing a single study, an artist would want a pose to be held for much longer: sometimes many hours.

Both deliberate and accidental abuses occurred. There was a black model named Wilson, who had a near-death experience when Haydon decided to make a plaster-cast of his body without allowing him room to breathe. And the sculptor Nollekins got more than he bargained for when he employed a prostitute from a brothel run by a tough madam called Mrs Lobb. He'd been using one of her girls, Bet Balmanno, to sit for a statue. Mrs Lobb turned up on his doorstep berating him for making her girl hold a position for eight hours without food or drink and only paying her two shillings. Under the onslaught the stingy Nollekins coughed up another five shillings!

But artists weren't the only people interested in looking at bodies. The late eighteenth century saw enormous scientific advances on all fronts. Scrutiny and experimentation were the order of the day. If medical science were to develop, the human form had to be studied – inside and out. Which meant someone had to provide a constant supply of corpses.

Resurrection Man

'Father,' said Young Jerry, as they walked along: taking care to keep at arm's length and to have the stool well between them: 'what's a Resurrection-Man?'

Mr Cruncher came to a stop on the pavement before he answered, 'How should I know?'

'I thought you knowed everything, father,' said the artless boy.

'Hem! Well,' returned Mr Cruncher, going on again, and lifting off his hat to give his spikes free play, 'he's a tradesman.'

'What's his goods, father?' asked the brisk Young Jerry.

'His goods,' said Mr Cruncher, after turning it over in his mind, 'is a branch of Scientific goods.'

'Persons' bodies, ain't it, father?' asked the lively boy.

'I believe it is something of that sort,' said Mr Cruncher.

'Oh, father, I should so like to be a Resurrection-Man when I'm quite growed up!'

Charles Dickens, *A Tale of Two Cities*

THE BEST & WORST OF TIMES

1760 George II dies. His grandson, George III, becomes King.

1769 James Arkwright invents the water frame, making possible a continuous cotton-spinning process powered by water, and leading to the factory system.

1769 David Garrick organizes the first Shakespeare festival at Stratford-upon-Avon.

Surgery had come some way since the days of the Barber Surgeon (see page 51), but it still had relatively low status. (Incidentally, the reason that consultant surgeons in hospitals today are called 'Mr' rather than 'Dr' is a relic of the time when only physicians were properly trained and the lower ranks who performed operations were simple 'sawbones'.) The advance of surgical knowledge was hampered by the lack of fresh bodies available for anatomical dissection. Which led to another black-market job in the dark underbelly of Georgian life: the Resurrection Men or, as they are now known, the Bodysnatchers.

Virtually the only legitimate anatomical subjects available were the bodies of executed criminals. Popular Christian belief in the resurrection of the body meant that people dreaded being dissected after death – it was thought you had to be whole in your grave to have a chance of rising in one piece on the Day of Judgement. (This was why the old punishment of hanging, drawing and quartering was so terrible. It not only ended your life but ruined your chances of getting to heaven in one piece.) A law of 1752 expressly stated that dissection by the Company of Surgeons should be part of the punishment for murder in London. But by the end of the eighteenth century pressure was growing for more bodies. In 1793 there were 200 medical students in London; by 1823 there were over 1,000. And every one wanted a cadaver to work on.

Resurrection Men were essentially criminals. Also known as 'Sack-em-up' men, they raided churchyards, put the bodies in sacks and sold them to doctors. No questions were asked, but a diary attributed to Joshua Naples of Crouch's Resurrection Gang in London reveals the scale of the trade:

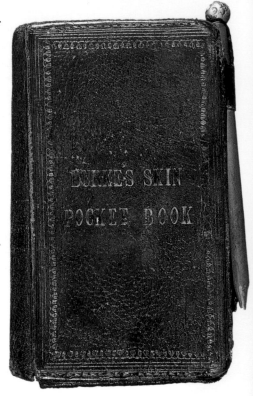

The earthly remains of William Burke, the 'bodysnatcher': his skin tanned (see the Worst Job of All on page 201) and made into a pocket book.

Sunday, 5th [January 1812]

At home all day. Met at 5, whole [gang] went to Newin Got 3 [bodies] *Jack and me took them to Wilson* [James Wilson of the Great Windmill Street Anatomy School]*, Came home, met at 12, got 5* [adult bodies] *and 2 small* [children] *at Harps* [probably Harper, the name of a keeper of a burial ground]*, afterwards went to Big Gates* [probably the entrance to another London graveyard]*, got 3 adults, left Dan at home, took the whole to Barthom* [St Bartholomew's Hospital].

The trick was to get the bodies fresh. Bodysnatchers were often tipped off by gravediggers. But the job could be difficult. Friends of the deceased took to guarding graves for four or five weeks, until the body was rotten. And 'grave clubs' were formed to stop them being dug up. Mortsafes – metal frames padlocked on – were put round coffins. In Leeds, where grave-robbing was a serious problem, they started burying corpses twelve feet down with iron staves set into the earth at fixed intervals immediately above the coffin.

Which brings us to Burke and Hare. Strictly speaking, they weren't Resurrection Men at all. They were chancers who saw that a living could be

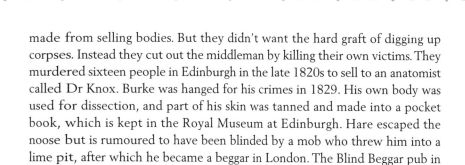

made from selling bodies. But they didn't want the hard graft of digging up corpses. Instead they cut out the middleman by killing their own victims. They murdered sixteen people in Edinburgh in the late 1820s to sell to an anatomist called Dr Knox. Burke was hanged for his crimes in 1829. His own body was used for dissection, and part of his skin was tanned and made into a pocket book, which is kept in the Royal Museum at Edinburgh. Hare escaped the noose but is rumoured to have been blinded by a mob who threw him into a lime pit, after which he became a beggar in London. The Blind Beggar pub in Whitechapel is said to be named after him.

As with smuggling, it was a change in the law that stopped the illegal trade. The 1832 Anatomy Act allowed bodies of the poor to be taken from workhouses for use in anatomical teaching. And given what the workhouses became in Victorian times, it's no wonder that they were able to supply all the corpses the surgeons needed.

Hermit

There can be no clearer example of people with more money than sense than the people who wanted to employ the candidates for the next Worst Job.

This was the age of the Grand Tour, when young men completed their education by doing the European cultural circuit. They came home imbued with the classical ideal. They wanted their houses and gardens to look like a painting by Poussin. They built neo-classical homes reminiscent of Roman temples and they employed landscape gardeners such as Capability Brown to reshape the countryside into an artful, classical version of itself.

Capability Brown was at the top of the landscape heap, but lurking in the undergrowth were the poor unfortunates contracted to be professional Hermits. Because if you were creating your own version of Arcadia, you needed a tasteful, wise ascetic at the bottom of your garden contemplating the brevity of life and the futility of riches to complete the picture.

The trouble is, real hermits weren't very thick on the ground in the eighteenth century, and genuine ascetics didn't come cheap. So landowners craving the ultimate neo-classical accessory hired eccentrics, mental defectives, poets, or the financially desperate to do the job. The vogue lasted for about a hundred years from around 1740. There was one at Hawkstone Park, near Shrewsbury until 1830, when popular pressure made Sir Richard Hill release his human hermit from his contract, and install a dummy instead.

To us it seems a little absurd, not to say contrived, that the rich would employ some old bloke so they could wander round their estate, catch sight of him and thus be reminded of the serious side of life. But even at the time there were those who saw the folly of this notion. The Prime Minister, Horace

Walpole, said, 'It is almost comic to set aside a quarter of one's garden to be melancholy in.'

This eccentric desire for a living, breathing, garden gnome frequently hit a common-sense snag. The job could drive you mad. Stephen Duck, the Royal Hermit installed at the Royal hermitage at Richmond Gardens (now part of Kew), was pressurized to the point of suicide. In order to avoid their employees throwing in the towel, landowners often designed contracts that tied the Hermit into a minimum period of time before money changed hands. At Pains Hill in Surrey, the owner, Sir Charles Hamilton, advertised for a Hermit who would:

continue in the Hermitage seven years, where he would be provided with a Bible, optical glasses, a mat for his feet, a hassock for his pillow, an hour-glass for his timepiece, water for his beverage and food from the house. He must wear a camlet [camel hair] robe, and never, under any circumstances, must he cut his hair, beard or nails, stray beyond the limits of Mr Hamilton' grounds, or exchange one word with the servant.

If these terms weren't bad enough, the Hermit had to carry on with his hermity life even when the owners weren't there to see him. If he obeyed these rules to the full for seven years then, and only then, would he receive £700. When you think that the Riding Officer got £40 per annum for turning out in all weathers, the hermit was potentially quids in, earning nearly three times the salary. But he had to complete his time to claim it.

Some employers required thoughtful positions for the hermit to assume when there were visitors.

The seemingly obvious drawbacks weren't always considered so by people at the time. George Durrant's hermit, an impoverished gentleman called 'Carlous', lived happily in a cave until his death, which was recorded in *Gentleman's Magazine*. A 'Mr Lawrence' from Plymouth coveted the prospect of a hermitage sufficiently to advertise for a position himself.

And some Hermits managed to negotiate better terms and conditions than the Hermit at Pains Hill. For instance, Hermit Finch at Burley was indulged with a sitting room complete with rustic chairs. And one Mr Rimbs from Preston was promised books, an organ and nourishing food. The downside was that he then had to live underground.

So, did Sir Charles get applicants for his Pains Hill job? Yes, of course he did. And did the Hermit last to the end of the seven-year period? Not exactly. He was sacked three weeks into his contract after being found down the local pub consorting with young women.

One can hardly blame him going AWOL. What could be worse for a red-blooded male? For the answer, see overleaf.

Not a Hermit per se, but the self-taught poet Stephen Duck, who was part of the same movement towards idealising the rural idyll for city folk. Lampooned by Jonathan Swift, Duck rhapsodised on the life of a thresher (hence the flail in his left hand). The real farm labourer looks none too impressed.

THE BEST & WORST OF TIMES

1782 James Watt patents his steam engine.

1790s Great Pump Room built at Bath.

1792 Britain declares war on France. The Royal Navy will be at war with France for twenty-three years.

Castrato

The Georgian equivalent of Robbie Williams or, perhaps more accurately, Charlotte Church, was the star of the new craze at the opera: the Castrato.

Strictly speaking, you could call this a non-British job because the Castrati were almost exclusively 'done' in Italy. But they sang all over Europe. The practice started out as a way of supplying voices for female roles, but the unearthly quality of the Castrato's voice was so popular that the main men's roles went to Castrati too. So in Monteverdi's *Coronation of Poppea*, the famous love duet at the end between Nero and Poppea was performed by two men, both castrati. Likewise the part of Julius Caesar in Handel's smash hit *Giulio Cesare* was sung by a eunuch.

The nearest we can get to the sound today is the refined falsetto of the counter-tenor. But this is very different from the timbre of the Castrato, which sounded almost like a strong woman's voice but with the strange, pure, sexless quality of the boy treble.

Above: clippers for severing the sperm duct.

Opposite: William Hogarth's illustration of a crowd at the opera. The banner portrays a cartoon version of a stage scene featuring Senesino, Handel's favourite castrato, the combined Pavarotti/ Charlotte Church of his day. (He's the tall one with a wide body, small head and thin legs.)

The young boys who were chosen for the operation had little choice in the matter. Mostly they came from very poor families who hoped it would lift them out of poverty. The practice of castration had actually been banned by the Vatican as barbaric but, despite the prohibition of both canon and civil law, a blind eye continued to be turned for centuries. To use contemporary parlance, the families of the victims often went 'into denial', alleging that their son had been castrated on account of illness, had suffered a riding accident or had been gored by a wild boar.

In adolescence the male vocal cords grow and thicken, and the voice deepens. Castration prevents the necessary flow of hormones, so growth of the vocal cords is arrested and the voice is prevented from breaking. The Castrato would have had the high voice of a boy soprano, but with the lung power of a full-grown man.

The operation was performed on boys between the ages of eight and ten. If you are a male reader you may wish to skip the next paragraph.

The boy was placed in a very hot bath until he lost consciousness. Some were also drugged with opium. Under this intense heat the testes were manipulated by hand and crushed until their structure began to break down. Then the sperm ducts leading from the testes were severed. The operation wasn't always successful and some boys died.

At the height of the Castrato craze an estimated 4,000 Italian boys were operated on. Unfortunately some were castrated in the mistaken belief that it would create a beautiful singing voice. But of course it only worked on boys who were good singers in the first place.

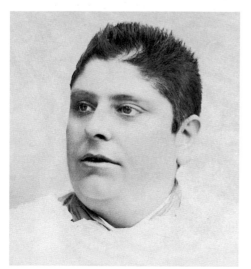

The last Castrato, Alessandro Moreschi.

Even when it was successful, there was often more bad news on the way. Your family put you through this brutal operation for fame and fortune. But the facts of stage life were the same in the eighteenth century as they are today. Very few of those castrated made it to the top of their profession. Only about one per cent of the 4,000 could expect to be successful. For the vast majority there was, at best, a life of occasional employment with no hope of a normal family life.

Worse than that, there were significant side-effects to the operation. Castrati were left with an infantile penis and an underdeveloped prostate. They may have looked tall and imposing on stage but their arms and legs were unusually long compared to their torso, and they were prone to excess fat on the hips, buttocks, breasts and eyelids. Quite apart from the physiological impact, the operation was said to affect their emotional state. Castrati were characterized as fat, volatile and conceited (in fairness these accusations are also applied to opera divas today). The composer Handel's notorious shouting matches with his Castrato Senesino were well known throughout England.

The heyday of the Castrato was between 1650 and 1750. But, despite being directly contrary to Catholic law, the practice continued until the end of the nineteenth century. There is actually a recording of the last Castrato, Alessandro Moreschi, who died in 1922. It was made when he was past his prime, but gives a clear idea of the voice behind a job which, thankfully, is now a mere historical footnote.

The Worst Jobs in the Navy

Rule, Britannia,
Britannia rules the waves
Britons never never never
Shall be slaves.

'Britannia' is a Georgian song. It expresses the confidence and aspirations of a buoyant, burgeoning empire. But, as a statement of fact, it is yet another Georgian sham.

The song expresses the determination of a free people determined to rule rather than be ruled, but the economic muscle of eighteenth-century Britain was founded on the misery of slaves forced to work in plantations of the New World. The slave route from West Africa produced a human horror to which we can't do justice in this book. None of our Worst Jobs compares to the terrible lives of those captured, crammed into slave ships, transported via Bristol and Liverpool and sold, if they survived, into lives of forced labour in the West Indies.

When Britain came to her senses, slavery was banned at home. The navy was despatched to disrupt the slavers operated by French and Spanish ships, and many slaves were freed and returned to freedom in Africa or were released in port. But some opted to enlist in the ships that liberated them. The lives of Nelson's sailors were clearly better than those of slaves; nevertheless they performed some of the toughest, most frightening jobs of the era.

The navy was the visible expression of Britannia's rule of the waves, but here, too, the confidence of the song rings hollow when compared to historical reality. For years Britain's supremacy at sea was touch and go. It wasn't just Napoleon who was the problem. The belligerence of Britain's foreign policy meant that for a generation the country was at war with varying combinations of France, Spain, America, Holland and Russia. Despite victories such as Trafalgar, the French continued to build new, better-designed warships, while the Royal Navy was overstretched and underequipped.

Success was due more than anything to the men who sailed and fought the frigates and ships of the line. They did so in miserable conditions, sustained by the desire to survive and the promise of prize money from captured vessels.

But the typical crew in Nelson's navy was very different from the jolly Jack Tar image you might expect.

To fight the American War and the Seven Years War required between 110,000 and 145,000 sailors and officers. There simply weren't enough home-grown seamen to fulfil these needs. So the ships of Nelson's navy were floating examples of multi-culturalism with just over half the crew coming from Britain, and the rest from Ireland, Poland, Malaya and the Far East, ex-slaves from the West Indies, Scandinavia – in fact anywhere with a coastline. But still this wasn't enough. Life aboard was so tough that volunteers were few and far between. Ships were reliant on the Impress Service or press gang that forced conscripts to enlist. The quota system instituted in 1795 meant that petty criminals could enlist as an alternative to jail. This brought a crop of mental defectives and jail-fever victims into the navy.

[Press warrant, issued to a ship's captain in 1809]

By the Commissioners for Executing the Office of Lord High Admiral of the United Kingdom of Great Britain and Ireland, &c. and of all His Majesty's Plantations, &c.

In pursuance of His majesty's Order in Council, dated the: Sixteenth Day of November, 1804. We do hereby Impower and Direct you to impress, or cause to be impressed, so many Seamen, Seafaring Men and Persons whose occupations and callings are to work in Vessels and boats upon Rivers, as shall be neccesary either to Man His Majesty's Ship under your Command or any other of His Majesty's Ships, giving unto each man so impressed One Shilling for Prest Money. And in the execution hereof, you are to take care that neither yourself nor any Officer authorised by you do demand or receive any money, gratuity, Reward or other Consideration whatsoever, for the sparing, Exchanging, or Discharging, any Person or Persons impressed or to be impressed as you will answer to it at your peril. You are not to intrust any Person with the execution of this Warrant, but a Commission officer and to insert his Name and Office in the Deputation on the other side hereof, and set your Hand and Seal thereto.

This Warrant to continue in Force till the Thirty First Day of December 1809, and in the due execution thereof, all Mayors, Sheriffs, Justices of the Peace, Bailiffs, Constables Headboroughs, and all other His Majesty's Officers and Subjects whom it may concern, are hereby required to be aiding and assisting unto you, and those employed by you, as they tender His Majesty's Service, and will answer the contrary at their Perils.

Given under our Hands and the Seal of the Office of Admiralty.

THE BEST & WORST OF TIMES

1792 Execution of Louis XVI – Reign of Terror starts in France.

1795 Lime juice is made compulsory in the Royal Navy to combat scurvy.

1799 Ten per cent income tax is introduced to help pay for the wars.

Once aboard, these landlubbers were known collectively as 'waisters'. Unlike the men rated 'able' seamen, they were confined to the waist, the middle part of the ship, and given menial work to do such as pulling on ropes until they had learnt the intricacies of the rigging. They were not allowed to perform more complex tasks until they had 'learnt the ropes'. (Welcome to Derivation City. Jobs in the navy, especially from the time of the Napoleonic Wars, seem to have contributed more to the English language than any other walk of life.)

But though they were unskilled, it didn't mean that the waisters couldn't be singled out for some really awful jobs aboard – such as the Loblolly Boy.

This depiction of the press gang turns it into a very gentlemanly affair. The reality involved a violent trawl through the underside of Britain's port towns.

Loblolly Boy

Like the Spit Boy (see page 81) in Tudor times, the Loblolly Boy wasn't necessarily young. And as for loblolly? Well, he took his name from one of the naval remedies he administered. Loblolly was the term for the dried lozenges of so-called 'portable soup' made of dried meat extract, the eighteenth-century equivalent of stock cubes, which were dissolved in hot water and given to patients. But making Bovril for sick sailors was the easiest part of the Loblolly Boy's job, which essentially involved assisting the ship's surgeon.

Medical men on board ships varied in skill and experience. Some, especially aboard the larger ships of the line such as Nelson's *Victory*, were genuine doctors, while lower down the naval pecking order a captain might be only too pleased to get an amateur quack with a talent for pulling teeth. While their land-bound compatriots were experimenting on supplies from the Resurrection Men, most ships' surgeons had only the most basic equipment, know-how and medicine to deal with a whole range of conditions.

The medical area was situated in the orlop, a lower deck above the stinking water of the bilges. This gave the workplace an unhealthy choking stench, but it kept patients and doctors safely out of the way in battle. Because it was close to the centre of gravity, there was less movement to disturb the surgeon's operations.

In the heat of a battle, this area was awash with blood. On a makeshift operating table, made of seamen's chests pushed together, and without the benefit of anaesthetic, the surgeon would stitch up the most savage wounds caused by wood splinters, musket balls and cannon shot. Where limbs were shattered, he would have to do emergency amputations. It was the only known treatment. This was the world of the Barber Surgeon gone mad.

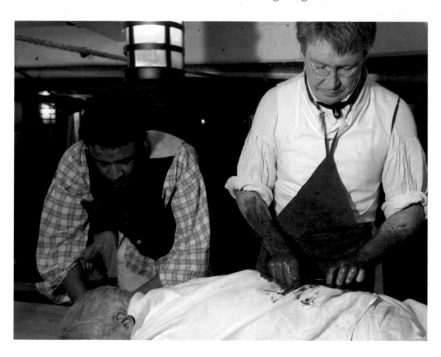

Reconstruction of eighteenth century surgery. Accurate in every respect apart from the pain.

The main problem for the Loblolly Boy was keeping the patient still. One way was to get him drunk to dull the pain. There was also the drug laudanum, an alcoholic tincture of opium, which was to become all the rage in the Victorian era. To stop the patient's screams, the Loblolly Boy would tie a leather strap across his mouth or give him a musket ball to clench in his teeth so he could 'bite the bullet'. And finally, once he'd pinned his patient down, often with the help of his messmates, the surgeon could begin his work.

The object was speed rather than neatness. Then, once the amputation had taken place, the arteries and veins were tied off, and left hanging from the wound. The plan was to remove them later when the wound had healed, but the dangling fleshy tubes left the patient vulnerable to infection, often with disastrous consequences.

The Loblolly Boy's final task at the operating table was to get rid of the severed limbs. In a full naval engagement he could easily fill a tub with the shattered bits of his fellow crew members.

But, as the table below shows, deaths and diseases weren't restricted to battle. Every day cannons rolled over feet and people fell from the rigging. With all the heavy work aboard ship, hernias were a particular problem. Nearly 4,000 trusses were issued to sailors in the Royal Navy every year.

FATAL CASUALTIES IN THE ROYAL NAVY IN 1810

CAUSE OF DEATH	NUMBER	PERCENTAGE
By Disease	2,592	50.0
By Individual Accident	1,630	31.5
By Foundering, Wreck, Fire, Explosion	530	10.2
By the Enemy, killed in action	281	5.4
By the Enemy, died of wounds	150	2.9
All Causes	5,183	100

The greatest health problem came from disease. Scurvy was a particular issue, and Loblolly Boys dispensed limes to counteract it. Indeed, British sailors earned the title 'Limeys' from their American counterparts, because of their partiality for the vitamin C-rich fruit. The consumption of limes on board ship was made compulsory in 1798, and the disease was contained. But jail fever, typhoid, yellow fever, malaria and cholera still took their toll. When the *Brunswick* went out to the West Indies in 1801, 287 men ended up on the sick list with the 'yellow jack' and malaria. And of course, when it came to deadly diseases, the Loblolly Boy, who had to nurse the sick, was especially at risk.

Working with the suffering, the bleeding and the terrified in fetid conditions can't have been much fun. The job was hazardous and the conditions fetid. It was a doddle compared to life up on deck.

THE BEST & WORST OF TIMES

1811 Luddite uprisings in the Midlands against weaving frames.

1811 George III is declared insane. The Prince of Wales (the future George IV) is made Regent.

1812 Start of war against America.

1814 Invasion of France by the Allies. Napoleon abdicates and is exiled to Elba.

Topman

Topmen were the elite of a ship's crew. They were the toughest and fittest aboard and were entrusted with the vital job of adjusting the sails.

The definition of a man o' war in the eighteenth-century navy was a ship with three masts: the foremast, the massive mainmast and the mizzen mast to the rear. These masts were crossed by yard arms, and the whole lot was supported by an incredible complexity of rigging. From these masts and yards, stretching down to the great bowsprit jutting out at an angle from the front of the ship, were hundreds of possible combinations of twenty-four different sails hung to make most efficient use of whatever wind and conditions were available.

Changing these sails quickly was a matter of life and death. In an Antarctic squall, reefing the sails ensured that the ship didn't capsize in the wind. An extra knot gained by the right combination could mean escape from a pursuing enemy in a sea chase, or, alternatively, could bring a vessel up to a valuable prize. Topmen were practised in scrambling up the horizontal ropes known as ratlins to the upper reaches of the masts. Once there, they'd run out on the yardarms to do their work with the sails.

The Topmen had to do the job at top speed with the boat pitching forwards and backwards as well as side-to-side. In a heavy swell the top of the mast would be moving like a pendulum. And, with the wind blowing and ice glazing the yards and the rigging, accidents could and did happen.

It wouldn't have been so bad if this was all they had to do. But it was just one part of a seven-day-a-week job, jam-packed with tough, unappealing tasks.

The ropes and rigging of a ship were coated in tar to prevent them from rotting, so Topmen would have had perpetually sticky hands from climbing. This is why sailors got the generic name Jack Tar.

These regulations were read periodically by the captain to his crew, often in place of a sermon at Sunday service. Punishments were harsh. The phrase 'shall suffer death' is a constant refrain. The most usual punishment was a flogging. The offender would be tied to a grating and given a specified number of strokes with the cat o'nine tails, a rope whip with metal weights in the lashes. This wasn't just six of the best. Floggings of 300 lashes are recorded.

1749 ARTICLES OF WAR

…19 *If any person in or belonging to the fleet shall make or endeavour to make any mutinous assembly upon any pretence whatsoever, every person offending herein, and being convicted thereof by the sentence of the court martial, shall suffer death: and if any person in or belonging to the fleet shall utter any words of sedition or mutiny, he shall suffer death, or such other punishment as a court martial shall deem him to deserve: and if any officer, mariner, or soldier on or belonging to the fleet, shall behave himself with contempt to his superior officer, being in the execution of his office, he shall be punished according to the nature of his offence by the judgement of a court martial.*

20 *If any person in the fleet shall conceal any traitorous or mutinous practice or design, being convicted thereof by the sentence of a court martial, he shall suffer death, or any other punishment as a court martial shall think fit; and if any person, in or belonging to the fleet, shall conceal any traitorous or mutinous words spoken by any, to the prejudice of His Majesty or government, or any words, practice, or design, tending to the hindrance of the service, and shall not forthwith reveal the same to the commanding officer, or being present at any mutiny or sedition, shall not use his utmost endeavours to suppress the same, he shall be punished as a court martial shall think he deserves.*

21 *If any person in the fleet shall find cause of complaint of the unwholesomeness of the victual, he shall quietly make the same known to his superior, or captain, or commander in chief, as the occasion may deserve, that such present remedy may be had as the matter may require; and the said superior, captain, or commander in chief, shall, as far as he is able, cause the same to be presently remedied; and no person in the fleet, upon any such or other pretence, shall attempt to stir up any disturbance, upon pain of such punishment, as a court martial shall think fit to inflict, according to the degree of the offence.*

22 *If any officer, mariner, soldier or other person in the fleet, shall strike any of his superior officers, or draw, or offer to draw, or lift up any weapon against him, being in the execution of his office, on any pretence whatsoever, every such person being convicted of any such offence, by the sentence of a court martial, shall suffer*

THE BEST & **WORST** OF TIMES

1815 Napoleon returns but is defeated at Waterloo.

1818 Cotton spinners in Manchester go on strike.

1819 Peterloo massacre: 60,000 orderly protesters at Peter's Fields in Manchester are ridden down by mounted troops wielding sabres.

1820 Accession of George IV.

death; and if any officer, mariner, soldier or other person in the fleet, shall presume to quarrel with any of his superior officers, being in the execution of his office, or shall disobey any lawful command of any of his superior officers; every such person being convicted of any such offence, by the sentence of a court martial, shall suffer death, or such other punishment, as shall, according to the nature and degree of his offence, be inflicted upon him by the sentence of a court martial.

23 If any person in the fleet shall quarrel or fight with any other person, or use reproachful or provoking speeches or gestures, tending to make any quarrel or disturbance, he shall, upon being convicted thereof, suffer such punishment as the offence shall deserve, and a court martial shall impose.

24 There shall be no wasteful expence of any powder, shot, ammunition, or other stores in the fleet, nor any embezzlement thereof, but the stores and provisions shall be careful preserved , upon pain of such punishment to be inflicted upon the offenders, abettors, buyers and receivers (being persons subject to naval discipline) as shall be by a court martial found just in that behalf.

25 Every person in the fleet, who shall unlawfully burn or set fire to any magazine or store of powder, or ship, boat, ketch, hoy or vessel, or tackle or furniture thereunto belonging, not then appertaining to an enemy, pirate, or rebel, being convicted of any such offence, by the sentence of a court martial, shall suffer death.

26 Care shall be taken in the conducting and steering of any of His Majesty's ships, that through wilfulness, negligence, or other defaults, no ship be stranded, or run upon any rocks or sands, or split or hazarded, upon pain, that such as shall be found guilty therein, be punished by death, or such other punishment, as the offence by a court martial shall be judged to deserve.

27 No person in or belonging to the fleet shall sleep upon his watch, or negligently perform the duty imposed on him, or forsake his station, upon pain of death, or such other punishment as a court martial shall think fit to impose, and as the circumstances of the case shall require.

28 All murders committed by any person in the fleet, shall be punished with death by the sentence of a court martial.

29 If any person in the fleet shall commit the unnatural and detestable sin of buggery and sodomy with man or beast, he shall be punished with death by the sentence of a court martial.

30 All robbery committed by any person in the fleet, shall be punished with death, or otherwise, as a court martial, upon consideration of the circumstances, shall find meet.

The sailor's square meal. The barrels of salt pork and beef that provided the main (but incredibly salty) constituent, could have crossed the Atlantic two or three times and be months' or even years' old. This meal was best by 1815.

However, the sailors did get a 'square meal' a day, literally. Their square mess tins were filled with a plentiful supply of monotonous and pretty disgusting food. The weekly menu of supplies hardly ever varied. It was a diet based on meat, preserved by being salted and placed in barrels. This had to be soaked in fresh water to make it edible. Carbohydrate came in the form of hard tack or ship's biscuit. This flour-and-water long-life bread often became infested with weevils: more protein but not very appetizing. Vegetables were absent from the diet, apart from dried and soaked peas.

To an eighteenth-century working-man's palate, this cuisine might not have seemed as bad as it does to us. Nevertheless, the fact that one of the articles of war deals with complaints about the food shows that all was not always well in the ship's kitchen.

The silver lining was that there was plenty to drink. Along with a pound of biscuit and a pound of dried meat a day, the men were allowed a gallon of beer. Yes, eight pints. But this was small beer – not very alcoholic. The real damage was done by the grog.

Every man on board ship received a half-pint rum ration per day. This was mixed with water to make grog. So the men went about their work with the equivalent of eight pints of low-alcohol lager and twelve rum and cokes swilling around inside them. The Topmen would be leaping round the rigging in a constant state of inebriation.

But all the furling and unfurling of sails was for one reason only: to fight. The wooden three-masters were floating gun batteries, and one of the most important parts of the Topman's job was to operate the great guns.

A captain, however, dined in style, particularly if he worked for the East India Company. In this Gillray cartoon you can tell the captain is entertaining his guests in his cabin by the broad sweep of windows running across the rear of the ship.

Crews learnt to aim their cannons and time their broadsides with the rhythm of the rise and fall of the waves. They had to be able not only to blast away randomly, but to aim for a mainmast or, before an enemy ship was boarded, rake her decks with deadly small-calibre canister-shot to decimate the waiting defenders.

If they weren't properly handled, a ship's own guns could be as deadly as the enemies'. One of the main dangers was the recoil. The guns were on wheels. When fired, the force of one shot from a fully loaded 32-pounder would send it springing back 50 feet, more than the width of a ship. So the cannon were restrained with ropes to restrict the recoil to 10 feet. The gun captain had to arch himself over the barrel to fire the gun, and hold steady on the roll as it shot underneath him. Any foot or finger in the way was crushed. In battle, the ropes could be shot away. A 'loose cannon' was a deadly risk to everyone else on the gun deck: tons of metal rolling up and down with the waves, ploughing through the other gun crews.

Each gun was operated by a crew of six in which each member knew his place and had to obey the order of firing. In the heat of battle, if gunpowder was shoved into a heated gun without being damped down before reloading, it would spell the end for the whole crew. So gun crews were numbered to avoid

Battle	British			Enemy (estimated)			
	killed	wounded	total	killed	wounded	total	Prisoners
First of June 1794	287	811	1,098	1,500	2,000	3,500	3,500
Cape St. Vincent 1797	73	227	300	430	570	1,000	3,157
Camperdown 1797	203	622	825	540	620	1,160	3,775
The Nile 1798	218	677	895	1,400	600	2,000	3,225
Copenhagen 1801	253	688	941	540	620	1,160	3,775
Trafalgar 1805	449	1,241	1,690	4,408	2,545	6,953	7,000
Total	1,438	4,266	5,749	9,068	7,245	16,313	22,657

British and Enemy Casualties in the Six Major Victories

This table of casualties shows the cost of naval supremacy.

errors. Number One, the gun captain, primed the cannon, looked through the sight, gave orders for aiming the gun and fired it. With the aid of a handspike, Number Two turned and raised the gun barrel. Three loaded it with the required ammunition – large roundshot, grapeshot, chainshot or canister. Four damped down sparks in the barrel with a swab before reloading. And Five moved the gun barrel and passed the ammunition.

Then there was Number Six.

The gundeck was coated in sand to soak up blood and give the crews their footing, but accounts tell of blood flowing through the scuppers in some engagements. The casualty figures even on the winning side were huge. In the confined space of the gundeck, the shattering noise of guns going off, the screaming of the injured and dying and the pounding of the enemy's broadsides against the hull must have been terrifying. It's hard to imagine a worse job than being a man working under those conditions.

Except being a boy.

Powder Monkey

Number Six was the Powder Monkey, responsible for supplying the gun captain with the gunpowder he needed to prime the gun. Because the gunpowder was so flammable, the gun crew kept very few cartridges close to their cannons. The Powder Monkey had to run a deadly relay race from the killing ground of the gundeck down to the magazine into the bowels of the ship.

For this speedy work, ship's boys as young as six were employed. In fact, anyone not manning a gun helped out. There were more women on board than you might have imagined and they too did this work. We know this because

This boy from a naval reconstruction group is already getting on a bit for a Powder Monkey.

when the government handed out naval medals to those who'd fought in the Battle of the Nile, many women applied (and, given the traditional machismo of the Senior Service, were predictably turned down).

The magazine was a copper-lined room in the heart of the ship. The copper kept the powder dry but, unlike iron, did not give off sparks. Here, in the handling chamber, the Master Gunner filled cartridges of gunpowder and handed them over to the Powder Monkeys through wet curtains known as 'fear-not' or 'dreadnought' screens that guarded against incoming heat and flame. These elaborate precautions didn't always work. At the Battle of the Nile, a red-hot cannonball rolled into the magazine of the French ship *L'Orient*. No bodies were ever found.

Powder Monkeys knew only too well what gunpowder could do. The most terrifying part of their job was to make their way back from the handling chamber, along the narrow gangways and ladders, to the butchery of the guns, clutching a cartridge of gunpowder that could kill them instantaneously. For the youngsters who'd joined up in the hope of glory or out of sheer poverty, the realities of war must have brought a shocking and swift end to childhood.

There was one consolation. If they survived and captured an enemy ship, even Powder Monkeys shared in the prize money. They also had the pride of knowing they were part of Britain's greatest claim to fame: the Royal Navy. Some working children didn't even have that consolation.

Which brings us to what must be the Worst Job of all in Georgian times.

The Worst Job of All: Mule Scavenger

The cotton and wool mills of northern England were the driving force behind the Industrial Revolution. The eighteenth century saw a quantum leap in technology that enabled mass production to take place. The invention of Hargreaves's spinning jenny in 1765, Arkwright's water frame in 1769 and Crompton's mule in 1779 revolutionized the spinning industry. Many mill owners were radical and far-sighted in their use of the new technology. They seized on every innovation that came along to streamline and increase production. So when James Watt invented an effective steam engine, they used it to supplement the water power that drove their looms.

But when it came to employment, they were far from forward-thinking. They were closer to a feudal lord than an enlightened employer. The lower echelons of mill workers had some of the sorriest jobs of all time. And at the bottom of the heap were the mill apprentices, the most junior of whom was the Mule Scavenger.

The apprentices who did this kind of work were regarded as a mere commodity. You can see this clearly through the history of just one cotton mill, Quarry Bank at Styal, just outside Manchester. Quarry Bank is now a fascinating museum of the industrial age, and contains not only the machinery of the time but also a living record of the people who worked there.

In 1791 its owner, Samuel Greg, by no means the harshest employer of the age, came up with a novel solution to his labour shortage. He decided to purchase some child apprentices from the local workhouse. He built an Apprentice House costing £300 and housing ninety children. This investment made good business sense. Parishes offered mill owners sweeteners of two to four pounds a child to get them off the workhouse books, so he got most of his money back before they even started work. These apprentices made up half Quarry Bank's workforce. There were sixty boys and thirty girls. Some were as young as eight. But there were no concessions to age when it came to the working day. They woke in their two-to-a-bed dorms at the crack of dawn to begin a twelve-or fourteen-hour shift, for which they received their board and lodging and pocket money of a couple of pence a week.

The entry-level jobs were the worst: 'piecing', which involved leaning over the looms to twist broken ends of cotton together, and 'scavenging' on the looms invented by Crompton, known as the 'mules'.

Mule Scavenging combined the risk of accident with severe long-term health problems. The job was tedious but unrelenting. And it was carried out in a newly created alien environment: the factory.

Quarry Bank Mill in full flow would not have been as noisy as the gundeck of a ship, but you knew that the great guns would eventually stop. The thump

THE BEST & WORST OF TIMES

1835 Christmas becomes a national holiday – a break for everyone.

1835 Darwin studies the Galápagos Islands on his voyage in the *Beagle*.

1837 William IV dies. Accession of Queen Victoria.

This drawing from 1823 shows the machine that the Piecers and Scavengers had to work round for twelve hours a day. On the left is a Scavenger crouched underneath the machine as she collects bits of dropped cotton. In black and white it looks harmless enough, but a moment's inattention, and this mule could maim and kill.

and clatter of the machines were perpetual. It created a confusing din that made human contact almost impossible.

This was compounded by the oppressive heat and air in the mills. To stop the cotton drying out, the atmosphere was kept warm and humid. The cotton dust flying around caused eye infections and the lung disease bissinosis. Our phrase for being used up, chewed up and spat out – 'gone through the mill' – came from the effect on people's appearances of working in this fledgling industry.

The Scavenger's job was simple. The mule moved forwards and backwards, weaving thread together. As it did so, bits dropped off and cotton fluff collected underneath and on its moving parts. This had to be harvested for recycling and also to prevent accidents.

Weavers were on piece rates so the looms stopped for nothing. Armed with a brush and a sack, the young Scavenger worked underneath the machine

itself, scampering in and out on all fours between the metal runners, crouching low to keep out of the way of the machinery. The choking cotton dust that pervaded the mill rooms was highly flammable. The Scavengers worked in bare feet rather than in their normal clogs, as hobnailed soles might strike a spark.

The safety of the children depended on timing their movements with the rhythm of the Mule. If they got a hand caught in the threads of the

The workers' dormitory at Quarry Bank. You can imagine the size of the child workers from the tiny beds.

loom or ended up in the wrong place as the heavy metal frame slid back into place, it could spell disaster. In the memoranda of the mill only major accidents are recorded. A lost finger or even hand was not usually thought worth mentioning.

Scrambling around on hands and knees was exhausting, and young children can be inattentive at the best of times. After twelve hours in soporific heat it must have been almost impossible to concentrate. It's no wonder that accidents happened. At Quarry Bank the following was recorded:

> *On the 6th of March 1865 a very melancholy accident befell a lad named Joseph Foden about 13 years of age. While engaged sweeping under a Mule his head was caught between the Roller beam and the carriage – as the latter was putting-up – and completely smashed, death being instantaneous.*

But the overseers had little sympathy for their young charges. Any slacking was punished by a beating with a stick or belt. In one mill there was a cistern of water in which to dunk any child found nodding off.

There were runaways from this virtual prison. Thomas Priestly had already lost a forefinger in the mule. He and another apprentice, Joseph Sefton, made their bid for freedom. In testimony to a Middlesex magistrate after his escape, Priestly revealed that the apprentices weren't even allowed proper meal breaks: 'Our working hours were from 6 am in the summer and in winter until 7 in the evening … our breakfasts were always brought to the mill … two days a week we had an hour allowed us for dinner.'

In 1816 Quarry Bank produced 342,578 pounds of cloth. A decade later, output had doubled. Owners like Samuel Greg thought they had everything to lose and nothing to gain from treating their workers better and thus reducing their profits.

Nevertheless, in the nineteenth century the pendulum slowly started to swing. It began in 1818 when the Manchester cotton spinners went on strike. This dispute led to the dreadful Peterloo massacre. But once the move for workers' rights had started, it could not be stopped. By 1833 the Factory Act had banned the employment of workers under the age of nine. It seemed as though things could only get better.

Perhaps not. Working people may have been fighting for better conditions, but the Victorian Age was about to dawn with its own Worst Jobs.

CHAPTER SIX

Victorian Worst Jobs

T he pace of scientific and social progress in the years of Queen Victoria's reign was phenomenal. But the flipside of the Victorian economic and technological miracle was a life of degradation and despair for much of the ever-increasing population. Writers such as Charles Dickens, Mrs Gaskell and Sir Arthur Conan Doyle have left us a vivid picture of the grubby side of Victorian life. The bad news is that, however heart-rending the stories, the reality was much worse.

Driven by poverty, millions left the countryside for the burgeoning towns and cities, and became bit players in a great smoky world of the machine. The new life-style adopted by many of the urban poor was far from the respectable Victorian ideal. Opium dens and drug taking were widespread. Despite Victorian Christian rhetoric, fewer than 50 per cent of the population attended church.

The Victorians investigated and categorized everything they could lay their hands on. The most obvious effects of this methodical analysis can be seen in the great nineteenth-century scientific inventions and the quantum leap forward made by Charles Darwin and his theory of evolution. But their inquisitiveness also applied to the social sphere. For the first time in history, people started taking serious notice of what the poor did and how they lived. Charles Dickens had personal experience of Worst Jobs. When he was twelve he did the excruciatingly boring job of label-sticking in Warren's Blacking factory near the Strand in London. Later he vividly painted the horrors of Victorian society in his novels. But it was left to others to record the smallest details of workers' lives, most notably the journalist Henry Mayhew. He set himself the project of investigating the poor, collecting stories of the London

Hard-working men and child labourer – a snapshot of the Victorian employment scene.

VICTORIAN

labourers he met and describing the conditions they worked in. Here he describes Jacob's Island in Bermondsey.

As we passed along the reeking banks of the sewer the sun shone upon a narrow slip of water. In the bright light it appeared the colour of strong green tea, and positively looked as solid as black marble in the shadow – indeed, it was more like watery mud than muddy water, and yet we were assured this was the only water which the wretched inhabitants had to drink. As we gazed in horror at it, we saw drains and sewers emptying their filthy contents into it; we saw a whole tier of doorless privies in the open road, open to men and women, built over it; we heard bucket after bucket of filth splash into it … we asked if they did drink the water? The answer was, They were obliged to drink the ditch, without it, they could beg a pailful or thieve a pailful of water.

The railways sum up the best and the worst of the Victorian age. They dramatically changed the lives of those who could afford to use them. Middle-class town dwellers could now travel to the seaside; fresh country produce could be transported to the heart of the cities; industry could move its products more efficiently; the farther reaches of the British Isles were no

Three great Victorians. From left to right: Charles Dickens, Henry Mayhew and Charles Darwin.

THE BEST & **WORST** OF TIMES

1831 Stephenson's *Rocket* goes into service on the Stockton to Darlington railway, launching the age of steam.

1834 The Poor Law Amendment Act creates the workhouse, a place of punishment.

1834 Fire destroys the Houses of Parliament. They are rebuilt with a new tower housing the bell known as Big Ben.

1836 Charles Dickens, the man who more than any other has given us our picture of Victorian life, publishes the first chapters of *The Pickwick Papers*.

longer isolated. But this radical transformation was only possible because thousands of men worked long hours in constant danger and suffered appalling casualties.

Navvy

'Navvy' derives from the word 'navigator', a reference to the men who had built the great navigation canals. But digging the canal network was just a rehearsal for the gargantuan task of creating the vast network of railways that soon covered Britain.

In 1830, there were 97 miles of railway track. By 1840, this had increased to 1,497 miles. By the time Queen Victoria died, there were 22,000 miles, far more than we have today. And every inch of every line had been laid and dug by hand. Or rather by millions of hands.

The Navvies had to literally reshape the land, building it up where it dipped and digging it out or tunnelling where it rose. Their tools were the wheelbarrow, shovel and pick. It was an almost unimaginable task.

By the mid-nineteenth century, there were 250,000 Navvies in Britain. They came from Lancashire, Yorkshire, Scotland and, predominantly after the great potato famine, from Ireland. They shacked up in huts by the lines they were building. A big hut could house twenty men. A bed cost a penny ha'penny a night. Whole shanty towns sprang up from these little settlements, acquiring names like 'Batty Green' or 'Jericho'. In 1845, at Woodhead between Manchester and Liverpool, 1,100 men were living in these temporary townships.

They were like an invading army, and were hated and feared by local people. As early as 1838, Lieutenant Peter Lecount of the London and Birmingham Railway declared the Navvies were 'the terror of the surrounding country; they are as completely a class by themselves as the gypsies … their ferocious behaviour can only be equalled by the brutality of their language'.

They revelled in their outsider status. They wore distinctive clothes: moleskin trousers and double canvas shirts for hard wear, velveteen square-tailed coats, hobnail boots, piratical rainbow waistcoats, gaudy handkerchiefs and white felt hats off-duty.

They tended to be known by nicknames like 'Fighting Jack' or 'Gipsy Joe', rather than by their real names. And they had their own brutal laws and rules. They even invented their own marriage ceremony. The couple leapt over a broom in the presence of a room full of Navvies, and then consummated the marriage right there in the middle of the communal living space.

Their lives were harsh. On a daily ration of two pounds of beef and a gallon of beer, an experienced Navvy was expected to move 20 tons of earth each shift. Building embankments was an especially tough task. The barrows of earth and rock had to be pushed to the tops of cuttings via plank-walkways, with just a single perilous rope attachment. The rope was drawn by a horse over a pulley mechanism, and attached to the barrow and the man's belt. A signal was given, and the horse moved forward, drawing the barrow up the embankment. This was known as 'making a running'. Pulled by the horse, the Navvy would walk up the 45-degree slope guiding the heavy barrow. If the horse was steady, all was well. If it slipped or stumbled on the soggy ground, the barrow could tip. If this happened, the Navvy had to hurl it away to stop it falling on top of him, as he and his barrow tumbled down the slope.

But an even more dangerous part of the job was digging tunnels. The only light in the pitch black was from candles, so there was always the possibility that the naked flame would set off the explosives. Accidents were horrifyingly common. During the building of the Woodhead Tunnel in 1839–45, 32 men

THE BEST & WORST OF TIMES

1837 Euston Station built, bringing the railway age, and jobs, to London.

1837 William IV dies; succeeded by Queen Victoria. Samuel Morse develops the telegraph and Morse Code. Instant communication over vast distances is now possible.

1838 Charles Dickens publishes *Oliver Twist*, his satire on the workhouse.

The railways the navvies laid were an inch-perfect engineering miracle. Here a crafted incline passes under a massive viaduct.

were killed and 140 seriously injured, while 400 received lesser wounds. This was 3 per cent of the total labour force dead, and 14 per cent wounded. From 1839–41, 131 Navvies were hospitalized while building the Great Western Railway. The great Isambard Kingdom Brunel simply said, 'I think it is a small list.'

Navvies in their insanitary shanty towns were particularly susceptible to dysentery, cholera, smallpox, consumption, inflammation of the lungs and, in the heat of summer, sunstroke. If a Navvy died, a small payment from a contributory sick fund was all his wife (or the broomstick equivalent) might expect.

A Navvy was paid well to compensate for the danger and hard labour, but the system of payment was an economic trap. An inexperienced Navvy would get two shillings a day, paid monthly. During the month while he waited for his wage, he bought goods on credit from company shops, which charged extortionate prices. Monthly salaries were frequently handed out in a pub owned by the management. Drunkenness on the job was commonplace, but it ensured that the money the Railway paid out in wages came back via the alehouse.

VICTORIAN

Railway tunnels were dug from the middle. The Navvies would dig down from above to excavate the ventilation shaft and then, using explosives and brute force, carve out the tunnel in two directions, thus doubling the speed of the job.

A MAN CRUSHED TO DEATH BY AN ENGINE – On Thursday, the 8th inst., about 10.15 a.m., a terrible accident happened to Peter Miles, a mason, on the new line of railway at Batty Wife Hole. It appeared that the deceased, who had been drinking at the Railway Inn, left in a state of intoxication for Sebastapol, about 8.30 p.m. In the dark he wandered on the tunnel tramway, where it is supposed that he laid himself down and fell asleep. According to the evidence of Henry Bailey, the guard, the engine which crushed the poor man to death was returning from Jericho, and that when about 150 yards away from Batty Green Platform, feeling a jerk, he ordered the driver to stop the locomotive. Then he alighted, and went to ascertain the cause of the interruption. The feelings of the guard may be better imagined than described, when he found that the engine's course had been checked by a fellow being, whose skull had been cut through, and whose abdomen was sadly mutilated. Peter Miles, who was 30 years of age, was a native of Bootle, near Liverpool. An inquest was held on the body of the deceased, on the 12th inst., at the Railway Inn before T. Brown. Esq., deputy coroner, when the jury returned a verdict of 'Accidentally killed by being run over by a railway engine'.

Craven Pioneer, 17 February 1872

THE BEST & WORST OF TIMES

1838 Regular Atlantic steamship service begins. Isambard Kingdom Brunel's *Great Western* becomes the first ocean-going steamship.

1839 First meeting of the social reform movement, the 'Chartists', who attempt to get the vote extended and unfair trade restrictions lifted.

1840 A law is passed banning climbing boys (chimney sweeps) under the age of 21 from being sent up chimneys, but few take any notice.

Navvies talked of 'going on a randy' (a drinking binge), much to the terror of local people. The drinking could be fatal.

The countryside through which the railways passed was changing fast. The end of the Georgian era had seen vast areas of common land enclosed and riots in the countryside. Well-to-do Victorians living in the comfort of the towns and new suburbs liked to imagine rural England as a utopian idyll, but it was far from that. The Wessex of Thomas Hardy's novels only scratches the surface of how hard life was for many farm workers. And the most tedious, menial work was often done by women and children as young as six.

Stone Picker

Stone picking has to be one of the most thankless tasks ever. Gangs of children, forty or fifty strong, would leave their village at six in the morning. They often walked two or three miles to work, as part of a fourteen-hour day. When they finally arrived at the farm at which they were going to work, they were given pails or baskets to fill with stones, which they heaved into a cart. As they

V I C T O R I A N

crouched on the ground scrabbling at the earth for hour after hour, a man with a whip walked behind them, beating them if they slacked on the job. They were paid a penny for one big basket of stones. They were exposed to the wind, hail and sleet, and ate their cold food under a hedge. There were no holidays, except for wet days and Sundays.

In addition to the day-to-day harshness of their lives, rural workers in East Anglia were at risk from 'Fen Ague'. This mysterious illness caused violent shivering, sweating and pain in the limbs. It was thought to be brought about by the 'miasma' from rotting vegetation, but in fact it was a form of malaria caused by the bite from a mosquito that thrived in the warm damp of the Fens. To ease the pain, labourers took opium, which they called 'comfort'. It was smoked in powder form, or mixed into tablets.

The *Lincoln Mercury* reported in 1846:

The Practice of taking opium, laudanum, ether, and morphia has increased, and is increasing, amongst the population of the fens of Cambridgeshire and Lincolnshire to a frightful extent. It gains ground amongst the aged, the infirm, and the young … It is common to see the man or woman of 20, 30 or 40 years with cadaverous countenance, tottering frame, and palsied step, daily going for his or her sixpenny-worth of poison.

Kids in the countryside did a whole host of other jobs that involved long hours, boredom and dreadful conditions. Some worked as Bird Scarers, running around all day with a rattle, others as Herring Callers, freezing on top of a cliff waiting for signs of a shoal of herring, then summoning the fishermen.

But children in the towns weren't immune from appalling jobs. Factories produced tons of grime. The thrusting red-brick extravagances of Glasgow, Birmingham and Manchester and the terraced warrens of London were veiled in filth. Coal was to blame. The ever-growing population used it to heat their homes, and industry swallowed it relentlessly. Coal meant soot, and soot meant Chimney Sweeps.

THE BEST & WORST OF TIMES

1840 Queen Victoria marries her cousin Albert.

1841 Fifth national census names every working man, woman and child (until then, many people had just been statistics) in a population of 18.5 million.

1842 Act of Parliament passed forbidding women and children from working down the mines. It is proposed by Lord Shaftesbury.

Chimney Sweep

The image of a little sweep boy climbing into the murk of a chimney flue is one of the archetypes of Victorian life, and it truly was one of the Worst Jobs of the age. The children were kept hungry and skinny so that they wouldn't get stuck. But the spaces in a Victorian chimney were improbably tight and boys became trapped and died. In the tall stacks of town houses there was also the danger of falling. Broken limbs were common.

A chimney sweep and a climbing boy. A vivid illustration of how youngsters could scramble into the smallest of flues and what a terrible loss of innocence was involved in the trade.

The climbing boys were usually street children who were picked up by sweeps on the look-out for cheap labour. Charles Kingsley's Tom is a conscious attempt, like Dickens's own street child, Oliver Twist, to make his audience see an individual rather than a faceless category of worker:

He cried when he had to climb the dark flues, rubbing his poor knees and elbows raw; and when the soot got into his eyes, which it did every day in the week; and when his master beat him, which he did every day in the week; and when he had not enough to eat, which happened every day in the week likewise.

Charles Kingsley, *The Water Babies*

And did the Victorians care? Well, yes, they did. Legislation banning anyone under the age of twenty-one from being sent up a chimney was passed in 1840, just three years into Victoria's reign. But the fines for breaking this law were paltry, and it was widely flouted, particularly as the newly invented extendable brushes were far more expensive to replace than climbing boys. It wasn't until the serialization of Charles Kingsley's social satire *The Water Babies* in 1862–3 that the public ceased to turn a blind eye. Lord Shaftesbury introduced a new Act that upped the fine to a massive £10.

By the time Henry Mayhew was writing, still only twenty-five years into Victoria's reign, the move for reform was such that even sweeps were looking back to the 'bad old days'.

A master sweeper, who was in the habit of bathing at the Marylebone baths once and sometimes twice a week, assured me that, although many now eat and drink and sleep sooty, washing is more common among his class than when he himself was a climbing-boy. He used then to be stripped, and compelled to step into a tub, and into water sometimes too hot and sometimes too cold, while his mistress, to use his own word, scoured him. Judging from what he had seen and heard, my informant was satisfied that, from 30 to 40 years ago, climbing-boys, with a very few exceptions, were but seldom washed; and then it was looked upon by them as a most disagreeable operation, often, indeed, as a species of punishment. Some of the climbing-boys used to be taken by their masters to bathe in the Serpentine many years ago; but one boy was unfortunately drowned so that the children could hardly be coerced to go into the water afterwards.

Henry Mayhew, *London Labour and the London Poor*, Volume II

Rat Catcher

Rats were a big problem in the filthy streets and sewers of Victorian Britain, particularly in the cities. When the infestation got too bad, a Rat Catcher was brought in to deal with it. He'd turn up on the doorstep complete with the tools of his trade: a big bottle of arsenic-based poison and a crop-eared terrier dog.

Rat Catchers received around four shillings for ridding an area of rats and then filling up the holes. But the rats were not necessarily killed. They were often captured alive. At threepence per head, the sale of live rats swelled a Rat Catcher's income considerably.

A Rat Catcher with a cage considerably smaller than Jack Black's mammoth affair.

How was it done? Mayhew has left a vivid portrait of one particular Rat Catcher. Jack Black was a failed publican who rose to the pinnacle of his new profession catching rats for Queen Victoria. There was no doubting his trade. He dressed in corduroy trousers and a velveteen jacket, sported a leather belt painted with rats, and had a pet rat, which ran up his sleeve and into his pocket. He also smelt strongly of oil of thyme and oil of aniseed, which he rubbed into his clothes because the smell was supposed to attract rats.

He would turn up not only with his terriers but also with his ferrets, vicious creatures bought for fourpence each in Leadenhall Market. And he'd have with him his big iron cage capable of holding up to a thousand squirming rats. He'd block up all the rat holes except one, send his ferrets in to drive the rats into a single area, then reach into the one remaining hole to pull out the terrified rodents one by one. This hands-on method was highly successful. In Camden Town, he caught 700 live rats in one property alone.

And so getting bitten by rats was an occupational hazard for the Rat Catcher. Sewer rats and street rats carried infection. Jack was once

VICTORIAN

infected so badly that he was ill and off work for three months, which meant no pay coming in at all. His flesh swelled up, and he was only cured by drinking stout. Rats weren't fussy where they bit, including, according to Jack himself: 'where I can't name to you, sir, and right through my thumb nail too, which as you see, always has a split in it, though it's years since I was wounded'.

The irony is that the only reason the rat catcher risked pain and infection by catching rats alive was so that they could then be killed in public. To increase their trade, publicans held illegal rat-killing evenings, which took place in a wooden pit inside their pub. Terriers were set loose among a melee of frightened rats, and bets were placed on the amount of kills each dog would make, or even if the dogs would survive against the ravening rats. It was comparatively big business. One pub bought 26,000 a year, supplied by twenty different families. That's £325 – the cost of a modest house – spent on rats in one East End pub.

> Rats in London were an endemic problem, affecting rich and poor. Jack Black's customers included commercial companies and clergymen as well as the Queen. Rats are omnivores, and when hungry will take bites out of horses, cattle, their own young and even sleeping children.
>
> *Rats will eat each other like rabbits, which I've watched them, and seen them turn the dead one's skins out like pusses, and eat the flesh off beautiful clean. I've got cages of iron-wire, which I made myself, which will hold 1,000 rats at a time, and I've had these cages piled up with rats, solid like. No one would ever believe it; to look at a quantity of rats, and see how they will fight and tear one another about – it's astonishing, so it is! I never found any rats smothered, by putting them in a cage so full; but if you don't feed them every day, they'll fight and eat one another – they will, like cannibals.*
>
> *One night I had two hundred rats in a cage, placed in my sitting-room, and a gent's dog happened to get at the cage, and undid the door, snuffing about, and let 'em all loose. Directly I come in I knew they was loose by the smell. I had to go on my knees and stomach under the beds and sofas, and all over the house, and before twelve o'clock that night I had got 'em all back again into the cage, and sold them after for a match. I was so fearful they'd get gnawing the children, having sterminated them in a house where children had been gnawed.*
>
> **Henry Mayhew, *London Labour and the London Poor,* Volume III**

THE BEST & WORST OF TIMES

1846 In Andover Workhouse, inmates are so hungry that they fight over rotten bones. This scandal leads to the replacement of the Poor Law Commissioners. Reform includes establishment of Poor Law hospitals. A century later these in turn become the basis for the NHS. But the workhouse remains a place of shame.

1848 In Britain a Chartist march passes off peacefully. Publication of the hymn 'All Things Bright and Beautiful', including the lines 'The rich man in his castle,/The poor man at his gate,/He made them, high or lowly,/And ordered their estate'.

Ferrets and terriers were essential tools of the job, herding the terrified rats towards the aniseed-smelling hands of the Rat Catcher.

Rat Catchers also supplemented their income by exhibiting their wares. Jack let rats run up his arms and over his body, while stroking them and playing with them. Catchers had another sideline too. They sold poison, demonstrating its effectiveness to potential customers by feeding it to rats in cages and watching them drop dead.

But poison wasn't used only on rats. Captains of industry were happy to expose their workers to noxious substances if it helped them make a profit, and no group of employees can have suffered more as a direct result of their bosses' greed than the Match Makers.

Match Maker (Victorian style)

In the nineteenth century matches were made by dipping little wooden sticks into white phosphorus. The fumes from this poisonous chemical caused the dreadful condition known as 'phossy jaw', which blighted the lives of those who made the matches. Its first symptoms were toothache and painful swelling of the gums and jaw. Then came abscesses and a foul discharge. Like ghastly glow-in-the-dark toys, the victims' rotting jawbones would give off a ghostly light. The only treatment was an agonizing and disfiguring operation in which the jawbone was removed surgically. Although phosphorus was banned in Sweden and the USA, the British government refused to follow their example, arguing that such a move would be a restraint of free trade.

Lewis Waite's, Wharf Road, Bethnal Green … is a very small place, employing about six men and eighteen boys. It consists of two small sheds, one a mere lean-to, the other a cart hovel. The latter is, I should say, judging by the eye, about 20 by 11 feet only, with no ventilation whatever. The door is at one end, and the only window close by it. This place serves for both dipping room and drying room, as well as for mixing and heating the sulphur and the phosphorus composition. The dipper is helped in mixing by a small boy whom I saw beside him paddling the mixture, actually leaning over the dipping stone. The smell on entering this place is quite suffocating, and one would think unendurable for any length of time. The other shed … is much of the same kind, without any ventilation, and is perhaps 30 by 10 feet. In this all the remaining processes are carried on. A white vapour may be seen constantly rising from the matches.

**Mr White's *Report on the Lucifer Match Manufacturer;*
Children's Employment Commission, First Report (v.18), 1863**

The Match Girls unwittingly making industrial relations history.

VICTORIAN

For many people Victorian Match Girls conjure up the sentimental image of bare-footed waifs in the snow selling individual matches. But the Match Girls at the Bryant and May factory in London were pioneers of workers' rights. They worked up to fourteen hours a day for a wage of less than five shillings a week. That was before fines. For offences like talking, dropping matches or going to the toilet without permission, the girls would have their wages docked by anything from threepence to one shilling. Their hours were 6.30 a.m. in summer (8.00 a.m. in winter) to 6.00 p.m. If they were late, they were fined a half-day's pay.

These young women were feisty. A commentator described them off-duty: 'They have fashions of their own; they delight in a quantity of colour; and they

Annie Besant, the campaigner and journalist who took up the Match Girls' cause.

can no more live without their large hats and huge feathers than 'Arry can live without his bell-bottom trousers. They all sport high-heeled boots, and consider a fringe an absolute essential.'

Led by the campaigning journalist Annie Besant, the Bryant and May workers organized a successful strike for better wages and conditions. They were helped by the emergence of a safety-conscious competitor. In 1891 the Salvation Army opened its own match factory in Old Ford, East London. Here the matches were made with harmless red phosphorus. The Salvation Army paid their employees twice the Bryant and May rate of just over twopence a gross. But they still managed to sell six million boxes of matches a year under the brand-name 'Lights in Darkest England'.

A report three years after the strike shows how things had improved at Bryant and May:

> *The business is now much more humanely managed, and the labour of the workers has been considerably lightened by the introduction of improved machinery.*
>
> *Speaking generally, the factory hands are a healthy class. One woman who was interviewed had worked continuously in the same establishment for twenty years, and she was as robust as could be wished. Nevertheless, it is a mistake to suppose that phosphorus poisoning is a thing of the past. There is still a terrible amount of the disease, which is termed 'phossy jaw'. The first sign of the disorder is toothache, accompanied by swollen cheeks. As soon as these symptoms appear the sufferer has several teeth removed, in order, if possible, to save the entire jaw.*
>
> Montague Williams QC, **Down East and Up West**

The Bryant and May women risked everything by going on strike. This gives an indication of how desperate they must have been. For poor people with no job, that grim icon of the Victorian age beckoned: the workhouse.

THE BEST & WORST OF TIMES

1854 Bessemer invents the steel converter for making lightweight steel. Suspension bridges and skyscrapers are now a possibility.

1858 Parliament gives Joseph Bazalgette permission to build over 1,100 miles of street sewers and 83 miles of brick-built sewers to solve the 'stench of London', unwittingly creating the workplace of the Toshers.

1859 Charles Darwin publishes his theory of evolution in *On the Origin of Species*.

1861 Albert dies. Victoria retires into mourning.

Workhouse Jobs

For centuries most Poor Relief had been given to people in their homes. But in a spooky pre-echo of arguments about benefits today, early nineteenth-century legislators felt that the old system encouraged people to take charity rather than buckle down to work. So in 1834, three years before Victoria's reign began, the Poor Law Amendment Act was passed. This new legislation created the prison-like institutions we know from *Oliver Twist*.

The 15,000 parishes in England and Wales were formed into Poor Law

Two frightening images of the workhouse. Opposite: the pinched faces and sunken eyes belie the for-the-camera smiles. Above: a mountain of stone waiting to be broken by the workhouse men in order to earn a crust.

Unions, each with their own workhouse. These buildings were specially designed to provide segregated accommodation for the different categories of pauper – male and female, able-bodied and infirm, and children.

The Act intended workhouses to operate on the principle of 'less eligibility'. Conditions were to be made less preferable than those of the lowest-paid labourer. The jobs people were given in the workhouse were supposed to be punitive, sometimes worse than actual prison regimes.

Stone Breaker

The majority of inmates were either very old or very young and incapable of heavy work. But if a tramp or casual labourer turned up, he could expect a dose of hard physical graft.

Stone breaking provided the raw material for laying roads. With a sledgehammer, the Stone Breaker would set about great lumps of hard stone and break them into small fragments. The chippings had to be about a couple of centimetres square. If they were too big to be pushed through a wire grill

specially designed for the job, they were sent back to be smashed into smaller pieces. The job was never-ending. As soon as one stone had been hammered to bits, another was waiting. And the reward for hours of this hard labour was the barest of subsistence diets.

Oakum Picker

Smelly, dirty and sore on the fingers, this job was given to older male inmates. Oakum was the name for pieces of old rope from shipyards, heavily impregnated with tar to protect them from the rain. These filthy lengths of rope were broken up by hammering them with a mallet. The thinner strands were then unravelled into pieces of string-thickness. Only once all these layers had been unwoven could the individual strands of fibre be unpicked. They were

Above: Oakum Pickers in the workhouse. A pile this size could rub the toughest fingers raw.

Opposite: Headington Union was just one of the workhouses serving Oxford and the surrounding villages. Many of the inmates are old men in their sixties and seventies. But there's also a railway porter, a vet and a musician. Anyone could fall into the Poor House. It was a lot harder getting out.

Headington Union Workhouse 1881 Census return

Inmates	Status*	Age	Sex	Offence	Occupation	Note	Address
Thomas BAKER	U	69	M	Pauper	General Labourer		Oxford
Lucy BLAIR	U	56	F	Pauper	General Servant		Oxford
Robert BOWELL	M	81	M	Pauper	Farm Labourer		Cowley, Oxford
Rebecca CARTER	W	47	F	Pauper	Laundress		Windsor, Berkshire
George CARTER		1	M	Pauper			Headington, Oxford
Mary CHAPMAN	W	69	F	Pauper	Laundress		Oxford
William CLANFIELD	O	6	M	Pauper			Denton, Oxford
James CLANFIELD	O	4	M	Pauper			Chippinghurst, Oxford
Agnes CLANFIELD	O	8	F	Pauper	Scholar		Denton, Oxford
Lucy CLANFIELD	O	10	F	Pauper	Scholar		Denton, Oxford
Elizabeth CLANFIELD	W	43	F	Pauper	Housemaid		Cuddesdon, Oxford
John CLAY	M	69	M	Pauper	Farm Labourer		Elsfield, Oxford
Richard CLAYDON	W	80	M	Pauper	Road Labourer		Dorchester, Oxford
James COLLINS	U	21	M	Vagrant	General Labourer		Shrewsbury, Shropshire
Fernandow COOPER	W	80	M	Pauper	Farm Labourer		Wheatley, Oxford
Henry COOPER	U	63	M	Pauper	Farm Labourer		Fewcott, Oxford
Rebecca COX	W	70	F	Pauper	Laundress		Oxford
Richard CUMMINGS	U	75	M	Pauper	Farm Labourer		Oxford
William CURRILL	W	76	M	Pauper	Shepherd		Marsh Baldon, Oxford
Jane CURRILL	U	38	F	Pauper	Vil [Villager]	Imbecile	Littleworth, Oxford
William GRANT	W	77	M	Pauper	Shoemaker		Oxford
Maria HART	U	26	F	Pauper	Housemaid		Iffley, Oxford
Mary HEIDON	W	53	F	Pauper	Servant		Heythrop, Oxford
Robert HUMPHRIS	M	72	M	Pauper	Carpenter		Forest Hill, Oxford
Thomas HUNT	W	72	M	Pauper	Woodman		Long Itchinton, Warwick
William JUGGINS	U	67	M	Pauper	Farm Labourer		Horspath, Oxford
William KNIGHT		1	M	Pauper			Headington, Oxford
Mary Ann KNIGHT	U	19	F	Pauper	Domestic Servant		Holton, Oxford
Robert MARRY	W	54	M	Pauper	Railway Porter		Horton Cum Studley, Oxford
Edward MARSHALL	W	66	M	Pauper	Musician		Oxford
Herbert MARSTON		4	M	Pauper			Headington, Oxford
Thomas MATHEWS	M	65	M	Pauper	Gardener		Stanton St John, Oxford
William MUNT	W	81	M	Pauper	Farm Labourer		Wheatley, Oxford
Henry NEWMAN		4	M	Pauper			Oxford
Harriet NEWMAN	M	30	F	Pauper	Laundress		Littlemore, Oxford
John PHIPPS	U	77	M	Pauper	Farm Labourer		Garsington, Oxford
Charlotte PICKETT	W	82	F	Pauper	Charwoman	Blind	Beckley, Oxford
Phoebe PRATT	U	40	F	Pauper	General Servant		Headington, Oxford
Emma PRATT		2	F	Pauper			Headington, Oxford
Mary PRATT	W	68	F	Pauper	Charwoman		Horton Cum Studley, Oxford
Mary RAY	U	30	F	Pauper	Vil [Villager]	Imbecile	Forest Hill, Oxford
William RAY	U	37	M	Pauper	Farm Labourer	Imbecile	Forest Hill, Oxford
George SHIRLEY		1	M	Pauper			Headington, Oxford
Ellen SHIRLEY	U	20	F	Pauper	Domestic Servant		Cuddesdon, Oxford
Elizabeth SLATER	W	74	F	Pauper	General Servant		Great Hazeley, Oxford
Susannah SMITH	W	68	F	Pauper	Charwoman		Garsington, Oxford
Thomas SMITH	W	73	M	Pauper	Farm Labourer		Drayton, Oxford
Henry STOW	M	76	M	Pauper	Veterinary Surgeon		Wheatley, Oxford
Frank STUCKFIELD		14	M	Pauper	Scholar		Birmingham, Warwick
Thomas SUTT	W	81	M	Pauper	Labourer		Witham, Berkshire
Henry TIMMS		11	M	Pauper	Scholar		Headington, Oxford
William TOLLEY	M	66	M	Pauper	Farm Labourer		Headington, Oxford
Elizabeth WASHINGTON	U	24	F	Pauper	Vil [Villager]	Imbecile	Holton, Oxford
Robert WEBB	W	69	M	Pauper	Bricklayer's Labourer		Headington, Oxford
Henry WEST	W	79	M	Pauper	Farm Labourer		Cuddesdon, Oxford

* U = unmarried, M = married, W = widow/er, O = orphan. Others are the children of inmates.

VICTORIAN

sticky with tar. It's hard enough to get tar off your hands using modern detergents. Imagine the tediously difficult time the inmates must have had, besmirching everything they touched.

The tiny strands they finally produced were rolled into small balls and sent to the shipyards, where they were stuffed between the planks of ships and coated with pitch to create a waterproof seal. This process was known as 'caulking'.

Men were expected to pick one and a half pounds of oakum per day, women half a pound. Like all workhouse tasks, the job was unpaid except for board and food.

With the threat of the workhouse ever-present, especially for the old or disabled, people would do almost anything to earn a crust. Henry Mayhew describes a whole host of people on the streets engaged in desperate forms of busking: the 'blind performer on the bells', the 'French Hurdy-Gurdy player with Dancing Children', the 'Penny profile-cutter', comic characters such as 'Billy Barlow', the 'Penny-Gaff clown', the 'whistling man', the 'Gun-Exercise

Everything about the workhouse was regimented and unpleasant. Even meals were designed to be functional rather than social.

Exhibitor – one-legged Italian', and even, towards 5 November, human 'Guy Fawkses' who dressed up but presumably weren't put on a bonfire.

He also records a number of scavenging jobs. In our ecologically minded age, it's tempting to think that we have invented recycling. In Victorian times they pumped pollution into the air and rivers like there was no tomorrow, but almost nothing went to waste, because there was always someone who could make a few pence by collecting it and selling it on.

Cigar End Finder

The Cigar End Finder looked for dog-ends unspoiled by spit in order to recycle the tobacco inside.

Women in a dustyard sifting filth and soot for the odd treasure.

We know from Mayhew of Irish children who scoured Ratcliff Highway, Commercial Road and Mile End Road in London looking for cigar ends and scraps of bread. Once they had a handful of cigar tips they'd trade them in

for a halfpenny to buy oatmeal. This was boiled with the scraps of bread to form the most frugal of meals.

In the Strand and Regent Street, cigar ends were easier to find. Experienced hunters worked there until they had about a kilo or more in weight, which is a hell of a lot of dog-ends. They then took these to a buyer in Rosemary Lane, who paid them sixpence per 500g. This middleman sold them back to the tobacco manufacturers, who mixed the recycled tobacco in with the new crop, either for cigars or snuff.

Tea Hawker

There was also a market for used tea-leaves. Tea Hawkers went from door to door collecting the leavings from the genteel teapots of respectable London, which they bought from servants in the big houses for a pittance.

They then placed the leaves on hot plates and dried them, and finally sold the newly recycled tea to unscrupulous shopkeepers who mixed it with genuine new tea to thicken out the load. If it was going to be part of a batch of green tea, it was first dyed with a preparation of copper. Tea was very expensive, and adulterating it was a thriving trade. It's said that nearly 4,000 tons of old tea-leaves were sold in London in one year!

Dustman

Today the word 'Dustman' means a general refuse collector, but in Victorian times it was a specialist occupation.

Coal was king. London alone consumed three and a half million tons of it every year. This made for a lot of ash and cinders. It was the duty of Parish Officers to ensure that it was removed quickly, by 'dust-contractors' with horses, carts, baskets and shovels and access to a patch of waste-ground on which to dump the refuse. There was money to be made out of dust. The finer 'soil' was sifted from the coarser portion and sold on as agricultural fertilizer. The coarser stuff was used in brick-making. Each contractor shifted about 10,000 loads of dust a year. And in order to do that, they employed Dustmen.

These were men born to the job. They began as children sifting the dust-heaps, and graduated to being fully fledged Dustmen. The 'Fillers' and 'Carriers' toured the streets with heavily built high box carts, which were normally coated in filth. They shouted 'Dust-oy-eh!' to announce their arrival. The Filler filled his basket with dust, which was carried off by the Carrier to

A Dustman either calling to announce his presence or dreaming of a cool pint of beer to wash the grime from his throat!

VICTORIAN

the cart. He then climbed up a ladder, tipped the basket into the cart, came back, picked up the next newly filled basket and so on. When each cart was full, it was driven to the dust-yard and its contents were discharged on to the heap.

Dustmen would collect dust one day, and clean the streets the next. They also had private arrangements with landlords to empty cesspools. Pay was low but regular. They got eightpence a load for their dust, so it was in their interest to bring as many cart-loads as possible back to the yard. Once there, it was sifted by women and children who, not surprisingly, had the worst part of this Worst Job.

> *In a dust-yard lately visited the sifters formed a curious sight; they were almost up to their middle in dust, ranged in a semi-circle in front of that part of the heap which was being 'worked'; each had before her a small mound of soil which had fallen through her sieve and formed a sort of embankment, behind which she stood. The appearance of the entire group at their work was most peculiar. Their coarse dirty cotton gowns were tucked up behind them, their arms were bared above their elbows, their black bonnets crushed and battered like those of fish-women; over their gowns they wore a strong leathern apron, extending from their necks to the extremities of their petticoats, while over this, again, was another leathern apron, shorter, thickly padded, and fastened by a stout string or strap round the waist. In the process of their work they pushed the sieve from them and drew it back again with apparent violence, striking it against the outer leathern apron with such force that it produced each time a hollow sound, like a blow on the tenor drum. All the women present were middle aged, with the exception of one who was very old – 68 years of age she told me – and had been at the business from a girl. She was the daughter of a dustman, the wife, or woman, of a dustman, and the mother of several young dustmen – sons and grandsons – all at work at the dust-yards at the east end of the metropolis.*
>
> **Henry Mayhew, *London Labour and the London Poor,*
> Volume II**

The main downside to this life was that you spent it in a welter of filth. But it wasn't as unhealthy or dangerous as a lot of other Victorian jobs. Dustmen were a surprisingly healthy group of men, according to Mayhew. There are no figures available, but tales circulated of Dustmen who survived into their nineties and one man, called Wood, lived to be a hundred.

THE BEST & WORST OF TIMES

1869 Suez Canal opened, making trade and communication with India and Australia much easier.

1873 Population of the United Kingdom: 26 million.

1876 Great Britain: school attendance made compulsory, thus helping to outlaw child labour.

VICTORIAN

Rag Man

Steptoe and Son ran a sophisticated second-hand business compared to the original Rag Men, who wandered for miles, carrying their wares in a greasy bag and holding a stick. This was used for prodding through the piles of rubbish left outside houses, in the hope of finding something to sell. The job was competitive. They got up as early as two in the morning to scour their chosen area before other Rag Men got there. Some of the best sites in London were in Petticoat Lane and Mayfair where the Jewish clothes makers threw out piles of discarded rags. Rag Men tramped round London for around eight hours a day, by which time they had walked a marathon, twenty or thirty miles, with a quarter to a half hundredweight of rags on their backs.

Rags were in great demand – 10,000 tons were imported in 1851. They fetched a halfpenny per pound from the street buyer. Before the advent of wood-pulp, paper was made from cloth. Early editions of Dickens's novels would have been printed on paper made partially by rags grubbed by the Rag Men. (This was robust, long-lasting paper. The British Library has huge problems preserving modern books, especially paperbacks printed on wood-pulp paper which is acidic and rots, but the early Victorian books are still almost as good as new.)

THE BEST & **WORST** OF TIMES

1876 America: Alexander Graham Bell patents the telephone.

1877 America: Thomas Edison invents the phonograph.

1879 America: Edison invents the electric light bulb.

1884 Third Reform Act: universal male suffrage in England; women must wait another forty years!

Bone Grubber

Bone grubbing is precisely what it sounds like – grubbing for old bones. It wasn't a job people did by choice. The filthy, rotting bones stank, and the work was poorly paid. People became Bone Grubbers after falling on hard times. Some were agricultural labourers who were out of work after the harvest. Many were unemployed Navvies. Henry Mayhew met one Grubber, whose 'ragged coat – the colour of the rubbish among which he toiled – was greased over, probably with the fat of the bones he gathered, and being mixed with the dust it seemed as if the man were covered in bird lime'.

The bones were sold to dealers, who had several uses for them. The large ones were sorted out and sent to France to be made into handles for tooth and shaving-brushes, children's teething-rings, knife handles and cheap combs. The rest were boiled to remove the gelatine and the fatty substances used to make soap. What was left was crushed into bone-meal fertilizer.

What could be worse than working in a dust-yard or starting out at two in the morning to walk twenty-odd miles in search of rotten bones or rags? Well, try being a Tosher.

Tosher

Toshers were the Kings of the Scavengers. They practised an illegal and disgusting profession deep within that most Victorian of locations, the sewers.

In 1850 London was producing 31,650,000,000 gallons of sewage every year, and it all went straight into the Thames. In 1853 cholera killed over 10,000 Londoners. Something had to be done, but Parliament showed no urgency until

When Bazalgette created the engineering marvel of the London sewers, he couldn't have imagined he was also building a workplace for the kings of scavengers, the Toshers.

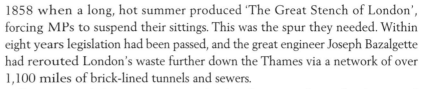

VICTORIAN

1858 when a long, hot summer produced 'The Great Stench of London', forcing MPs to suspend their sittings. This was the spur they needed. Within eight years legislation had been passed, and the great engineer Joseph Bazalgette had rerouted London's waste further down the Thames via a network of over 1,100 miles of brick-lined tunnels and sewers.

But it wasn't just excrement and urine that went down the drains and lavatories. All sorts of weird things found their way into the sewers. In spite of a law banning their dangerous trade, the Toshers, or Sewer Hunters, spent their lives in the network of tunnels looking for coins, jewellery, cutlery, coal, bits of iron and lumps of old metal.

All Toshers were male. They had to be physically strong enough to handle the tool of their trade – a pole, over 2 metres long, with an iron hoe at one end to plunge into the turbid waters. They wore a canvas apron and trousers, and a long greasy coat with big pockets for carrying valuables. Every Tosher had a bag slung on his back and a lamp strapped to his chest.

Toshing was not only illegal, it was also highly dangerous. After rain, the sewers would be awash, and there was the risk of drowning. In hotter weather, the fumes and chemicals given off by the sewage could kill. There was the occasional fall of brickwork. But the greatest worry was the sewer rats. They were known to be particularly aggressive. Toshers never went in groups of less than three, and tried not to get separated in case they were attacked by angry rodents.

Financially, Toshers could do very well. There were large quantities of coins to be found, which they divided among their group. A Tosher could make thirty shillings from one trip, but on average it was six shillings per day. This was better money than a clerk could make! And, in spite of the smell, they were never stigmatized in the same way that Sweeps or Bone Grubbers were. Perhaps the danger and illegality turned them into local heroes.

The deposit has been found to comprise all the ingredients from the brewery, the gasworks and the several chemical and mineral manufactories; dead dogs, cats, kittens and rats; offal from slaughterhouses, sometimes even including the entrails of the animals; street pavement dirt of every variety; vegetable refuse; stable dung; the refuse of pig-sties; night soil; ashes; tin kettles and pans; broken stoneware, as jars, pitchers, flowerpots, & bricks; pieces of wood; rotten mortar and rubbish of different kinds; and even rags.

Henry Mayhew, ***London Labour and the London Poor,***
Volume II

VICTORIAN

Mud Lark

Toshers operated in comparatively pleasant surroundings. The sewage that provided their living was generally carried along by flowing water. But once discharged into the tidal waters of the Thames, it was sufficiently exposed to provide the Mud Larks with their workplace. Despite their somewhat lyrical name, Mud Larks engaged in a far from pleasant activity.

'Mud lark' is a generic name for any bird that paddles at the river's edge. The name was consequently applied to the people who scavenged for the few scraps that the Toshers had missed. But it wasn't an accurate description. The job was far from being a lark, and the nineteenth-century Thames wasn't mud, it was excremental waste.

These were the Victorian equivalent of the children you see on television in the Developing World, picking over rubbish heaps. Mud Larks had equally slim pickings. A prize find might be a copper nail from a ship refitting in Wapping.

According to Henry Mayhew, the Mud Larks were 'the most despicable in their appearance of any I have met with in the course of my enquiries.'

THE BEST & WORST OF TIMES

1885 Germany: the first car run on the internal combustion engine is developed by Herr Benz.

1889 Match girls strike for better conditions and sixpence an hour.

1894 Tower Bridge is completed.

1900 Sigmund Freud lays the foundations of psychoanalysis with the publication of *The Interpretation of Dreams*.

1901 Queen Victoria dies; Edward, Prince of Wales, succeeds to the throne.

But even treasures like this were rare, because Mud Larks were usually chased away from ships. Their lives were made doubly difficult by the fact that the time they had to scavenge was controlled by the tide. If they hadn't filled their kettle or pail when the waters rose, they simply went hungry.

From the age of six, they crawled among the barges at the various wharfs along the Thames, shoe-less and half-covered in rags. They paddled in the mud, bent double. They rarely spoke to each other, but worked in silence. In cold weather, they warmed their frozen feet in the hot water that ran down the riverside from the out-flows of factories with their steam-driven machines. When the tide came in and their work was cut short, they would try to earn extra money by going to the city and opening cab doors for passengers.

Mayhew interviewed a fourteen-year-old Mud Lark. He had no shirt, only trousers, and chilblains on his bare feet. His father had been a coalwhipper, and had died on the barges. His mother's business had collapsed because of the potato blight. He rolled his trousers up, and regularly waded into the mud knee-deep and always barefoot. Nails and pieces of glass would stick in his feet but, having dressed the wounds, he would return quickly before the tide came back. 'For should the tide come up without my having found something, why I must starve till next low tide.' A copper nail in the foot made him lame for three months.

You might think we have now crashed to the bottom of the lift-shaft of Victorian employment. Trudging barefoot through raw sewage was terrible. Not as terrible, though, as using your bare hands? If you ever meet a Pure Collector, don't greet them with a handshake.

Pure Collector

Pure adj. clean; unsoiled, unmixed; chaste etc – n. dog's faeces or any similar substance *(Chambers Dictionary)*.

It's the last bit of this definition which was the stock-in-trade of the Pure Collector. Perhaps it started as a joke, but 'pure' as a noun means dog poo. The Pure Collector literally went round the streets with a bucket picking up shit. (And they didn't necessarily have a shovel.)

Surely this must be the Worst Job of all? Well, no, because the Pure Collector wouldn't have bothered if someone hadn't been willing to pay for it. Technically dog faeces only become 'pure' when used as an ingredient by another trade. The Pure Collector may have had the worst scavenging job, but the stench of dog faeces was only one part of a grim cocktail of smells and experience that epitomize our Worst Job of all time, and the job that receives the ultimate accolade: our Worst Job Oscar.

The Worst Job of All Time

It may be that you've flicked straight through to the back of the book to see what the Worst Job is. But if you've taken your task seriously and dutifully followed the worst job trail down the ages, scraping the very dregs of the employment barrel, by now you'll have a good idea of the depths of awfulness that the very Worst Job of all has to plumb.

There have been five recurring qualities that our Worst Jobs have shown in varying degrees. There has been **tough**, tiring work like turning over the Anglo-Saxon soil with a light plough (page 22), or sedan-chair carrying (page 110), or digging out the Victorian railways (page 171).

Then there are horrible **messy** jobs of various kinds, whether it's diving into sheep's innards to get the gut for violin-string making (page 130), or standing ankle-deep in a fulling tub (page 70).

For **low pay** it is hard to match the destitution of the Mud Larks (page 198), unless you were the poor thrall who sat stamping coins for no pay at all (page 33).

Danger comes in two basic forms: the gut-churning chance of sudden death in combat that faced the Petardier's Assistant (page 108) and the Powder Monkey (page 162), or the insidious danger of job-related diseases suffered by Match Makers (page 182) or Boy Actors (page 94).

And finally, there's **boredom**. Today it's the most common complaint that people make about their jobs, but working at a supermarket-checkout or staring at a computer screen has to be infinitely less tedious than the job of the Pipe Roll Transcriber (page 67) or the Hermit (page 147).

The Worst Job of all is a triumphant mixture of four of the qualities listed above. On the up-side it was comparatively well paid, but the financial reward was more than negated by an excess of everything else. It was messy, boring and exhausting, and caused long-term health problems. It also featured a bizarre mixture of smells so disgusting that having no nose should have been on the job spec. If there was a Worst Jobs World Cup, these workers would be the Brazilians. Ladies and gentlemen, please put solariums completely out of your mind as we explore the extraordinary world of the Tanners.

Tanner

The Tanner could have featured as the Worst Job in any one of the chapters of this book. However, there are good reasons for his appearance at the end of the Victorian chapter.

Tanners made leather, which was more important than ever in the Victorian age. Before the appearance of synthetic materials, it made the aprons, belts and workboots of the Navvies, Toshers, Rat Catchers and factory workers. It provided the tooled saddles, the halters, reins, blinkers and all the paraphernalia of the horse-drawn age. And it was the material used for the belts that drove the steam-machines. These in turn powered all the factories and mills underpinning the leading industrial world economy.

Compare this sixteenth-century engraving of a Tanner at work with the photo over the page and you'll see how little the job has changed in five hundred years or more.

Tanning has always been a job to avoid. The pioneering Italian medical author Ramazzini observed the unhealthy look of Tanners in the late seventeenth century.

The same is true of tanners, who steep the hides of animals in pits with lime and gallnuts, tread them with their feet, wash and clean them, and smear them with tallow for various purposes; I mean that they are distressed in the same way by the incessant stink and foul exhalations; one can see them with cadaverous complexions, swollen bodies, ghastly looks, and oppressed breathing; they are nearly all splenetic. I have observed many cases of dropsy in workers who follow this trade. How, indeed, could it be otherwise when they spend nearly all their time in a damp place and in air vitiated by those horrible emanations from rotting hides? How, I ask, could the storehouses of the spirits, both animal and vital, fail to be poisoned and therewith the economy of the whole body deranged? I have often noticed that horses could not be driven by spur or whip to pass close to such workshops; the moment they could smell that peculiar odour they galloped at full speed toward home, like mad things, paying no heed to the reins. For these reasons the buildings in which hides are dressed are placed, as are other dirty trades, either near the city walls, or, as at Modena, outside them to prevent pollution of the air.

Bernadino Ramazzini, *De Morbis Artificum – On the Diseases of Workers*, 1700

This early twentieth-century image shows men in Bermondsey, London de-hairing and scraping the fatty tissue off the hides. This is still the least-favoured job at the Colyton Tannery in Devon, the only place in Britain still using the same traditional methods as the Victorians. When I tried it, I found the knife slides over the skin, the fat sticks to it, and has to be removed from the blade, impregnating your hands with the same revolting odour. And, of course, your hands get slippery with the fat, making the job of holding the knife firmly that much more difficult.

But, at the same time, the Tanner's status in the Victorian age took a nosedive. The process by which raw hides were preserved from decay had always been disgusting. Tanning had long been one of those trades relegated to the outskirts of cities. And like Gong Farmers, Woad Dyers and Fullers, Tanners had been forced to look to other Tanners for love and marriage. But in the Victorian age their status as pariahs became greater.

> *Then supremacy of leather is, and ever was, maintained by the working Englishman almost as strenuously as Magna Charta, 'An Englishman's house is his castle', and 'God save the Queen'. He regards it with the same implicit confidence as he regards his beer, and will no more accept gutta-percha or india-rubber as a substitute for the former than light French wines or lemonade for the latter. No matter in what shape the material appears, it elicits an equal amount of respect; and that the passion is deeply implanted in the Englishman is evident from the fact that it is one of the earliest to develop itself in the youthful mind. Long before the boy is out of pinafores and strap shoes he is anxious for a whip with a real leather thong, or choice is divided between that and one of those oozy leathern abominations known as a 'sucker' and if his first cap be furnished with a real leather peak, in place of a mean affair of japanned cardboard, he holds his head all the higher. True, we have degenerated from the ancient custom of casing our nether limbs in buckskin, but we still show an affectionate leaning thereto by miscalling our trouser-stuffs doeskin, and swathing our legs knee high in a refined and dandified preparation of horse or cow skin. Even the low-minded costermonger, to whom 'wellingtons' are objects of contempt and derision, and who laughs to scorn galligaskins and knickerbockers, evinces the national tendency for leather by stipulating for 'anklejacks' with 'tongues' ample enough to overlap the lacings by at least three inches. There is no surer passport to the best room of an inn than a portmanteau of the orthodox brown colour, and branded 'warranted leather'; if it should happen to bear the additional recommendation 'solid', your high respectability is at once established.*
>
> **James Greenwood, *Unsentimental Journeys; or Byways of the Modern Babylon*, 1867**

Because so much leather was needed, almost every town in Victorian Britain had its tannery. Where raw materials were plentiful, there might be a cluster of them. The Oxfordshire market-town of Wantage had more than its fair share. At one stage there were 300 tan-yards pumping out their overpowering smell, casting a pungent pall over the community.

In Victorian London the Tanners were pushed out east.

Bermondsey Leather Market. This great leather, or rather hide, market, lies in Weston Street, ten minutes' walk from the Surrey side of London-bridge. The neighbourhood in which it stands is devoted entirely to thinners [fleshers] and tanners, and the air reeks with evil smells. The population is peculiar, and it is a sight at twelve o'clock to see the men pouring out from all the works. Their clothes are marked with many stains; their trousers are discoloured by tan; some have apron and gaiters of raw hide; and about them all seems to hang a scent of blood … The warehouses round are all full of tanned hides; the yards behind the high walls are all tanneries, with their tens of thousands of hides soaking in the pits. Any visitor going down to look at the Bermondsey hide-market should, if possible, procure beforehand an order to visit one of the great tanning establishments. Unless this be done the visit to the market itself will hardly repay the trouble of the journey, or make up for the unpleasantness of the compound of horrible smells which pervade the whole neighbourhood.

Charles Dickens Jr, *Dickens's Dictionary of London*, 1879

Tanners got their hides direct from local butchers or abattoirs. From the time of the Ancient Egyptians, the skins of cows, calves, bulls, oxen, pigs, horses, sheep and even dogs had been tanned for leather. Each sort of skin had its qualities. Calf skin produced the most supple leather (like the vellum of the Lindisfarne Gospels), whereas ox, bull and cow hides gave a tougher leather suitable for boots and hard wear.

Human skin too was not without its merits. We've already seen the famous body-snatcher Edmund Burke end up as a pocket book in an Edinburgh museum. The Scottish hero William Wallace ('Braveheart') was also reputed to have flayed one of his English enemies and had him turned into a belt.

Nevertheless, Tanners tended to avoid the temptation of pickling their friends and relations, and instead concentrated on four-legged hides. The hides were carted en masse from the abattoir, still reeking of blood, where they were trimmed, salted and washed. They were then placed in a sickly-sweet-smelling pit to loosen the hair and soften the tissues. The solution in these pits was made from slaked lime and water. In medieval times Tanners may well have added urine, a handy substance as ubiquitous then as WD-40 is today. The hides would stay in the lime pits for weeks, gently rotting and softening. Then when the Tanner judged they were ready, they would be hefted out and put on a great curved bench known as a fleshing beam for de-hairing and removing the rotting flesh from the other side.

Victorian Tanners with their tools. Presumably the young lads are the next generation of Tanners, still coming to terms with the realisation that they've been born into the messiest trade of all time.

This was far tougher work than it sounds. The lime-drenched hides were immensely heavy and slimy. As soon as the Tanner began to manhandle them, great clumps of hair reeking with the acrid smell of the lime came away in his hands.

Then, once the hide was in place on the bench, he began the tedious job of de-hairing with a curved two-handled knife (see pictures on pages 201 and 202). This task achieved the difficult feat of combining physical hard work and monotony while still requiring intense concentration. Every single little bit of stubble had to be removed at this stage because, once leather is tanned, the hairy bits won't come out. No one wants shoes or handbags with a five-o'clock shadow.

When all the hair had been removed, the hide was turned over, and the same sharp knife was used to scrape off the fatty tissue which, after its long immersion, was swollen and bloated with lime liquid. This fat was then saved and sent away to be made into soap.

So far so bad. But now the job really went downhill. It's at this stage that the dog-shit appeared. The de-haired and scraped hide had to be put in another pit,

VICTORIAN

this time of 'bate' to get rid of the lime and soften the material still further. Health and Safety regulations now insist on an artificial substitute, but in Victorian times the bate would have been a revolting gravy of water and dog dung, constantly festering at the edge of the de-hairing room.

Why dog dung? The faeces contain residual elements from the dog's stomach. These strong acids and enzymes are designed by nature to break down and digest meat and skin. A brief soaking in the dung gravy removed the lime from the hides and impregnated them with just enough bacteria and enzymes to make them lithe and flexible.

Although the hides soaked in the pit for a relatively short time, the dung in the pit was sometimes kept brewing for weeks. Old dung was preferred by the Tanners. And, as if the natural stench of the lime and the bating pits wasn't bad enough, the Victorian Tanners added their own form of enhancement. In order to speed up the tanning process, they heated the various liquids with steam pipes laid under the pits. The dog poo sludge became a warm soup, spreading an excremental pall over the tannery and surrounding area.

Tanners couldn't rely on the Pure Collector for a regular supply of dog faeces. Bull mastiffs at the yard served a triple function as guard dogs, rat catchers and bate suppliers.

The skill of the Tanner lay in keeping the hides in the bate for just the right amount of time, before giving them their final treatment, a year-long soaking in tanning fluid. Tanning needed tannin like you get in tea. Except that in the tan-yard the tea-leaves were chippings of oak bark the size of your hand. The hides were soaked in increasingly strong brews of this tea, until finally they were rinsed, and slowly and carefully dried out under cover.

To keep them in a dry atmosphere, fires were constantly smouldering away. So there was smoke, the smell of the tanning pits, the stink of the lime pits and the rancid whiff of the bate all mingled together. This combination of smoke, bacteria and chemicals led to all sorts of poor health and degenerative illnesses. The workers must have been extraordinarily resilient, as must their wives who had to steel themselves every night for the after-work reek.

Because of the multiple processes involved, tanning has given us two British surnames: Tanner and Barker. As mentioned above, tanneries needed quantities of bark for the tanning process. This is an advertisement from the *Derby Mercury* in 1793:

> *Bark Peelers Wanted – To peel this season 1793 a large quantity of oak coppice timber at Bradley near Ashbourne. As the timber stands in five coppices any person may be treated with to peel any one lot or the whole by applying to Mr Buxton, Tanner, Ashbourne, or Mr Fearn, Timber Merchant, Bradley.*

The trade of tanning epitomizes the Worst Jobs concept. It was astonishingly hard work and to the squeamish modern mind utterly revolting. Not only that, Tanners were outcasts from the own communities. And yet it was a skilful trade. In the Victorian period it kept thousands of people employed. More importantly, without the Tanners and the leather they made, there would have been no horse-drawn ploughs, no cavalry, no knights on chargers, no illuminated manuscripts, no pipe rolls. Society and history would literally have ground to a halt.

But then that's true of so many of the jobs outlined in this book. Without the Arming Squire, the Powder Monkey or the Gong Scourer we may not have had Agincourt, Trafalgar or Hampton Court Palace. We owe a huge debt to all those faceless people who did the Worst Jobs throughout the ages. They have shaped our world.

VICTORIAN

What's in a Name?

Have you got an ancestor who did a Worst Job?

Surnames began to appear in Britain between the thirteenth and fifteenth centuries. There were four main types of surname: those that described a relationship to a family or individual, e.g. Robinson; nicknames describing physical or emotional characteristics, e.g. Brown (colouring or hair) or Root – meaning 'cheerful'; names relating to places (London); and those that describe occupations.

Some job names are self-explanatory: Barber, Plumber, Baker and so on. Some refer to obscure trades long since disappeared. And some apparently obvious occupational names aren't what they seem at all. A Farmer did not work in agriculture but collected taxes; and Banker is not an occupational surname – it means 'dweller on a hillside'. Others, like Slaughter or Glass, have dual derivations. They could mean that you had a slaughterer/glass maker in the family; alternatively they could indicate that you came from one of the boggy villages known as sloughs, or that you had Scottish relatives with 'glas' – 'blue' eyes. Tricky. There's no definitive way of telling but, with that caveat, here is a list of some of the hundreds of British surnames – some common, some more obscure – that come from the jobs our ancestors did. I've indicated some of the wider variations on the names. More obvious spelling variations like Smith, Smyth or Smythe, I leave to common sense.

Not all our Worst Jobs had been invented when these surnames came into use. So you won't find anyone called George Mule Scavenger or Zoe Sedan Chair Carrier. However, where medieval surnames refer to jobs that I've dealt with in a later century I've highlighted them anyway.

Archer – a longbowman

Arkwright/Hattrick – a maker of arks or chests

Bachelor – a young knight or novice in arms, i.e. an arming squire

Bacon – a pork butcher

Badger – either a peddler or hawker, or a maker of bags

Bailey – a bailiff

Baker/(female form) Baxter – a baker

Bannerman (Scottish) – an ensign bearer

Bannister – a basket maker

Barber/Barbour – a barber surgeon

Barker/Barkis – a tanner

Booker – either a scribe or a bleacher

Bowman – an archer

Bowyer/Bowers – a maker or trader in longbows

Brenner – a burner, either of lime or charcoal

Brewer/(female form) Brewster – a brewer of ale

Buckman – either a goat keeper or from 'books', a scholar

Bullinger/Pullinger – a baker, cf. French *boulanger*

Bullman – a bull keeper

Butcher/Bowcher/Bowker – a butcher

Butler – a servant in charge of the wine cellar

Byers – one employed in the cow house

Callender – a man who rolls and smoothes woollen cloth

Cantor – a precentor or cantor at a monastery or cathedral

Carboner – a maker and seller of charcoal

Carl – a countryman (from Churl)

Carpenter – a carpenter

Carter – a cart driver

Cartwright – a maker of carts

Carver – a wood carver (sometimes stone)

Cash – a maker of boxes and chests

Chafer – a lime burner

Chamberlain – an officer of the private chambers of a monarch or lord (the role later played by the Groom of the Stool)

Chandler – a maker of candles

Chaplin – a chaplain or chantry priest

Charman – a carter or carrier

Chaucer – a shoemaker (from the French *chauces*, clothing for the legs; cf. modern French *chaussures*)

Checker – a clerk who worked in the Exchequer

Cheeseman/Cheesewright – a cheese maker

Clark – a man in minor religious orders, a scholar or recorder

Cleaver – one who split wood with wedges instead of sawing

Cockerell – cock seller, poultry dealer

Coleman/Collier – both refer to the men who burnt and sold charcoal

Conner – an ale inspector

Constable – a household, castle or parish official

Cook(e)/Cock – a cook

Cooper/Cowper – a maker of barrels, buckets and tubs

Coward – a cowherd

Creek – a basket maker, from the Middle English *creke*, a basket

Cripps – a maker of (Middle English again) *crippes*, pouches

Cropper/Crapper – a reaper

Currier – a leather dresser

Cutler – a maker, repairer and seller of knives

Dauber – a plasterer making buildings in wattle and daub

Deacon – a deacon

Delver – a quarryman

Dower – a maker of dough, a baker

Draper – a maker or seller of woollen cloth

Driver – a driver

Drover – a herdsman

Dyer – a dyer (not necessarily with woad)

Ewer – a servant who gives guests water to wash their hands

Falkener – a falconer

Fisher – a fisherman

Flaxman/Flexer – a dresser and seller of flax

Fletcher – a maker and seller of arrows

Forester/Forster/Foster – a forester or woodman

Forward/Foreman – a swineherd, from the Old English *for*, a pig

Fowler – a hunter of wild birds

Frear/Friar – a friar

Fuller/Voller – a fuller

Furmage/Firminger – a cheese maker and seller (from French *fromage*)

Garden/Gardiner – a gardener

Garlic – a seller of garlic

Garner – a keeper of the granary

Gilder – a gilder

Glass/Glazier/Glaisher – a glass maker

Glassman – a dealer in glassware

Gleeman – a singer

Glover – a maker of gloves

Goater – a goatherd

Goldsmith – a goldsmith

Grange – one in charge of a grange, a farm bailiff

Grassman – a seller of grease

Graves/Grieves – a steward or overseer

Greensmith – a coppersmith

Groom – a serving man

Hall – a worker at the hall (manor house)

Hamer/Hammer – a maker of hammers

Hanger – a hangman

Haster/Hastler – a spit boy; from Old French *haste*, a spit

Hatter – a maker or seller of hats

Hawker – a falconer

Hayward – a man who kept the fences round the hay to stop the cattle getting in

Heard/Hurd/Horder/Herdman – a herdsman

Heckler – a dresser of flax

Heffer – a keeper of the heifers

Henman – the man in charge of the hens (or in modern English – a perpetual runner-up)

Hermitte/Armette – a hermit (though if he had children he must have taken early retirement)

Hewer – a stone cutter

Hoggard – a swineherd

Hollister – a female brothel keeper!

Homer – a maker of helmets

Hood/Hodder – a maker of hoods

Hooker – a maker of hooks

Hooper – a maker and fitter of hoops on barrels

Hornblower – a man paid for blowing the horn to call people to work

Horner – a maker of horn spoons and horns as instruments

Horrocks – nickname for a shipwright

Hunt/Hunter/Huntsman – a hunter

Husband – a farmer

Hussey – the mistress of a house

Inman – an inn keeper

Jaggar – a carrier or carter

Jenner – an engineer, maker of military machines

Jewell – a jeweller or goldsmith

Joiner – a joiner

Keat – a herdsman

Keeble – a seller of cudgels

Kellogg – a butcher, from 'Kill hog'

Kidman – one who looks after the kids (baby goats, not a childminder)

Kitchen/Kitchener – a worker in a kitchen

Knight – a servant of a knight

Last – a maker of lasts for shoemakers

Lavender – a washerwoman or man

Leach – a physician or doctor

Leachman – a servant of the physician

Leadbetter – a worker in lead

Leader – a driver or carter

Legat – an ambassador

Limmer – an illuminator of manuscripts

Lister – a dyer, from the Middle English *lite*, to dye

Lockyer – a locksmith

Lorimer – a maker of spurs

Luther – a lute player

Marber – a hewer of marble

Marchant – a merchant

Mariner – a seaman
Marshall – one who tends horses and treats their diseases
Mason – a stonemason
Mayle/Mailer – an enameller
Mercer – a merchant dealing in silks and fine fabrics
Messenger – a messenger
Miller (Millar in Scotland**)** – a miller. Other related Miller names include **Millman, Milward, Milne** and **Milner**
Miner – a miner
Minter – a monier at the mint
Monier – the man who could lose his hand at the mint
Monk – originally an occupation name, later also a nickname for monkish looks
Monkhouse/Monks – a servant at the monastery

Napier/Napper – one who has charge of the table linen in a household
Naylor – a maker of nails
Naysmith – a maker of knives
Neat – a cowherd, from the Old English for ox or cow
Nutman/Notman – a seller of nuts
Nutter – a secretary (one who takes notes)

Osler – a seller of game or poultry
Ostler – a stableman, but more often an innkeeper

Ovens – one who worked with a (probably charcoal-fired) furnace

Packer – a woolpacker
Page – a page boy
Painter – a painter
Panther – a panter, a household officer in charge of the bread
Parsons – a servant at the parson's house
Partner – a pardoner, a seller of indulgences
Patten – a patten maker, a patten being either an ecclesiastical vessel or the overshoe worn by peasants
Pease – a grower or seller of peas
Peck – a maker of vessels used as a peck measure of dry goods
Pepper – a dealer in pepper or spices
Pinder – an officer responsible for impounding stray beasts
Pinner – a pinner
Piper – a player on the pipes
Planter – a gardener
Plater – either a maker of plate armour, or an advocate or pleader
Plowman – a Ploughman
Plowright – a maker of ploughs
Plum/Plummer – a plumber, from the Latin for lead, *plumbum*
Porter – a doorkeeper
Pottinger – a soup maker (from potage)

Potts/Potter – a potter
Prentice – an apprentice
Priestman/Pressman – a servant at the priest's house
Purves – a servant who acted as purveyor or provider of supplies for an institution
Pye – a pie maker

Quiller – a maker of spoons
Quilter – a maker of mattresses

Ratner – a rat catcher (not a jeweller!)
Reader/Redman – a collector of reeds, or thatcher
Reeve – a tax collector
Rimmer – a rhymer, poet
Rooker – a spinner, from the Middle English for distaff, *rocke*
Roper/Raper – a maker of rope

Saddler – a maker of saddles
Salter – a maker or seller of salt, but also a harpist – from the psaltery, a stringed instrument
Sargeant – a servant
Sawyer – a worker in a timber yard
Scorer – a scourer or cleanser
Scrimgeour/Scrimshaw – a fencing master (same root as 'scrimmage')
Scudder – a seller of second-hand clothes
Seaman – a sailor

Sellers – three possibilities here: a general
    salesman, a sadler, or a cellarer in charge of
    the pantry in a monastery
Shakespeare – a spearman in the army
Sharman – a sheep shearer
Shepherd – a shepherd
Sheriff – from the Shire Reeve, the sheriff who
    collected taxes for the county
Shipman – a sailor
Shooter/Shotter – an archer
Singer/Sanger/(female form) Sangster – a
    chorister
Skinner – a skinner at the abattoir
Slater – a slater
Slipper – a sword-sharpener
Smith/Smithers – a blacksmith
Soper – a maker of soap
Souter/Sewter/Sutor – a shoemaker
Spears – a spearman
Spenser – a dispenser of provisions, a butler
Spicer – a dealer in spices
Spinner – a spinner of wool yarn
Spooner – a maker of shingles for roofing
    ('spoon' only later came to mean an eating
    utensil)
Stamper – a stamper of coins or worker at the
    mint
Steward/Stuart – an estate manager
Stonier/Stanyer – a stone hewer
Summers – a servant of the sumpter
Sumpter – a driver of a packhorse
Surgenor – a surgeon
Surman – a preacher
Swain/Swan – a servant boy or swineherd

Tailor/Taylor – a tailor
Tanner – the worst job of all
Tapper – a tavern keeper, beer seller (on tap)
Taverner – an inn keeper
Thatcher/Thacker – a thatcher
Thrower – one who 'throws' silk, converting it
    into silk thread
Tiler – a maker of tiles

Topper – one who put the *toppe* on the distaff
    for spinning
Trinder – a braider
Trotter – a messenger
Tucker – a fuller
Turner – a worker on a lathe, but also possibly a
    turnspit

Vickers – a servant of the vicar

Wader – a woad dyer and seller
Wainwright – a wagon builder
Waites (and variations) – a watchman
Walker – a fuller
Waller – a builder of walls
Weaver/Webber/(female form) Webster – all
    names for a weaver
Weller – a salt boiler
Wetherhead – a shepherd from the old English
    wether, a sheep
Wheeler – a wheel maker
Woodman/Wadman – a woodsman
Workman – exactly what it says on the tin
Wright – a carpenter or joiner

Yates – a gate keeper

Worst Jobs Career Guide

The twenty-first century offers a bewildering range of career options. If you live in the developed world it's a fair bet that anything you do, whether you're a student, pork-belly-futures dealer or even an underpaid field archaeologist, will be infinitely better than any of our historical Worst Jobs. But what would you have ended up doing if you'd been born 100, 500, or 1,000 years ago? The following rigorously scientific[1] questionnaire will enable you to assess what Worst Job would have suited you best.

1. **You've popped into your local newsagent to buy a paper and some mints, when through the shop window you see masked men emerging from the building society opposite. What do you do?**
a) Rush out of the shop and bring down the man with the sawn-off shotgun, thus winning 'Have-a-go-hero' headlines.
b) Get the tobacconist to phone the police while you take down the number of the getaway car.
c) Quickly look down and pretend to be engrossed in *Angling Times*.
d) Genuinely get distracted by *Angling Times*, in particular the photo of a prize-winning carp weighing a massive 64 lb.

[1] *Tony Robinson, GCE Chemistry Grade 5*

2. **It's the weekend. A friend suggests a day's walking in the Welsh mountains. What do you take with you?**
a) Stout boots, all-weather gear, crampons, ice-pick, Kendall mint cake and 100 metres of high-tensile rope.
b) A waxed jacket, some walking boots, a flask of coffee and the RSPB *Guide to European Birds*.
c) Trainers, a pair of old jeans in case you have to slide down the steep bits on your bottom, and a copy of *The Good Pub Guide*.
d) A copy of *The Good Pub Guide* and enough money to last while your friend goes off walking.

3. **You're throwing a stick for your dog in the park. By the sort of fluke that only happens in questionnaires, it lands in a stagnant, disused pond. The dog follows and gets into distress in a mass of stinking mud, goose-droppings and slime. What do you do?**
a) Nothing. You believe that a dog is for Christmas and not for life.
b) Wade right in with no thought about whether you might get stuck.
c) Wade in, but take off your Levi's and T-shirt first.
d) Call the park attendant and offer encouragement while he wades in.

4. **A new telephone directory flumps heavily on to your doormat. What do you do?**
a) Fail to realize because of the mass of bills, free newspapers and unsolicited mail already piled high round your front door.
b) Immediately replace your old one with it.
c) Put it on top of the old one, which has valuable numbers scribbled all over it.
d) Transfer your valuable numbers into the new one, then read the front pages to see what exciting new features have been included and learn all the freephone numbers by heart.

5. **Your mother-in-law has given your name to TV's *How Clean Is Your House* team. A researcher turns up to assess your suitability for a visit from Aggie and Kim. First stop is your loo and bathroom. How does she react?**
a) Goes green and shaky, and requires bringing round with a stiff whisky.
b) Says that you'd be ideal, but advises you to clear up a bit first.
c) Rejects you on the grounds that you aren't dirty enough.
d) Tries to sign you up for a new spin-off show called *Hygiene Hitlers*.

6. **Your firm is trying to cope with an extra order from a potentially vital customer. It's created a backlog of work for everyone. What do you do?**
a) Tell your boss you'd be happy to work day and night until the job is done.
b) Pitch in with everyone else but take some work home instead of doing overtime.
c) Carry on as normal. It's not your problem and there's no incentive to do more.
d) Bring a spare jacket into work to put on the back of your chair, so you can take a long lunch while everyone thinks you're in another office working hard.

7. **Your local pub has a Friday Nite Quiz Nite. What do you do?**
a) Refuse to have anything to do with any misspelt leisure activity.
b) Go once as a matter of interest, but prefer your drinking unimpeded by questions about John Wayne's real name (Marion Morrison).
c) Form a team, ironically called The Cheating Bastards, and compete regularly.
d) Go on your own every week and spend the other six nights reading trivia books.

8. **In a fit of enthusiasm at a party you've agreed to do a bunjee jump for charity. What do you do?**
a) Go ahead because it's a great excuse for a laugh, but don't bother too much about getting sponsors.
b) Feel obliged to go through with it. Raise as much money as possible, and wear elasticated pants on the day in case you get too frightened.
c) Ring up to wheedle your way out on the grounds that drunken promises can't be substantiated in a court of law.
d) Change your name and emigrate.

9. **There's a job that you want. It's in the gift of your immediate superior. How far will you go to get it?**
a) You work hard, and believe your track record will speak for itself.
b) You take your boss out for a drink to chew over old times and make sure he/she remembers your track record.
c) You take your boss out for a drink and, as you both have the same sexual orientation, 'jokingly' offer your body.
d) All the above *plus* a five-course meal at a posh restaurant, craven flattery, deliberately losing at golf, and offering up yourself and your partner in a sordid sex-slave scenario.

10. **By another fluke, a pearl from a precious pair of earrings that has been in the family for generations has fallen into your accident-prone dog's dinner and been eaten. What do you do?**
a) Shoot and disembowel the dog to make certain of getting your jewel back.
b) Let it go (*c'est la vie*), claim on the insurance, and keep the other earring for sentimental reasons.
c) Poke around hopefully with a stick in your dog's poo for the next couple of days in case it comes through.
d) You collect dog faeces as a hobby anyway, so it's an easy job squeezing it through your fingers to check for pearls.

Scoring

If you answered a) to question 3 or 10, ignore the scoring. You are perfectly suited for a plague Dog and Cat Killer (page 125). If you answered d) on question 10, look no further than Pure Collector (page 199). Otherwise, score the following points:

1. a) 10 b) 5   c) 0   d) -5
2. a) 10 b) 5   c) 0   d) -5
3.   b) 30 c) 10 d) 0
4. a) 20 b) 5   c) 0   d) -10
5. a) 40 b) 20 c) 0   d) -10
6. a) 0   b) 5   c) -5 d) 10
7. a) 5   b) 0   c) -10 d) -20
8. a) 10 b) 5   c) 0   d) -5
9. a) 5   b) 0   c) 10 d) 30
10.   b) 0   c) 10.

How did you do?

100 and above: There's not much that you're afraid of – especially mucky stuff. In fact, if you've ever wondered what that funny smell is, it may be you. You're ideally suited to some of our tougher, grimier jobs. Try Fulling (page 70), building your house with poo as a Churl (page 20), rootling around inside a sheep as a Violin String Maker (page 130), Nit-picking (page 117), Tanning

(page 201) or, for the upwardly mobile, Groom of the Stool (page 84).

70 to 100: You're bold as brass and brave as a lion, but not such a messy pup. You might be prepared to cope with being an Arming Squire (page 47) for the potential of becoming a knight, but you're ideally suited to some of the high-risk Worst Jobs like Topman or Powder Monkey (pages 157 and 162), fish-fingered Portager (page 37), out-numbered Riding Officer (page 134), Petardier's Assistant (page 108), or even Guillemot Egg Collector (page 40).

30 to 70: You don't mind doing your fair share of hard graft, but you'd prefer not to be killed doing it. If tough is your bag, try Sedan Chair Bearer (page 110), Scavenging for bones or cigar ends or Toshing (pages 195, 191 and 196), Roman Gold Mining (page 16), operating a Treadmill (page 65) or working as a Navvy (page 171).

0 to 30: No one is saying you're work-shy, but you'd suit a more sedentary occupation, even if it gets a trifle monotonous. Executioner (page 76) is a little messy, but won't put huge demands on your time. If you don't mind getting wet or sitting still, Bath Guide (page 137) or Artist's Model (page 142) might suit you, or, if you're not too squeamish about the sight of blood, pus or the odd taste of urine, try putting in an application form for some of the medical jobs: Leech Collecting (page 56), Barber Surgeon (page 51) or Loblolly Boy (page 154).

Below 0: Oh dear, I hate to have to say it, but you are doomed to a life of boredom. Dull, repetitive, uninspiring: these are the adjectives people use about you behind your back. Most of the suitable jobs for you are solitary, but don't worry about that. You're used to being on your own, especially at social occasions. Illuminating manuscripts (page 27) may be too racy for you, so consider Pipe Roll Transcribing (page 67), Pinning (page 97), Charcoal Burning (page 30) and Oakum Picking (page 188). Or for the truly dedicated, what about the long-term boring commitment of a Hermit (page 147).

Index

Bibliography

Printed sources

Black, Maggie, *A Taste of History* (English Heritage in association with British Museum Press, 1993)

Bignamini, Alaria and Postle, Martin, *The Artist's Model* (University Art Gallery, Nottingham, 1991)

Blawer, Dian, *John Peck of Parson Drove, an Exceptional Fenman* (Friends of the Wisbech & Fenland Museum, 1997)

Booth, Charles, *The Life and Labour of the People of London* (Research publication, 1994)

Cahill, Thomas, *How the Irish Saved Civilisation* (Doubleday New York, 1995)

Chaucer Geoffrey, *Canterbury Tales* (Haughton and Mifflin, 1987)

Coleman, Terry, *The Railway Navvies* (Pimlico, 2000)

Cowper, Letters, p. 43, S. Cowper to his brother, 2nd Earl Cowper, 10 April 1745

Cresswell, Paul, *Bath in Quotes – A Literary View from Saxon Times Onwards*

Cunliffe, Barry, *The Extraordinary Voyage of Pytheas the Greek* (Penguin, 2002)

Derby, H.C., *The Changing Fenland* (Cambridge University Press, 1983)

Dickens, Charles, *A Tale of Two Cities*

Dronsfield, A. and Edmonds, J., *The Transition from Natural to Synthetic Dyes* (John Edmonds, 2001)

Dyer, Christopher, *Making a Living in the Middle Ages – The People of Britain 850-1520* (Penguin, 2003)

Dyer, Christopher, *Everyday Life in Medieval England* (Hambledon and London, 2000)

Dyer, Christopher, *Standards of Living in the Middle Ages: Social Change in England c.1200-1520* (Cambridge University Press, 1989)

Erlande-Brandenburg, Alain, *Cathedrals and Castles: Building in the Middle Ages* (Abrams, 1993)

Forster, John, *The Life of Charles Dickens* (Everyman, 1970)

Greenwood, James. *Byways of the Modern Babylon 1867*, taken from the *Victorian Directory* by Lee Jackson

Hosie, Robin S. (ed), *Reader's Digest Book of British Birds* (Reader's Digest, 1969)

Hunt, Tony, *The Medieval Surgery* (Boydell Press, 1992)

(For Autun Cathedral expenses) Icher, Francois, *Building the Great Cathedrals* (Abrams, 1998)

Keevil, Lloyd *Medicine and the Navy 1200-1900* (Churchill Livingstone, 1963)

Labistour, Patricia, *A Rum Do! Smuggling in and around Robin Hood's Bay* (Marine Arts Publications, 1996)

Laing, Lloyd and Laing, Jennifer, *The Picts and Scots* (Sutton, 1993)

Langland, William, *The Vision of Piers Plowman* (Open University Press, 2000)

Latham, Robert (ed) and Latham, Linnet (ed), *The World of Samuel Pepys* (Harper Collins, 2000)

Lloyd, Christopher, *The Health of Seamen: Selections from the Works of Dr James Lind, Sir Gilbert Blane and Dr Thomas Trotter* (Navy Records Society, 1965)

Mayhew, Henry, *London Labour and the London Poor* (Four volumes first published London Griffin Bohn and Co 1861, a selection is available in Penguin Classics)

Miller and Sketchley, *The Fenland Past and Present*

O'Brian, Patrick, *Master and Commander* and nineteen subsequent naval novels (HarperCollins, 1996)

Picard, Liza, *Restoration London* (Weidenfeld & Nicolson, 1997)

Picard, Liza, *Dr Johnson's London* (Weidenfeld & Nicolson, 2000)

Picard, Liza, *Elizabeth's London* (Weidenfeld & Nicolson, 2003)

Pliny the Elder, *Natural History*, tr. John F. Healy 1991 (Penguin Classics, 1991)

Porter, Roy, *English Society in the Eighteenth Century* (Penguin, 1982)

Porter, Roy, *Blood and Guts: A Short History of Medicine* (Allen Lane, 2002)

Ramazzini, Bernardino, *The Diseases of Workers*, tr. Wilmer Cave Wright (The University of Chicago Press, 1940)

Rawcliffe, Carole, *Medicine and Society in Later Medieval England* (Sutton, 1997)

Reaney, P. H. (ed) and Wilson, R. M. (ed), *The Dictionary of English Surnames* (Open University Press, 1997)

Richardson, Ruth, *Death, Dissection and the Destitute: The Politics of the Corpse in Pre-Victorian Britain* (Weidenfeld & Nicolson, 2001)

Savage, Anne (translator), *The Anglo-Saxon Chronicles,* (Harper & Collins, 1982)

Sawyer, P. H., *The Age of the Vikings* (E Arnold, 1975)

Sawyer, P. H., *From Roman Britain to Norman England* (Methuen, 1978)

Sim, Alison, *The Tudor Housewife* (Sutton, 1996)

Smith, Adam, *The Wealth of Nations* (First published 1776, Penguin Classics, 1991)

Smith, Graham, *Smuggling in Yorkshire 1700-1850* (Countryside Books, 1994)

Smollett, Tobias, *The Expedition of Humphrey Clinker*, 1771

Stenton, Frank, *Anglo-Saxon England* (Open University Press, 1971)

(For Aelfric's Colloquy) Michael Swanton (ed), *Anglo-Saxon Prose,* (Everyman, 1975)

Thompson, Denys (ed), *Change and Tradition in Rural England, An Anthology of Writings on Country Life*

Thompson, Flora, *Lark Rise to Candleford* (Penguin Modern Classics, 2000)

Tiller, Kate, *English Local History – An Introduction* (Sutton, 1992)

Vaughan, William, *British Painting – The Golden Age* (Thames and Hudson, 1999)

The Venerable Bede, *The Ecclesiastical History of the English Peoples*, (Oxford World Classics, 1999)

The Venerable Bede, 'The Life and Miracles of St. Cuthbert', in *The Age of Bede: Bede's 'Life of St.Cuthbert', 'Eddius Stephanus' 'Life of Wilfrid' and Other Works* (Penguin Classics, 1998)

Waller, Maureen, *1700: Scenes from London Life* (Hodder & Stoughton, 2000)

Wilson, A. N. *The Victorians* (Hutchinson, 2002)

Wilson, D. (ed) *The Archaeology of Anglo-Saxon England* (Methuen, 1976)

Wilson, Geoffrey, *Poles Apart: The Public Sedans of Bygone London*, a pamphlet (Connor & Butler Ltd, 2002)

Wood, Michael, *In Search of the Dark Ages* (BBC Books, 1981)

Wordsworth, William, 'Resolution and Independence' from *Poems of the Imagination, Wordsworth Poetical Work* (Open University Press, 1978)

(For worm stew recipe) Weald and Downland Museum

Internet sources

Arming Squire translations from the Hastings Document by Brian Price from Archeologia 57, Vol 1 – http://www.chronique.com/Library/Armour/armyd1.htm

Athelstan's Law Codes and Richard Fitznigel of Bath's *Dialogue De Scaccario* – Internet Medieval Sourcebook www.fordham.edu/halsall

Guillemot Eggs – www.genuki.org.uk (look at 'Climmers' in Google). Also www.lore-and-saga.co.uk

All you ever needed to know about leeches at www.biopharm-leeches.com

The Naval Articles of War – http://www.io.com/gibbonsb/articles.html

On-line exploration of the Lindisfarne Gospels – http://www.bl.uk/collections/treasures/lindis.html

Plague information – http://uhaweb.hartford.edu/bugl/histepi.htm

Rule of St Benedict, translated by Rev. Boniface Verheyen – www.kansasmonks.org/RuleOfStBenedict.html

Trimalchio's Dinner from Petronius – http://depthome.brooklyn.cuny.edu/classics/course/dinner.html

Viking bog iron and ships – www.valhs.org/history/articles/manufacturing (look at 'Hurstwic' in Google)

Acknowledgements

Much of the information for this book was gleaned while trying out jobs for the Channel 4 television series of the same name. Without the knowledge and practical experience of a whole host of academics, museum curators, experimental historians and craftsmen and craftswomen too numerous to mention, the whole project would have ground to a halt.

So thanks are due to them, and thanks to everyone at Spire Films who gave me the dubious privilege of coming face to face with fulling, tanning, guillemot egg collecting and the scold's bridle. Not only Jo Foster, Andrew Gray and Lucy Vernall who distilled knowledge and decanted wee, but also Brendan Hughes, Patricia Murphy, Nigel Walk, Linda Flanigan, Jenny Matheson, Carrie Tooth, Andrea Wellington, Philip Bonham Carter, Robin Cox, Gerry Dawson, Rob Goldie, Steve Bowden, Rob Alexander, and Paul Jackson.

Thanks also to Emma Marriott – at last a decent editor! And to Dan Newman, our designer, who can make fulling look stylish.

But most of all thanks are due to Heledd and Janine who, in putting up with everything from writer's cramp to the raw materials for pure-collecting, have at least a claim to sharing the Worst Jobs in history.